The Economic Theory
of Organization and the Firm

The Economic Theory of Organization and the Firm

Richard M. Cyert
President, Carnegie Mellon University

NEW YORK UNIVERSITY PRESS
Washington Square, New York

First published 1988 in the USA by
NEW YORK UNIVERSITY PRESS
Washington Square
New York, NY10003

Library of Congress Cataloging-in-Publication Data

Cyert, Richard Michael, 1921-
    The economic theory of organization and the firm/Richard M.
Cyert.
      p.   cm.
    Bibliography: p.
    Includes index.
    ISBN 0-8147-1427-7
    1. Industrial organization (Economic theory) I. Title.
HD2326.C94 1988
338.5—dc 19   88-17688
                                                     CIP

To M.S.C.

Contents

Contents

List of Figures

List of Tables

Introduction

These articles represent an evolution of thought that began when I was an undergraduate at the University of Minnesota and, I hope, is continuing to this day.

My major focus from the time I became interested in economics has been in micro theory and, particularly, in the theory of the firm. Under the influence of George Stigler I became a student of oligopoly theory. This field is essentially a series of special cases. A number of extremely insightful models have been developed over the years, beginning with Cournot's work. All of these models are in essence duopoly models, even in cases such as the "kinked-demand curve" or "dominant firm", where more than two firms are assumed. The solutions are derived by lumping together all the firms but one and then determining a solution from the tension between the group, which is treated as one firm and the single firm remaining.

The firms involved in these models are all built in the same way as the firm in the theory of the firm. That is to say, the firm consists of a decision rule which is to determine price and output at the point of intersection of the marginal revenue and the marginal cost curves. It is a firm that would not be recognized by a businessman, nor does it have a prototype in the real world.

Specifically, there is no internal structure to the firm and there is no place in the theory for any influence on decisions stemming from the behaviour of individuals within the organization. The external market forces are assumed to be dominant. Thus, the behaviour of the firm is predictable regardless of size, industry, organizational structure and so on. This approach gives the theory great powers of generalization. All that is necessary in any model is to find the marginal cost and marginal revenue curves. Once that task is accomplished, the behaviour of the firm can be predicted.

This view of the firm can be justified under the conditions of perfect competition, as giving great insight into the way that resources are allocated in an economy based on a price system. Studying oligopolies, I began to question the validity of the conventional model for markets consisting of a small number of large firms. There, it seemed to me, that the way information was gathered and processed within the organization had to be incorporated into the decision-making process. I had become sensitized to the importance of organization theory by my colleague, Herbert Simon, but had not incorporated any of the theory into my own work up to that point. I had not studied any organization theory in graduate school and, in fact, was negative about attending to anything that went on inside the firm. At the same time, I was dissatisfied with continuing along the path that seemed to be the mainstream in economic theory.

As I thought more about oligopoly, I came to the conclusion that the organizational structure and the information flow within that structure had to be influential in the decisions that the firm made. I went to my colleague, James March, to discuss the idea and was met with great enthusiasm. With that meeting, we began an association that lasted approximately ten years and ended with the publication of *A Behavioral Theory of the Firm*.

We began to explore the possibilities of bias in the information flow within the firm and to examine the ways in which that bias might affect the decisions that the firm made. That work led to a publication in the *American Economic Review* and later resulted in several experiments with graduate students that were also published.

With the number of publications and increased interest on the part of our colleagues, we began in earnest to look for ways of doing more empirical work to determine how decisions, particularly on price and output, were made in firms. Our work received a boost with a large grant from the Ford Foundation. That grant made it possible for us to hire graduate students to assist us in the empirical side of our work. We were able to make connections with a number of firms in the Pittsburgh area, and these connections enabled us and the graduate students to get inside the firm to observe and study actual decision-making processes.

At the same time the computer had begun to play a bigger role in scientific research. Carnegie Mellon was one of the first schools in the country to get a computer, and it so happened the computer centre was located in the same building as our offices. With the help of some of our graduate students who had earlier become involved with the computer, we began to experiment with simulation. We became particularly interested in simulation because of our findings from the direct observation of decision making.

It was clear that decision makers were not actually using the simple marginal calculus that is embedded in most mathematical models of the firm and of markets. In fact, the actual decision-making process appeared too complex to be handled manageably in the models that we wanted to develop. We began to experiment with some theoretical models of duopoly markets and then began to simulate some of the actual decision processes that we were observing. The paper with Kalman Cohen in this volume is one of the earliest discussions on simulation in the literature analysing the strengths and weaknesses of that approach.

Thus, we were developing a methodology for a study of the firm that had never been used before to the best of our knowledge. We were, on the one hand, observing actual decision processes and, by a combination of interviews and analysis of actual data, trying to determine the decision rules that were being used by the decision-maker. The interviews gave a kind of framework in which to analyse the data which we were allowed to examine, and between the two we began to get a good understanding of the way the actual decision was made. Then, after constructing a model, we were able to get the same types of inputs that the decision maker used and, through a simulation of the process, feed the computer model the same data as the decision-maker had actually used—although on new decisions. We were then able to make a test of how accurate our model was by comparing the prices that the computer predicted with the actual prices that were set by the decision-maker.

This was an exciting time at the Graduate School of Industrial Administration generally, but, in particular, with our project. We attracted a number of excellent graduate students who were interested in the project. A number of theses developed as a result of the research, several of which eventually won an award given by the Ford Foundation at that time and were published as books.

While this empirical work was going on, March and I continued to worry about the theoretical aspects of the firm and tried to draw inferences as rapidly as we could from the observations that were coming to us. This period was one in which I concentrated on the decision-making process in organizations and attempted to relate all of the economic and organizational factors that seemed relevant to the decision-making process. It was in this milieu that *A Behavioral Theory of the Firm* was born.

Jim March and I published our book in 1963 and that brought to a close this phase of the research. In 1962, I had become dean of the Graduate School of Industrial Administration at Carnegie Mellon, and shortly after that March became a dean at the University of California at Irvine. There were a number of concepts in *A Behavioral Theory of the Firm*, however, that I wanted to pursue further. Among them was the xiv The Economic Theory of Organization and the Firm

concept of organizational learning. It had always been my belief that economic theory, in developing as it did, distilled the decision rules into behaviour that was too simple in relation to the real world. In particular, I believed that firms could learn, and that there are many ways of signalling to one another the intentions that would make models like the "kinked-demand curve" fail to conform to reality. I had uncovered some evidence of this kind while doing research for my thesis. As I explored these ideas further with some of my colleagues at Carnegie Mellon, it seemed as though Bayesian analysis was a framework that held promise for building some of the ideas of *A Behavioral Theory of the Firm* into a more formal framework.

Morris DeGroot, a distinguished statistician and one of the outstanding Bayesians in the field, became interested in trying to relate Bayesian analysis to economic theory. He and I began to develop this work in the late 60s. We continued under a number of NSF grants during the 70s after I became president of Carnegie Mellon University in 1972. We began to publish a number of papers that incorporated concepts of learning in duopoly markets and utilized Bayesian analysis. During this period I became a director of a number of corporations and had some opportunity to observe further decision-making first hand as well as to participate in it. I continued to incorporate some of my observations into the models that Morris and I developed. Our work eventually culminated in a book, *Bayesian Analysis and Uncertainty in Economic Theory*, published in 1987.

This work is a continuation of my interest in oligopoly and my interest in developing a theory of the firm that can better describe and predict actual firm behaviour. I was attracted to Bayesian analysis, in particular, because it represents a framework in which organizational learning can be effectively represented. By introducing a learning component into the traditional duopoly models, it is possible to get solutions that are more realistic than the traditional models that assume no learning even after repeated trials.

As part of our joint work, DeGroot and I have developed a model of the firm that is based on the concept of control. The notion is that the top management of the firm is essentially trying to keep the firm on a path that will better its previous year's record on the variables it considers important, including earnings per share, and will make corrections as necessary to bring the firm into control when it fails to meet its targets. The concept is one that is based in part on my observations as a board member, and attempts to integrate the role of strategic planning in the firm, as well as to analyse the various actions that are possible for management to utilize to bring the firm into control. This concept of the firm can be modelled reasonably well by the use of control theory and is, in my view, a direction that economics should be steered into with respect to building models of the firm.

In addition to the work with DeGroot, I have been influenced by my role as president to work on management problems of universities. I was a pioneer in introducing the concept of strategic planning into university management. By applying a number of concepts, particularly that of seeking comparative advantages, we were able at Carnegie Mellon University to strengthen our organization significantly. Through writing and speaking about this concept, the whole area has been opened up significantly, and many universities see themselves as doing strategic planning in a significant way.

More currently, I have been deeply involved in the analysis of the impact of technology on employment. I have recently chaired a national panel for the Committee on Science, Engineering, and Public Policy known as COSEPUP. This is a committee that is jointly sponsored by the National Academy of Sciences, National Academy of Engineering, and the Institute of Medicine. The report has been issued, and I have been involved in explaining it to a number of Congressional Committees and labour union leaders. I was willing to be involved because I am deeply concerned about the manufacturing sector in the United States and, in particular, its ability to reduce costs and improve the quality of the product. I have become convinced by my own analysis of the manufacturing problem that automation is the key for American manufacturing if it is to compete effectively on an international level. Clearly, for American industry to move in this fashion, chief executive officers have to know a lot more about automation than most of them do. I have been trying to participate in this educational process through my writings and a number of talks that I have given.

It is my ultimate intent, however, to return to the ideas described in this essay. I want to contribute to making micro economics an empirical science rather than a deductive one.

In particular, the idea of developing a control theory of the firm is an appealing one. It fits the empirical observations and the approach has the capability of being formalized. Within that context, also, the theorems of organizational theory can be utilized. Thus, the ultimate aim would be to develop a behavioural control theory of the firm that would merge organization theory and economic theory. That development would set the theme for a microtheory that could be integrated with macrotheory. It is this latter development that ultimately must be the goal of economic theory.

March 2, 1988

Part I
Some Empirical Studies

1 Oligopoly Price Behaviour and the Business Cycle*[1]

Work in the area of oligopoly falls into two broad classes. One of these is theory; the other might be called the industry or case-study approach. In general, these two streams of work have not merged to any great extent. The reasons for this are not difficult to discover, but they are not the concern of this chapter. As a result of this condition, economists find themselves with few propositions on oligopoly behaviour that have any empirical basis.

In the theoretical literature there has frequently been speculation about the manner in which oligopolistic firms determine prices during various phases of the business cycle.[2] These speculations, as might be expected, are in some instances at odds with one another. Professor Mitchell described the trough of the business cycle as a period in which formal and informal price agreements broke down, intensifying competition. The prosperity period, on the other hand, he viewed as a time when broken agreements were healed and new ones made, with the result that prices were maintained or advanced. Professor Lange, though he approached the problem from the framework of the kinked demand curve, generally agreed with Mitchell that a period of rising demand leads to higher prices, though not necessarily to increased output. Lange made no propositions about the downswing of the business cycle. Professor Abramovitz, while emphasizing the tentativeness of his argument and the need for empirical work, concluded that the recession stage of the business cycle is most likely to produce prices appropriate to monopoly, whereas in the upswing forces are present that make prices tend toward a position appropriate to competition.

This chapter is an empirical study of price behaviour in three industries—cigarettes, automobiles, and potash—that are commonly

* Reprinted by permission from *The Journal of Political Economy*, Vol. LXIII, No. 1, February 1955.

considered oligopolies. Utilizing time-series data for each of these industries, it tests the (null) hypothesis that "oligopoly" price behaviour is independent of the phase of the business cycle—in particular, that price behaviour is the same during the downswing and the upswing.

"Oligopoly price behaviour" is, of course, an ambiguous expression. The four different aspects of price behaviour examined in this paper can be summarized in the following questions: (1) Does the phase of the cycle affect the likelihood that the firms in an oligopoly will change their prices in the same or different directions? (2) Does the phase of the cycle affect the likelihood that the dispersion of prices will be increased, decreased, or the same after a price change? (3) Is the amount of dispersion of prices independent of the cycle? (4) Is the number of months of unchanging prices independent of the cycle?

Wherever possible, for each of these criteria a null hypothesis is stated and tested for each of the three industries; nine tests are made altogether. In eight of the nine tests the data do not reject the hypothesis that price behaviour is independent of the cycle. The exception concerns the first question for the automobile industry.

I. METHODS OF MEASURING PRICE CHANGES

A. Price-change Patterns

The *first criterion* depends upon the price-change pattern among the firms in each phase of the cycle. Price-change pattern means here the sequence of response to a given price change within a particular time period. Assume that one of the firms initiates a price increase. The other firms then have three alternatives—to follow the price increase, to maintain the old price, or to reduce the price. If any of the firms chooses the second or third alternatives, the pattern will be classified as "Type C". If all firms follow the price increase, the pattern will be classified as "Type S". Now assume that one of the firms initiates a price decrease. Again, the other firms in the industry have three alternatives—to follow the decrease, to maintain the price, or to increase the price. If all firms follow the decrease, the pattern is "Type S". If any of the firms selects the second or third alternatives, the pattern will be called "Type M". Clearly, a time period has to be defined which distinguishes between the reaction to a price change and the initiation of a price change. The length of the period will depend primarily on the characteristics of the particular market. It may be, for example, that the nature of the market is such that firms react within a day to a competitor's change, or they may take a month or an irregular time period. For the industries analysed in this study a month seems to be a satisfactory period.

B. Dispersion of Prices

The *second criterion* is based on the statistical dispersion of prices. The coefficient of variation is used as a measure of dispersion.[3] At each point of price change the dispersion of prices will be calculated and used to classify price changes as resulting in increased, decreased, or constant dispersion in relation to the previously existing situation.

C. Statistical Distribution of the Coefficients of Variation

The coefficient of variation can also be used in another way. The method of classification discussed above will not disclose differences in the absolute amount of dispersion between the phases of the cycle. By appropriate statistical techniques, it can be determined whether the statistical distributions of the measures of dispersion are different between the phases. This is the *third criterion*.

D. Periods of "No Price Change"

Up to this point, I have concentrated on observations of actual price changes in the search for criteria. Yet it is quite clear that "not changing price" is also a definite decision and is in one sense equivalent to the case of all firms changing at the same time for the *first criterion* and to the case of a constant coefficient of variation for the *second criterion*. If specific information could be obtained, showing when firms made a decision to maintain price, these cases could be handled as cases of price change. Unfortunately, however, this information is not available.

The problem of the *fourth criterion* is essentially one of discovering whether the number of periods in which no firm changed price differs between phases of the cycle. The time unit that will be used to define a period of no change will be the same as for the *first criterion*—one month.

II. EMPIRICAL TESTING

On the basis of these four criteria the price behaviour of the major firms in three industries will be tested for differences over the business cycle. The general hypothesis being tested is that the phase of the business cycle has no effect on the price behaviour of oligopolistic firms. In each section a more precise statement will be made of the specific hypothesis being tested.

A. The Cigarette Industry

The analysis of the cigarette industry will be conducted in terms of three leading brands—Camel, Lucky Strike, and Chesterfield. It is not possible to develop here the historical and institutional material necessary for a full appreciation of the pricing problems of the industry.[4] A study of the industry makes it clear that manufacturers' list prices are a significant factor in the price structure of the industry, although the retail price is not completely determined by the list price. The statistical analysis will be made on the announced manufacturers' list prices. These prices, for the period examined, are given in Table 1.1.

The second piece of information necessary for the analysis is the business-cycle pattern of the industry. In the terminology of the National Bureau of Economic Research, this is the specific cycle dates of the industry. Because of the tremendous growth in cigarette consumption,

Table 1.1.; List prices of Camel, Lucky Strike, and Chesterfield cigarettes, 1917–48 (Dollars per thousand)

Date of Price Change	Camel	Lucky Strike	Chester-field	Date of Price Change	Camel	Lucky Strike	Chester-field
February 28, 1917....	$4.10	$4.00	$3.90	October 28, 1922	$6.40	....	....
October 4, 1917.......	4.55	....	4.45	October 30, 1922	....	....	$6.30
October 19, 1917	....	5.00	....	October 31, 1922	....	5.80	....
November 2, 1917....	5.25	....	4.85	January 15, 1923	....	....	6.40
March 1, 1918........	6.00	....	....	August 8, 1923	....	6.45	....
March 9, 1918........	....	5.833	....	April 21, 1928	6.00	6.00	....
March 28, 1918	....	....	5.25	April 23, 1928	....	....	6.00
May 15, 1918.........	....	....	6.00	October 5, 1929......	6.40	6.40	6.40
July 27, 1918........	....	6.00	....	June 24, 1931........	6.85	6.85	6.85
September 27, 1918..	....	7.50	....	January 2, 1933......	....	6.00	6.00
November 11, 1918..	....	6.00	....	January 3, 1933......	6.00	....	....
February 25, 1919....	8.00	7.50	7.50	February 11, 1933...	5.50	5.50	5.50
March 2, 1919........	7.30	....	....	January 9, 1934......	6.10	6.10	6.10
October 15, 1919	....	....	7.80	January 19, 1937	6.25	6.25	....
November 1, 1919....	....	7.80	....	January 20, 1937	....	....	6.25
November 22, 1919..	8.00	....	....	July 1, 1940..........	6.53	6.53	6.53
November 24, 1919..	....	....	8.00	December 28, 1941..	....	7.10	....
November 27, 1919..	....	8.20	....	December 30, 1941..	....	6.53	....
December 18, 1919...	....	8.00	....	November 1, 1942...	6.81	6.81	6.81
December 5, 1921	....	7.75	....	April 25, 1946........	7.09	7.09	7.09
December 31, 1921...	7.50	....	....	August 1, 1946	....	....	7.31
January 3, 1922......	....	....	7.50	August 5, 1946	....	....	7.09
January 19, 1922	....	7.50	....	October 8, 1946......	....	7.38	....
March 4,1922.........	6.80	....	....	October 10, 1946	....	....	7.38
March 7, 1922........	....	6.80	....	October 14, 1946	7.35	....	....
March 8, 1922........	....	....	7.20	July 28, 1948	....	7.78	....
August 1, 1922.......	....	....	6.90	July 29, 1948	7.75	....	....
August 24, 1922	....	6.20	....	July 30, 1948	....	....	7.78

* Source: W. H. Nicholls, *Price Policies in the Cigarette Industry* (Nashville: Vanderbilt University Press, 1951), pp. 46–7, 80, 152.

Table 1.2*: Reference-cycle dates

Peak	Trough
....	December, 1914
August, 1918	April, 1919
January, 1920	July, 1921
May, 1923	July, 1924
October, 1926	November, 1927
June, 1929	March, 1933
May, 1937	June, 1938
February, 1945	October, 1945
November, 1948	....

* Source: National Bureau of Economic Research.

however, the National Bureau has not been able to develop specific cycle dates for this industry. It is possible to establish, nevertheless, through the use of first differences in the time series of annual sales of the three leading brands, that the fortunes of the industry have followed quite closely the schedule of reference-cycle dates developed by the Bureau. These dates will therefore be used in testing the hypotheses of price behaviour for the cigarette industry; they are given in Table 1.2.

First criterion. The hypothesis tested by use of the *first criterion* is that the pattern of price change does not vary between the phases of the business cycle. The data necessary for testing this hypothesis are derived by superimposing the reference-cycle dates on the price series for each brand of cigarette. The level of prices is not relevant at this stage, but only the direction in which the firms changed price. The result of superimposing the two tables is given in Table 1.3.

By applying the *first criterion* of measurement to Table 1.3 the following contingency table was constructed:

	Type C	Type M	Type S	Total
Upswing.....	6	3	15	24
Downswing	2	2	5	9
Total.........	8	5	20	33

Chi square was then computed for this table and the hypothesis tested, using a probability of .05 as the critical level.[5] The test led to the conclusion that the hypothesis should not be rejected. This means that,

Table 1.3*: Dates and direction of changes in the prices of three leading brands of cigarettes, 1917–48

	Upswing					Downswing				Upswing		
Cigarette	1917	1917	1918	1918	1918	1918	1918	1919	1919	1919	1919	1919
	Oct.	Nov.	Mar.	May	July	Sept.	Nov.	Feb.	Mar.	Oct.–Nov.	Nov.	Dec.
Camel	+	+	+					+	−	+	+	
Lucky Strike	+		+		+	+	−	+		+	+	−
Chesterfield	+	+	+	+				+		+	+	

	Upswing	Upswing				Down-swing	Up-swing	Downswing			
Cigarette	1921	1922				1923	1923	1928	1929	1931	1933	
	Dec.–Dec.	Jan.	Mar.	Aug.	Oct.	Jan.	Aug.	Apr.	Oct.	June	Jan.	Feb.
Camel	−	−			−			−	+	+	−	−
Lucky Strike	−	−	−	−	−		+	−	+	+	−	−
Chesterfield	−	−	−	−	+			−	+	+	−	−

	Upswing			Upswing		Upswing			
Cigarette	1934	1937	1940	1941	1942	1946			1948
	Jan.	Jan.	July	Dec.	Nov.	Apr.	Aug.	Oct.	July
Camel	+	+	+		+	+		+	+
Lucky Strike	+	+	+	+	+	+		+	+
Chesterfield	+	+	+		+	+	+	+	+

* Source: Adapted from Table 1.

on the basis of the evidence available and the criterion of measurement used, the phase of the business is not a significant variable in determining the pattern of price changes followed by firms in the cigarette industry.

Second criterion. The specific hypothesis tested by the *second criterion* is that the phase of the business cycle does not affect the dispersion of prices. The coefficient of variation was computed for the prices prevailing after each price change. The values of the coefficient of variation are shown in Table 1.4. The following contingency table was formed, using the *second criterion*:

	Decreased Dispersion	Increased Dispersion	Constant Dispersion	Total
Upswing.....	10	7	5	22
Downswing	3	2	4	9
Total.........	13	9	9	31

Table 1.4*: Coefficients of variation of prices of three leading brands of cigarettes, 1917–48

Date	$\overline{X}$	δ	$\dfrac{\theta}{\bar{x}}$
February, 1917 ...	4.00	.0819	.02048
October, 1917.....	4.67	.2387	.05111
November, 1917..	5.03	.1649	.03278
March, 1918.......	5.69	.3209	.05640
May, 1918	5.94	.0900	.01347
July, 1918..........	6.00	.0000	.00000
September, 1918..	6.50	.9576	.14732
November, 1918..	6.00	.0000	.00000
February, 1919 ...	7.67	.2358	.03074
March, 1919.......	7.43	.0980	.01319
October– November, 1919..	7.43	.0943	.01220
November, 1919..	8.07	.0980	.01214
December, 1919 ..	8.00	.0000	.00000
December, 1921 ..	7.58	.1179	.01555
January, 1922.....	7.50	.0000	.00000
March, 1922.......	6.93	.1887	.02723
August, 1922......	6.63	.3092	.04664
October, 1922.....	6.17	.2625	.04254
January, 1923.....	6.20	.2828	.04561
August, 1923......	6.42	.0245	.00382
April, 1928	6.00	.0000	.00000
October, 1929.....	6.40	.0000	.00000
July, 1931..........	6.85	.0000	.00000
January, 1933.....	6.00	.0000	.00000
February, 1933 ...	5.50	.0000	.00000
January, 1934.....	6.10	.0000	.00000
January, 1937.....	6.25	.0000	.00000
July, 1940..........	6.53	.0000	.00000
November, 1942..	6.81	.0000	.00000
April, 1946	7.09	.0000	.00000
October, 1946.....	7.37	.0141	.00191
July, 1948..........	7.77	.0141	.00181

* Source: Computed from Table 1.

The hypothesis was again tested by computing chi square, and the conclusion was that the hypothesis should not be rejected. Thus there is no evidence of a trend of increasing or decreasing dispersion of prices in either phase of the business cycle.

Third criterion. A second and different type of test was conducted on the calculated measure of dispersion. Despite the result of the previous test, it is still possible that the coefficients of variation are distributed differently over the phases of the cycle. It is possible, for example, that the location of the distribution is different in the two phases; that is, the values may be generally higher in one phase than in the other. The median test, a nonparametric test that is sensitive to differences in location, was used to test the hypothesis that the sample of coefficients of variation in the downswing comes from the same distribution as the sample of coefficients of variation in the upswing.[6] The conclusion drawn from the test was that the two samples could have come from the same distribution. This means that the spread of the firm's prices, as measured by the coefficient of variation, does not on the average vary with the phase of the cycle.

Fourth criterion. The last test concerns the periods in which no firm changed price. The testing procedure is to calculate the proportion of months of no price change observed in the upswing of the cycle and in the downswing of the cycle. The hypothesis to be tested is that the phase of the cycle does not affect the proportion of periods of no price change. The test was conducted as follows:

Let

$\bar{p}_1$ = the proportion of months of no price change in the downswing sample = $113/122$ = .9262;

$\bar{p}_2$ = the proportion of months of no price change in the upswing sample = $229/254$ = .9016;

p_1 and p_2 = the true proportion of months of no price change in the downswing and upswing, respectively; and

$\bar{p}$ = the estimated proportion of months of no price change in the distribution on the assumption that $p_1 = p_2$.

Then

$$\bar{p} = \frac{(122)\,(.9262) + (254)\,(.9016)}{122 + 254}$$

$$= .9096.$$

The test of significance at the 5 per cent level is whether or not

$$|\bar{p}_1 - \bar{p}_2| \geq 1.96 \sqrt{\left[\frac{(.0914)\ (.9096)}{122} + \frac{(.0914)\ (.9096)}{254} \right]} = .0619;$$

$$|\bar{p}_1 - \bar{p}_2| = .0246 < .0619.$$

Therefore, the hypothesis that the phase of the cycle has no effect on the number of periods of no price change cannot be rejected. This means that on the basis of the evidence we can conclude that the firms producing the three leading brands of cigarettes do not maintain their prices a higher proportion of the time in one phase of the cycle than in the other.

B. The Automobile Industry
The second industry analysed is the automobile industry, which is generally considered to be an oligopoly with a differentiated product. The product is best classified on the basis of price. The low-price class, since 1931, has consisted primarily of the Ford, Chevrolet, and Plymouth automobiles. The hypotheses constructed will be tested by price data for the low-price class.

The prices analysed are the manufacturers' list prices. The business-cycle dates used are the specific cycle dates established for the industry by the National Bureau of Economic Research from the series on automobile passenger-car production. The relevant data for the tests conducted are presented in Tables 1.5 through 8; in general, the tests for the automobile industry are the same as those for the cigarette industry.

First criterion. As before, the hypothesis being tested concerns the differences in price-changing patterns over the business cycle. The contingency table constructed from the data is as follows:

	Type C	Type M	Type S	Total
Upswing.....	9	5	6	20
Downswing	2	11	1	14
Total.........	11	16	7	34

The results of the statistical analysis indicate that there is a significant difference between the phases of the cycle in the pattern of price change among the firms in the automobile industry. The typical pattern seems to be that all firms do not follow price changes initiated by one of the firms—whether the change is an increase or a decrease. In the upswing most of the changes not followed are price increases, and in the

Table 1.5*: List prices of three leading bands of low-price four-door sedans, 1926–41†

Date of Price Change	Chevrolet	Ford	Plymouth
January, 1926	$645	....	....
February, 1926	....	$565	....
June, 1926............	....	545	....
January, 1927	595	....	....
December, 1927.....	....	570	....
January, 1928	585	....	....
September, 1928	....	....	$735
December, 1928.....	675	....	....
February, 1929	....	625	695
November, 1929	....	600	....
February, 1930	675	....	....
May, 1930............	....	....	625
December, 1930.....	635	....	....
February, 1931	....	590	....
July, 1931	....	....	635
April, 1932...........	590	590	....
December, 1932.....	....	....	575
March, 1933	565	560	....
May, 1933............	....	....	510
February, 1934	645	585	585
April, 1934...........	675	....	610
July, 1934	640	575	600
January, 1935	....	575	570
November, 1935	....	580	....
December, 1935.....	575	....	590
December, 1936.....	600	555	595
April, 1937...........	....	604	....
August, 1937	....	639	....
September, 1937	697	....	....
November, 1937	730	685	730
November, 1938	689	665	726
November, 1939	689	685	740
August, 1940	....	....	744
October, 1940	767	735	780
November, 1940	754	....	....
July, 1941	....	750	800

* Source: *Automobile Trade Journal and Motor Age,* 1926–41.
† These prices include federal tax for the Chevrolet and the Plymouth but not for the Ford. Ford prices were always quoted in this way in the trade journals, and, since it was not necessary, I have not attempted to adjust them.

Table 1.6*: Dates and direction of changes in the prices of three leading brands of low-price automobiles, 1926–41

Automobile	Downswing		Upswing			Downswing			Upswing	
	1926	1927	1927	1928	1929	1930	1931	1932	1932	1933
	Jan. Feb. June	Jan.	Dec.	Jan. Sept. Dec.	Feb. Nov.	Feb. May Dec.	Feb. July	Apr.	Dec.	Mar. May
Chevrolet...........	–	...	...	– ... +	... –	–	... –	...	...	... –
Ford................	... – ...	+	...	... ...	+ –	... ...	... –	...	–	– ...
Plymouth..........	... ...	...	+	... ... +	... –	... ... –	... +	...	–	...

Automobile	Upswing				Downswing				
	1934	1935	1936	1937	1937	1938	1939	1940	1941
	Feb. Apr. July	Jan. Nov. Dec.	Dec.	Apr. Aug.	Sept. Nov.	Nov.	Nov.	Aug. Oct. Nov.	July
Chevrolet...........	+ + ...	... ... –	+	... +	+ +	–	+	... + –	...
Ford................	+ ... +	... + ...	+	... –	... +	–	+	... + +	+
Plymouth..........	+ ... +	... – ...	+	... ...	... +	–	+	... + +	+

* Source: Adapted from *Automobile Journal* and *Motor Age*, 1926–41.

downswing most of the changes not followed are decreases. Only 20 per cent of the price changes observed are those in which all firms changed price in the same direction in the same period. These results are in sharp contrast with those for the cigarette industry.

Second criterion. The hypothesis tested by this criterion concerns the dispersion of the firms' prices over the cycle. Applying the criterion of measurement to the computed measures of dispersion produces the following contingency table:

	Decreased Dispersion	Increased Dispersion	Total
Upswing	14	10	24
Downswing...	6	7	13
Total...........	20	17	37

The results indicate that the hypothesis should not be rejected. This means that the dispersion does not tend to increase in one phase of the cycle and to decrease in the other. However, as indicated earlier, this result does not demonstrate that the dispersion in one phase cannot, on the average, be different from the dispersion in the other. This possibility is investigated in the next test.

Third criterion. The hypothesis being tested is that the coefficients of variation in the upswing sample and those in the downswing sample come from the same distribution. The Wald-Wolfowitz run test, a nonparametric test, was used to test this hypothesis.[7] The first step is to merge the two samples and rank them from the lowest to the highest value. The values coming from the upswing are marked with a "1" and those coming from the downswing with a "0". A run is defined as a sequence of numbers of the same kind bounded by numbers of the other kind. The test can then be conducted as shown below.

Let

m = the sample size of the downswing sample = 14;

n = the sample size of the upswing sample = 24;

U = the number of runs in the total sample = 21;

$E(U)$ = the number of runs on the assumption that the two samples come from the same distribution; and

$\sigma^2(U)$ = the variance of the distribution of U.

Then,

$$E(U) = \frac{2mn}{m+n} + 1 = 19;$$

$$\sigma^2(U) = \frac{2mn(2mn - m - n)}{(m+n)^2(m+n-1)} = 7.9742;$$

$$\sigma(U) = 2.824;$$

$$\frac{U - E(U)}{\sigma(U)} = .708.$$

Table 1.7*: Specific cycle dates, automobile passenger-car production

Peak	Trough
December, 1925	November, 1927
January, 1929	October, 1932
August, 1937	August, 1938

* Source: Unpublished work of the National Bureau of Economic Research

Table 1.8*: Coefficients of variation of prices of three leading brands of automobiles in ranked order

Rank	Value	Sample No.	Rank	Value	Sample No.
1........	.0099	1	20........	.0355	1
2........	.0110	1	21........	.0356	0
3........	.0115	0	22........	.0362	1
4........	.0121	1	23........	.0381	1
5........	.0130	1	24........	.0439	0
6........	.0194	1	25........	.0442	1
7........	.0215	1	26........	.0443	0
8........	.0237	0	27........	.0452	1
9........	.0244	1	28........	.0456	1
10........	.0248	1	29........	.0467	1
11........	.0266	1	30........	.0492	0
12........	.0289	1	31........	.0616	1
13........	.0296	1	32........	.0623	0
14........	.0297	0	33........	.0623	0
15........	.0301	1	34........	.0661	0
16........	.0313	0	35........	.0840	0
17........	.0321	1	36........	.1033	1
18........	.0342	0	37........	.1114	1
19........	.0351	0	38........	.1183	1

* Source: Table 5.

On the basis of this result the hypothesis would not be rejected, since the probability is high (.39) that a deviation this large (.708) or larger may be obtained by chance when the hypothesis is true. This result means that the phase of the business cycle has no effect on the dispersion of prices of rivals, as far as can be determined from the available evidence.

Fourth criterion. The test of the hypothesis that the phase of the business cycle does not affect the proportion of periods of no price change was conducted in the same manner as before. The result was again the same—the available evidence would not admit of rejection of the hypothesis.

C. The Potash Industry

The third industry studied is the potash industry. The potash industry differs from the other two industries studied in that there is no branding of products. The product varies according to the concentration of the salts and is not differentiated among sellers. The industry differs in one other respect from automobiles and cigarettes. It is primarily a producers' goods industry. The bulk of the output goes to the fertilizer industry; a small portion goes to the chemical industry.

There are two aspects of pricing in the potash industry that should be mentioned before the testing of hypotheses is discussed. The first is the seasonal character of the major consumer, the fertilizer industry. Fertilizer production is primarily a spring activity, whereas potash production is spread evenly throughout the year. As a result, a system of discounts from the list prices has been used in an attempt to encourage the delivery of orders in seasons of slack demand. Therefore, a change in price may take the form of a change in the discounts or a change in the list prices. The second relevant aspect of pricing is the issuance of price schedules. Price schedules are issued annually, regardless of whether or not there are any changes in prices or discount terms. They are usually issued in April, May, or June and hold for about a year; in any event, a termination date is stated in the schedule.[8] The dates and amounts of price changes are recorded in government and trade publications.

The problems of testing hypotheses for potash are in general the same as in the other industries. The only difference is that the decision to maintain price has been recorded in the table as a "0". This was done because of the industry practice of issuing annual price schedules. Firms must make a definite decision to act in a particular way each year, since the old prices are not perpetuated automatically. Operationally, a new price has been established even though the price may not have changed. The price-change series begins in 1933 with the prices charged by two domestic producers and an importing firm. The price data and the business-cycle dates are given in Tables 1.9 and 1.2, respectively.

Table 1.9*: Dates and direction of changes in the price of potash produced by leading firms, 1933–49

Company	Upswing					Down-swing		Upswing	
	1933	1934	1935	1936	1937	1938	1939	1940	1941
	May Nov.	June June July July (1, 26, 7, 27)	May July	June July	May	May	May June	June	June
American potash and Chemical Corp.	0	– +	+ +	– –	+	0	0 –	+	0
U.S. Potash Co.	0	+	+ +	– –	+	0	0 –	+	0
N.V. Potash Export M.Y., Inc.	0	–	+	–	+	0	0	...	...
Potash Company of America	...	...	+	–	+	0	0 –	+	0
International Minerals and Chemicals Corp.	...	...	...	...	...	...	...	+	0

Company	Upswing			Down-swing		Upswing		
	1942	1943	1944	1945	1946	1947	1948	1949
	June	Apr.	Apr.	May	June	May	Feb. Mar.	May
American Potash and Chemical Corp.	0	0	0	0	0	0	+ –	0
U.S. Potash Co.	0	0	0	0	0	0	...	0
N.V. Potash Export M.Y., Inc.	0	0	0	0	0	0	...	...
Potash Company of America	0	...	0	0	0	0	...	0
International Minerals and Chemical Corp.	0	0	0	0	0	0	0	0

* Source: Bureau of Mines *Minerals Yearbook*, 1933–49.

First criterion. Using the *first criterion* of classification, as before, the hypothesis can be tested that the phase of the business cycle has no effect on the pattern of price change:

	Type C	Type M	Type S	Total
Upswing	3	5	16	24
Downswing	0	0	3	3
Total........	3	5	19	27

The probability had to be computed directly because of the small number of observations.[9] The probability calculation leads to the conclusion that the evidence is not strong enough to warrant rejection of the hypothesis.

Other criteria. The same results were obtained when the decisions to maintain price were treated as in the other industries. The tests involving the coefficient of variation were not possible for the potash industry, since prices are not differentiated by firms. The test of the hypothesis that the phase of the business cycle does not affect the number of price changes was made, and the hypothesis was not rejected. However, because of the small number of observations in the downswing, the test is of little significance and is not shown here.

III. CONCLUSIONS

The results of the statistical testing in the three industries indicate that the phase of the business cycle affects price behaviour in only one case. It should be clear that these results are limited by the small number of industries investigated and by the observations available in each industry. However, I believe that only through a quantitative approach to the problem is it possible to construct a theory of oligopoly price behaviour that will have empirical substance. By investigations of this type it may be possible to isolate variables that are significant and patterns of behaviour that need to be explained. The task of the theorist is then to discover the mechanisms by which the relevant variables produce the observed behaviour.

NOTES

1. I wish to express my indebtedness to Professors M. Abramovitz, A. F. Burns, E. S. Grunberg, and G. J. Stigler for their criticisms of an earlier draft.
2. Cf. W. C Mitchell, *Business Cycles and Their Causes*, new edition of

Mitchell's *Business Cycles, Part III* (Berkeley: University of California Press, 1941), pp. 10 and 134; O. Lange, *Price Flexibility and Employment* (Bloomington: Principia Press, 1944), pp. 41–3; and M. Abramovitz, 'Monopolistic Selling in a Changing Economy', *Quarterly Journal of Economics*, LII (February, 1938), 191–214.

3. See H. Cramér, *Mathematical Methods of Statistics* (Princeton: Princeton University Press, 1946), pp. 357–8.

4. See R. B. Tennant, *The American Cigarette Industry* (New Haven: Yale University Press, 1950).

5. For the method of computation of chi square see Cramér, *op. cit.*, pp. 441–5.

6. See A. M. Mood, *Introduction to the Theory of Statistics* (New York: McGraw-Hill Book Co., 1950), pp. 394–5. The median test was selected rather than the run test (which is used later) because of the number of "ties" in the data. The run test is somewhat more satisfactory because it is sensitive to differences in shape as well as in location.

7. Mood, *op. cit.*, pp. 391–4.

8. J. W. Turrentine, *Potash in North America* (New York: Reinhold Publishing Corp., 1943), pp. 95–8.

9. For the method used see Paul R. Rider, *An Introduction to Modern Statistical Methods* (New York: John Wiley & Sons, 1939), pp. 112–15.

2 Observation of a Business Decision*

with Herbert A. Simon and Donald B. Trow

Decision-making—choosing one course of action rather than another, finding an appropriate solution to a new problem posed by a changing world—is commonly asserted to be the heart of executive activity in business. If this is so, a realistic description and theory of the decision-making process are of central importance to business administration and organization theory. Moreover, it is extremely doubtful whether the only considerable body of decision-making theory that has been available in the past—that provided by economics—does in fact provide a realistic account of decision-making in large organizations operating in a complex world.

In economics and statistics the rational choice process is described somewhat as follows:

1. An individual is confronted with a number of different, specified alternative courses of action.

2. To each of these alternatives is attached a set of consequences that will ensue if that alternative is chosen.

3. The individual has a system of preferences or "utilities" that permit him to rank all sets of consequences according to preference and to choose that alternative that has the preferred consequences. In the case of business decisions the criterion for ranking is generally assumed to be profit.

If we try to use this framework to describe how real human beings go about making choices in a real world, we soon recognize that we need to incorporate in our description of the choice process several elements that

* Reprinted by permission from *The Journal of Business of the University of Chicago*, Vol. XXIX, No. 4, October 1956. This is a preliminary report on research carried out under a grant from the Ford Foundation for studies in organization and decision-making. The authors are grateful to the Foundation for its support, to the executives of the company that opened its doors to them, and to colleagues and graduate students who have assisted at various stages of data collection and analysis.

are missing from the economic model:

1. The alternatives are not usually "given" but must be sought, and hence it is necessary to include the search for alternatives as an important part of the process.

2. The information as to what consequences are attached to which alternatives is seldom a "given", but, instead, the search for consequences is another important segment of the decision-making task.

3. The comparisons among alternatives are not usually made in terms of a simple, single criterion like profit. One reason is that there are often important consequences that are so intangible as to make an evaluation in terms of profit difficult or impossible. In place of searching for the "best" alternative, the decision-maker is usually concerned with finding a *satisfactory* alternative—one that will attain a specified goal and at the same time satisfy a number of auxiliary conditions.

4. Often, in the real world, the problem itself is not a "given", but, instead, searching for significant problems to which organizational attention should be turned becomes an important organizational task.

Decisions in organizations vary widely with respect to the extent to which the decision-making process is *programmed*. At one extreme we have repetitive, well-defined problems (e.g., quality control or production lot-size problems) involving tangible considerations, to which the economic models that call for finding the best among a set of pre-established alternatives can be applied rather literally. In contrast to these highly programmed and usually rather detailed decisions are problems of a non-repetitive sort, often involving basic long-range questions about the whole strategy of the firm or some part of it, arising initially in a highly unstructured form and requiring a great deal of the kinds of search processes listed above. In this whole continuum, from great specificity and repetition to extreme vagueness and uniqueness, we will call decisions that lie toward the former extreme *programmed*, and those lying toward the latter end *non-programmed*. This simple dichotomy is just a shorthand for the range of possibilities we have indicated.

It is our aim in the present chapter to illustrate the distinctions we have introduced between the traditional theory of decision, which appears applicable only to highly programmed decision problems, and a revised theory, which will have to take account of the search processes and other information processes that are so prominent in and characteristic of non-programmed decision-making. We shall do this by recounting the stages through which an actual problem proceeded in an actual company and then commenting upon the significance of various items in this narrative for future decision-making theory.

The decision was captured and recorded by securing the company's permission to have a member of the research team present as an observer in the company's offices on substantially a full-time basis during the most active phases of the decision process. The observer spent most of his time with the executive who had been assigned the principal responsibility for handling this particular problem. In addition, he had full access to the files for information about events that preceded his period of observation and also interviewed all the participants who were involved to a major degree in the decision.

THE ELECTRONIC DATA-PROCESSING DECISION

The decision process to be described here concerns the feasibility of using electronic data-processing equipment in a medium size corporation that engages both in manufacturing and in selling through its own widely scattered outlets. In July, 1952, the company's controller assigned to Ronald Middleton, an assistant who was handling several special studies in the accounting department, the task of keeping abreast of electronic developments. The controller, and other accounting executives, thought that some of the current developments in electronic equipment might have application to the company's accounting processes. He gave Middleton the task of investigation, because the latter had a good background for understanding the technical aspects of computers.

Middleton used three procedures to obtain information: letters to persons in established computer firms, discussions with computer salesmen, and discussions with persons in other companies that were experimenting with the use of electronic equipment in accounting. He also read the current journal literature about computer developments. He informed the controller about these matters principally through memorandums that described the current status of equipment and some of the procedures that would be necessary for an applications study in the company. Memorandums were written in November, 1952, October, 1953, and January, 1954. In them, in addition to summarizing developments, he recommended that two computer companies be asked to propose possible installations in the company and that the company begin to adapt its accounting procedures to future electronic processing.

In the spring of 1954 a computer company representative took the initiative to propose and make a brief equipment application study. In August he submitted a report to the company recommending an installation, but this was not acted upon—doubt as to the adequacy of the computer company's experience and knowledge in application being a major factor in the decision. A similar approach was made by another computer company in September, 1954, but terminated at an early stage without positive action. These experiences convinced Middleton and other executives, including the controller, that outside help was needed to develop and evaluate possible applications of electronic equipment.

Middleton drew up a list of potential consultants and, by checking outside sources and using his own information, selected Alpha as the most suitable. After preliminary meetings in October and November, 1954, between representatives of Alpha and the company accounting executives, Alpha was asked to develop a plan for a study of the application of electronic data-processing to sales accounting. Additional meetings between Alpha and company personnel were held in February, 1955, and the proposal for the study was submitted to the controller in March.

Although the proposal seemed competent and the price reasonable, it was felt that proposals should be obtained from another consulting firm as a double check. The controller agreed to this and himself selected Beta from Middleton's list. Subsequently representatives of Beta met with Middleton and other department executives. Middleton, in a memorandum to the controller, listed criteria for choosing between the two consultants. On the assumption that the written report from Beta was similar to the oral proposal made, the comparison indicated several advantages for Beta over Alpha.

After the written report was received, on May 2, the company's management committee authorized a consulting agreement with Beta, and work began in July, 1955. The controller established a committee, headed by Middleton, to work on the project. Middleton was to devote full time to the assignment; the other two committee members, one from sales accounting and one from auditing, were to devote one-third time.

The consulting firm assigned two staff members, Drs Able and Baker, to the study. Their initial meetings with Middleton served the purpose of outlining a general approach to the problem and planning the first few steps. Twenty-three information-gathering studies were defined, which Middleton agreed to carry out, and it was also decided that the consultants would spend some time in field observation of the actual activities that the computer might replace.

During July, Middleton devoted most of his time to the twenty-three studies on volume of transactions and information flow, obtaining data from the sales department and from the field staffs of the other two committee members. Simultaneously, steps were taken to secure the co-operation of the field personnel who would be visited by the consultants early in August.

On July 22 Middleton submitted a progress report to the controller, describing the data-gathering studies, estimating completion dates, and summarizing the program's objectives. On July 25 the consultants met with Middleton and discussed a method of approach to the design of the data-processing system. The field trip took place early in August. The consultants obtained from field personnel information as to how accounting tasks were actually handled and as to the use actually made of information generated by the existing system.

On August 8 Middleton submitted another progress report, giving the status of the data-gathering studies and recording some ideas originating in the field trip for possible changes in the existing information-processing system. On August 10 he arranged with the assistant controller to obtain clerical assistance on the data-gathering studies, so that the consultants would not be held up by lack of this information, and on August 17 this work was completed.

On the following day the consultants met with the company committee to review the results of the twenty-three studies. They then listed the outputs, files, and inputs required by any sales accounting system the company might adopt and drew a diagram showing the flow of the accounting information. The group also met with the assistant controller and with the controller. The latter took the opportunity to emphasize his basic decentralization philosophy.

Upon returning from his vacation early in September, Middleton discussed the flow diagram in greater detail with Able and Baker, and revisions were made on the basis of information Middleton supplied about the present accounting system. Baker pointed out that all the alternative systems available to the company could be defined by the location of seven principal functions and records. Further analysis reduced this number to three: stock records, pricing of orders, and accounts receivable. The possible combinations of locations of these gave eighteen basic alternative systems, of which eight that were obviously undesirable were eliminated. Middleton was to make a cost analysis of the existing system and the most decentralized of the proposed systems, while the consultants were to begin costing the most centralized system.

Middleton reviewed these tentative decisions with the other members of the company committee, and the group divided up the work of costing. Middleton also reported to the controller on the conference, and the latter expressed his attitudes about the location of the various functions and the resulting implications for the development of executive responsibility.

During the next week, in addition to working on his current assignments, Middleton gave an equipment salesman a preliminary overview of the probable requirements of a new system. Next, there was a two-day meeting of the consultants and the company's committee to discuss the form and implications of a centralized electronic system. The consultants presented a method of organizing the records for electronic processing and together with the committee calculated the requirements which this organization and company's volume of transactions would impose on a computer. The group then discussed several problems raised by the system, including the auditing problems, and then met with the assistant controller to review the areas they had discussed.

On the following day, Middleton summarized progress to date for the controller, emphasizing particularly the work that had been done on the centralized system. The controller expressed satisfaction with several new procedures that would be made possible by an electronic computer. During the next several days the committee members continued to gather the information necessary to determine the cost of the present system. Middleton also checked with the assistant controller on the proposed solutions for certain problems that the consultants had indicated could not be handled readily by a computer and relayed his reactions to the consultants.

A week later the consultants returned for another series of meetings. They discussed changes that might be necessary in current practices to make centralized electronic processing possible and the way in which they would compare the centralized and decentralized proposals. The comparison presented some difficulties, since the data provided by the two systems would not be identical. A general form for a preliminary report was cleared with the assistant controller, and a date was set for its submission. The processing, outputs, and costs for the two alternatives would be described, so that additional information required for a final report could be determined.

During the next week Middleton continued collecting cost data. He phoned to the consultants to provide them with important new figures and to inform them of the controller's favourable reaction to certain proposed changes in the system that had implications for the company's policies.

On October 17 Baker met with Middleton to review the content of the accounting reports that would be produced by the centralized system, to discuss plans for the preliminary report, and to discuss the relative advantages and disadvantages of the centralized and decentralized systems. On the next day, Middleton checked on their decisions relative to the report with the controller and assistant controller and raised the possibility of an outside expert being retained by the company to review the final report submitted by Beta. During the last days of this week, Middleton attended the national meeting of a management society, where he obtained information about the availability of computers and computer personnel and the existence of other installations comparable to that contemplated for the company.

Work continued on the planning and costing of the two systems— Middleton worked primarily on the decentralized plan, and the consultants on the centralized. On October 27 the two consultants met with Middleton and they informed each other of the status of their work. Baker discussed methods for evaluating system reliability. Plans for the preliminary report were discussed with the company committee and the assistant controller. Since the controller strongly favoured decentralization of authority, the question was raised of the compatibility of this with electronic processing in general and with the centralized system in particular. The groups concluded, however, that centralization of purely clerical data-processing operations was compatible with decentralization of responsibility and authority.

After several meetings between the committee and the consultants to iron out details, the preliminary report was presented to the company committee, the controller, and the assistant controller on November 3. The report was devoted primarily to the centralized system. The following points were made in the oral presentation: (1) that both the centralized and decentralized proposals would yield substantial and roughly equivalent savings but that the centralized system would provide more and better accounting data; (2) that the alternatives had been costed conservatively; (3) that the centralized system involved centralization of paper work, not of management; (4) that not all problems raised by the centralized system had been worked out in detail but that these did not appear insurmountable; (5) that the centralized system would facilitate improved inventory control; and (6) that its installation would require nine to twelve months at a specified cost. At this meeting the group decided that in the final report only the two systems already considered would be costed, that the final report would be submitted on December 1, and that investigation of other accounting applications of the system would be postponed.

In informal conversations after the meeting the controller told Middleton he had the impression that the consultants strongly favoured the centralized system and that he believed the cost considerations were relatively minor compared with the impact the system would have on executives' operating philosophies. The assistant controller told Middleton he thought the preliminary report did not adequately support the conclusions. The committee then reviewed with the assistant controller the reasons for analysing in detail only the two extreme systems: the others either produced less information or were more costly.

The next day the committee met with the controller and assistant controller to determine what additional information should be requested for the final report. The controller outlined certain questions of practicability that the final report should answer and expressed the view that the report should contain a section summarizing the specific changes that the system would bring about at various levels of the organization. He thought the comparison between systems in the preliminary report had emphasized equivalence of savings, without detailing other less tangible benefits of the centralized system.

Middleton reported these discussions to the consultants and with them developed flow charts and organization charts for inclusion in the final report, settled on some intermediate deadlines, and worked up an outline of the report. Within the company he discussed with the controller and assistant controller the personnel and organizational requirements for installation of an electronic system and for operation after installation. Discussion focused on the general character and organizational location of the eventual electronic-data-processing group, its relation to the sales accounting division, and long-term relations with manufacturing accounting and with a possible operations research group.

On November 14 the controller, on recommendation of Middleton, attended a conference on automation for company senior executives. There he expressed the view that three to five years would be required for full installation of a centralized electronic system but that the fear of obsolescence of equipment should not deter the company in making the investment. He also concluded that a computer installation would not reverse his long-range program for decentralizing information and responsibility.

Middleton, his suggestion being accepted, made tentative arrangements with an independent expert and with two large computer companies for the review of the consultants' report. Middleton presented to the controller and assistant controller a memorandum he had prepared at the latter's request, establishing a new comparison of the centralized and a modified decentralized system. The modification made the two systems more nearly comparable in data-processing capacity, hence clarified the cost comparison, which was now in favour of the centralized system. Consideration of the possibility of starting with a partially electronic decentralized system as a step toward a completely electronic system led to the decision that this procedure had no special advantages. The controller reported that conversations with the sales manager and the president had secured agreement with the concept of removal of stock record-keeping from field locations—an aspect of the plan to which it had been assumed there would be sales department opposition. The group discussed several other specific topics and reaffirmed that the final report should discuss more fully the relative advantages and disadvantages of centralized and decentralized systems.

Toward the end of November there was further consultation on the report, and final arrangements for its review were made with the two equipment companies and the independent expert. Each equipment company was expected to determine the method for setting up the proposed system on its computer and to check the consultants' estimates of computer capacity. During this week the controller informed the company's management committee that the report from the consultants would be submitted shortly and would recommend a rather radical change to electronic data-processing.

The final report, which recommended installation of the centralized system, was submitted on December 1. The report consisted of a summary of recommendations, general description of the centralized system, a discussion of the installation program, and six appendixes: (1) statistics on volume of transactions (the twenty-three studies); (2) costs of the present system; (3) the requirements of a fully centralized system; (4) changes in allocation of functions required by the system; (5) an outline of the alternative decentralized system; and (6) a description of the existing system in verbal and flow-chart form. When the report was received and reviewed initially, the company's committee members and the consultants made some further computations on installation costs.

At a meeting the following Monday the assistant controller proposed an action program: send copies of the report to equipment companies, send copies to the sales department, and await the report of the independent expert. The controller decided that the second and third steps should be taken before giving the report to the machine companies, and the assistant controller indicated to Middleton some points requiring further clarification and elaboration.

By January 7 Middleton had prepared an outline for a presentation of the report to the sales department. This was revised on the basis of a meeting with the other interested accounting executives. A final outline was agreed upon after two more revisions and three more meetings. The report was presented on January 28 to the president and to six of the top executives of the sales department. The presentation discussed large-scale computers briefly, described with flow charts the proposed system, emphasized the completeness and accuracy of the information produced, discussed costs and savings, and mentioned the current trend in other companies toward electronic data-processing.

At Middleton's recommendation the same presentation was made subsequently to top members of the accounting department and still later to a group from the manufacturing department. At the same time the preliminary report of the independent expert was received, agreeing that the electronic installation seemed justifiable and stating that there might not be any cost savings but that it would make possible numerous other profitable applications of the computer. The consultants' report was then distributed to the computer companies, and Middleton began more detailed planning of the installation.

Middleton, the assistant controller, and the controller now met with the independent expert, who reported his conclusions: the feasibility study was excellent, the estimates of processing time were probably optimistic, the installation program should provide for an early test run, and the two principal available computers were highly competitive. Independent confirmation had been obtained on the last two points from another outside source. Middleton now proposed that the company proceed with its planning while awaiting the final written report from the independent expert and the proposals of the equipment companies. The assistant controller preferred to wait until these reports were actually in hand.

During the next week the equipment companies proceeded with their analysis, meeting several times with Middleton. Baker sent a memorandum on his estimates of processing time to meet the criticism of the independent expert. Middleton prepared two charts, one proposing a schedule and the staffing requirements for the installation phase, the other proposing organizational arrangements for the computer centre. Middleton and the assistant controller presented these to the controller at the beginning of February, discussion centering on responsibility for accuracy of input information.

Middleton and the assistant controller also had a meeting with sales executives, who reported that on the basis of their own internal departmental discussions of the consultants' report they were in general agreement with the program. Middleton and one of the other committee members then spent two days inspecting computer installations in two other companies.

In the middle of February the two equipment companies presented their reports, each bringing a team of three or four men to present their recommendations orally. The two recommendations were substantially alike (except for the brand of the machine recommended!), but one report emphasized the availability of its personnel to give help during the installation planning stage.

Discussions were held in the accounting department and with consultant Baker about these reports and the next steps to be taken. The question was debated whether a commitment should be made to one equipment company or whether a small group should continue planning the system in detail, postponing the equipment decision until the autumn. Most of the group preferred the former alternative.

On February 15 the controller, in conference with the assistant controller and Middleton, dictated a letter to the company's president summarizing the conclusions and recommendations of the study and requesting that the accounting department be authorized to proceed with the electronics program.

On the following day the controller read the letter to the management committee. The letter reviewed briefly the history of the project and summarized the conclusions contained in the consultants' report: that there was ample justification for an electronic-data-processing installation; that the installation would warrant use of the largest computers; and that it would produce savings, many intangible benefits, and excess computer capacity for other applications. The letter quoted the consultants' estimate of the cost of the installation and their recommendation that the company proceed at once to make such a conversion and to acquire the necessary equipment. It then cited the various cross-checks that had been made of the consultants' report and concluded with a repetition of the conclusions of the report—but estimating more conservatively the operating and installation costs—and a request for favourable management committee action. Supplementary information presented included a comparison of consultant and equipment company cost estimates and a list of present and proposed computer installations in other companies. After a few questions and brief discussion, the management committee voted favourably on the recommendation, and the controller informed Middleton of the decision when the meeting ended.

THE ANATOMY OF THE DECISION

From this narrative, or more specifically from the actual data on which the narrative is based, one can list chronologically the various activities of which the decision process is composed. If we wish to describe a program for making a decision of this kind, each of these activities might be taken as one of the steps of the program. If the rules that determined when action would switch from one program step to another were specified, and if the program steps were described in enough detail, it would be possible to replicate the decision process.

The program steps taken together define in retrospect, then, a program for an originally unprogrammed decision. The program would be an inefficient one because it would contain all the false starts and blind alleys of the original process, and some of these could presumably be avoided if the process were repeated. However, describing the process that took place in terms of such a program is a useful way of organizing the data for purposes of analysis.

In order to make very specific what is meant here by a "program",

Figure 2.1 has been prepared to show the broad outlines of the actual program for the first stages of the decision process (through the first seven paragraphs of the narrative).

Subprograms. The various program steps of the decision process fall into several subprograms, some of which have been indicated in Figure 2.1. These subprograms are ways of organizing the activities *post factum*, and in Figure 2.1 the organizing principle is the method of approach taken by the company to the total problem. It remains a question as to whether this organizing principle will be useful in all cases. As in the present example, these subprograms may sometimes be false starts, but these must be regarded as parts of the total program, for they may contribute information for later use, and their outcomes determine the switching of activity to new subprograms.

In this particular case the reasons for switching from one subprogram to another were either the proved inadequacy of the first one or a re-definition of the problem. Other reasons for switching can be imagined, and a complete theory of the decision process will have to specify the conditions under which the switch from one line of attack to another will occur.

Common processes. In the whole decision-making program there are certain steps or "routines" that recur within several of the subprograms;

> Keeping-up program (paragraphs 1 and 2 of narrative):
> Search for and correspond with experts;
> Discuss with salesmen and with equipment users;
> Search for and read journals;
>
> *Procurement program* (paragraph 3):
> Discuss applications study with salesmen who propose it;
> Choice: accept or reject proposed study;
> (If accepted) transfer control to salesmen;
> Choice: accept or reject applications proposal;
> (If rejected) switch to consultant program;
>
> *Consultant program* (paragraphs 4 through 7):
> Search for consultants;
> Choice: best consultant of several;
> Transfer control to chosen consultant:
> Choice: accept or reject proposal;
> (If accepted): begin double-check routine;
> Request expenditure of funds;
> (If authorized) transfer control to consultants;
> And so on.
>
> *Figure 2.1:   Program steps from inception of*
> *the problem to selection of a consultant*

they represent the basic activities of which the whole decision process is composed. For purposes of discussion we have classified these common processes in two categories: the first comprises processes relating to the communication requirements of the organization; the second comprises processes relating directly to the solution of the decisional problem.

Communication processes. Organizational decision-making requires a variety of communication activities that are absent when a decision is made in a single human head. If we had written out the program steps in greater detail, many more instances of contacts among different members of the organization would be recorded than are now explicit in the narrative. The contacts may be oral or written. Oral contacts are used for such purposes as giving orders, transmitting information, obtaining approval or criticism of proposed action; written communications generally take the form of memorandums having the purpose of transmitting information or proposing action.

The information-transmitting function is crucial to organizational decision-making, for it almost always involves acts of selection or "filtering" by the information source. In the present instance, which is rather typical in this respect, the consultants and subordinate executives are principal information sources; and the controller and other top executives must depend upon them for most of their technical information. Hence, the subordinate acts as an information filter and in this way secures a large influence over the decisions the superior can and does reach.

The influence of the information source over communications is partly controlled by checking processes—for example, retaining an independent expert to check consultants—which give the recipient an independent information source. This reduces, but by no means eliminates, filtering. The great differences in the amounts and kinds of information available to the various participants in the decision process described here emphasize the significance of filtering. It will be important to determine the relationship of the characteristics of the information to the resultant information change and to explore the effects of personal relations between people on the filtering process and hence upon the transmission of information.

Problem-solving processes. Alongside the organizational communication processes, we find in the narrative a number of important processes directed toward the decision problem itself. One of the most prominent of these is the search for alternative courses of action. The first activities recounted in the narrative—writing letters, reading journals, and so on—were attempts to discover possible action alternatives.

At subsequent points in the process searches were conducted to obtain lists of qualified consultants and experts. In addition to these, there were numerous searches—most of them only implicit in the condensed narrative—to find action alternatives that would overcome specific difficulties that emerged as detail was added to the broader alternatives.

The data support strongly the assertion made in the introduction that searches for alternative courses of action constitute a significant part of non-programmed decision-making—a part that is neglected by the classical theory of rational choice. In the present case the only alternatives that became available to the company without the expenditure of time and effort were the systems proposals made early in the process by representatives of two equipment companies, and these were both rejected. An important reason for the prominent role of search in the decision process is that the "problem" to be solved was in fact a whole series of "nested" problems, each alternative solution to a problem at one level leading to a new set of problems at the next level. In addition, the process of solving the substantive problems created many procedural problems for the organization: allocating time and work, planning agendas and report presentations, and so on.

Examination of the narrative shows that there is a rich variety of search processes. Many questions remain to be answered as to what determines the particular character of the search at a particular stage in the decision process: the possible differences between searches for procedural alternatives, on the one hand, and for substantive alternatives, on the other; the factors that determine how many alternatives will be sought before a choice is made; the conditions under which an alternative that has tentatively been chosen will be subjected to further check; the general types of search strategies.

The neglect of the search for alternatives in the classical theory of decision would be inconsequential if the search were so extensive that most of the alternatives available "in principle" were generally discovered and considered. In that case the search process would have no influence upon the alternative finally selected for action. The narrative suggests that this is very far from the truth—that, in fact, the search for alternatives terminates when a satisfactory solution has been discovered even though the field of possibilities has not been exhausted. Hence, we have reason to suppose that changes in the search process or its outcome will actually have major effects on the final decision.

A second class of common processes encompasses information-gathering and similar activity aimed at determining the consequences of each of several alternatives. In many decisions, certainly in the one we observed, these activities account for the largest share of man-hours, and it is through them that subproblems are discovered. The narrative suggests that there is an inverse relation between the cost or difficulty of this investigational task and the number of alternative courses of action that are examined carefully. Further work will be needed to determine if this relation holds up in a broader range of situations. The record also raises numerous questions about the *kinds* of consequences that are examined most closely or at all and about the conditions under which selection of criteria for choice is prior to, or subsequent to, the examination of consequences.

Another set of common processes are those concerned with the choices among alternatives. Such processes appear at many points in the narrative: the selection of a particular consulting firm from a list, the choice between centralized and decentralized electronic-data-processing systems, as well as numerous more detailed choices. These are the processes most closely allied to the classical theory of choice, but even here it is notable that traditional kinds of "maximizing" procedures appear only rarely.

In some situations the choice is between competing alternatives, but in many others it is one of acceptance or rejection of a single course of action—really a choice between doing *something* at this time and doing nothing. The first such occasion was the decision by the controller to assign Middleton to the task of watching developments in electronics, a decision that initiated the whole sequence of later choices. In decisions of this type the consequences of the single alternative are judged against some kind of explicit or implicit "level of aspiration"—perhaps expressed in terms of an amount of improvement over the existing situation—while in the multiple-alternative situations, the consequences of the several alternatives are compared with each other. This observation raises a host of new questions relating to the circumstances under which the decision will be formulated in terms of the one or the other of these frameworks and the personal and organizational factors that determine the aspiration levels that will be applied in the one-alternative case.

Another observation derivable from our data—though it is not obvious from the condensed narrative given here—is that comparability and non-comparability of the criteria of choice affects the decision processes in significant ways. For one thing, the criteria are not the same from one choice to another: one choice may be made on the basis of relative costs and savings, while the next may be based entirely on non-monetary criteria. Further, few, if any, of the choices were based on a single criterion. Middleton and the others recognized and struggled with this problem of comparing consequences that were sometimes measured in different, and incomparable, units, and even more often involved completely intangible considerations. The narrative raises, but does not answer, the question of how choices are made in the face of these incommensurabilities and the degree to which tangible considerations are overemphasized or underemphasized as compared with intangibles as a result.

CONCLUSION

We do not wish to try to transform one swallow into a summer by generalizing too far from a single example of a decision process. We have tried to illustrate, however, using a large relatively non-programmed decision in a business firm, some of the processes that are involved in business decision-making and to indicate the sort of theory of the choice mechanism that is needed to accommodate these processes. Our illustration suggests that search processes and information-gathering processes constitute significant parts of decision-making and must be incorporated in a theory of decision if it is to be adequate. While the framework employed here—and particularly the analysis of a decision in terms of a hierarchical structure of *programs*—is far from a complete or finished theory, it appears to provide a useful technique of analysis for researchers interested in the theory of decision as well as for business executives who may wish to review the decision-making procedures of their own companies.

3   Competition, Growth, and Efficiency*[1]

INTRODUCTION

There is a growing awareness in the United Kingdom of a conflict between size of firm and competition. That is, the size of the United Kingdom market is such that in many industries the number of firms of minimum optimal size which the market could support is not large enough to ensure effective competition. The importance of this conflict is found in the fact that for capitalist economies competition has been the "control mechanism" in the system. In other words, competition has been relied upon to force the economy to achieve certain objectives which are desired by society.

It is not possible to state the objectives of the economic system without the intrusion of personal values, but there are three objectives which would probably command general agreement.

The first is efficiency in the production of a given set of outputs. That is, with a given capital stock, a given technology and a given set of resource prices, firms should be producing goods and services with a minimum expenditure of the economy's resources. This condition implies that firms should utilize capital embodying the latest technological improvements as soon as it is economical for them to do so. It also implies that there must be resources devoted to improving the production processes through technical research and development, or that there is an information system which has access to such activities in other countries. In addition, resources should be devoted to the improvement of the management and administrative processes within the firm so that progress in the techniques of co-ordinating resources keeps pace with technical advances in production.

---

* Reproduced from *The Economic Journal* March 1969 by permission of Cambridge University Press, New York, NY.

A second objective relates to the need for the system to devote resources to product innovation. This objective includes the improvement of existing products and the development of new ones in both the producers' and consumers' markets.

A third objective is to pass on the fruits of efficiency and innovation in the system to society as a whole. This means that the gains should not take the form of excess profits or an economic rent but should rather be converted to benefits to the consumer in the form of lower prices and improved quality.

CONTROL MECHANISMS

The essence of a control mechanism is that it constrains in some way the freedom of opportunity of the individual economic actors in the system. In the perfectly competitive world of neo-classical economics, control comes from the pressure exerted by competition in the market in which the firm is selling. The system is designed so that there will be many firms selling the same product. The number of firms is large enough to eliminate collusion on price as an alternative behaviour pattern, and at the same time the number of consumers is so large that they cannot collude to force a reduction in the market price. Any profits above the normal level that the firm may command are passed on to consumers in the form of lower prices by the pressures exerted from other resources entering the market. The exit of resources when price is "too low" functions as a control to protect society from the waste of resources. The market, an objective and neutral force, contains the power in the system. Competition serves to reduce the discretionary alternatives that are available to a firm or, in other words, serves as a control on the behaviour of business management.

Perfect competition as a control device can achieve objectives one and three as listed above, but will not necessarily achieve two. There is nothing in the competitive model viewed as a control mechanism that can force firms to innovate in the same way that the model forces firms to be efficient or to leave the industry: perfect competition is neither a necessary nor a sufficient condition for innovation.[2]

A greater difficulty with dependence on competition as a control mechanism is made manifest from an examination of market structures which demonstrate the fact that the conditions necessary for competition to be effective have disappeared from many markets or have never existed. The number and size distribution of firms is frequently inappropriate, and in many markets conditions of free entry do not prevail. The last full-scale investigation of market structure in Britain was made by Evely and Little using the 1951 census data.[3] Out of 219 trades 90 (41 per cent) were classified as monopolistic or oligopolistic because of a small number of firms, a large size ratio and a high concentration or some combination of these factors; 69 trades (32 per cent) were on the borderline between being competitive and oligopolistic, and 60 (27 per cent) were classified as being competitive. Since 1951 the evidence suggests, although not conclusively, that the structure of markets has in general become more oligopolistic. In a study of structural change from 1951 to 1958 Armstrong and Silberston found that concentration had increased in 36 out of 63 comparable trades.[4] In 16 trades concentration had declined, and in the remaining 11 it showed no change or was indeterminate. Furthermore, over the post-war years an increasing proportion of the total capital outlay of quoted companies has been expended on acquisitions. Over the years 1959–66, 15 per cent of the total capital outlay of non-financial quoted companies took the form of expenditure on acquisitions, as compared to 8 per cent over the years 1953–8 and 4 per cent in the period 1949–52. This increasing importance of take-overs has accelerated during the past two years as shown by the fact that for three months of 1967 expenditure by quoted companies on acquisitions was only about £85 million less than the *annual* average for 1964–6. A large percentage of the mergers have also been within the existing product lines of the acquiring company and have therefore probably tended to increase concentration.[5]

Recognition of the absence in many markets of the structural conditions necessary for atomistic competition led to the concept of workable competition which "in a primary sense is the result of whatever gives rise to reasonably satisfactory or workable performance".[6] The latter is defined in terms of a set of ideals or norms relating to the important dimensions of performance, such as the relationship of price to cost, the cost of production and the degree of product differentiation. There is also a derived meaning of workable competition which "refers to patterns of market structure and conduct which may be expected to give

Table 3.1:   Acquisitions by non-financial quoted companies 1949–66 manufacturing, distribution, construction (average annual expenditure or percentage)

	Total capital outlay, £ million.	Expenditure on acquisitions	
		£ million.	% of total.
1949–52	984	38	4·0
1953–58	1,331	108	8·0
1959–66	2,519	351	15·0

rise to or be associated with workable performance".[7] However, short of assuming the structural characteristics of perfect competition, it is not possible to predict a unique association between structure, conduct and performance. A given type of conduct or performance may in fact be associated with a number of different types of market structures. The concept of workable competition suffers from the lack of a control mechanism which forces firms to behave in such a way as to achieve the desired objectives of the economic system. The absence of the structural conditions needed for atomistic competition and the absence of an alternative form of organization which can produce a unique, and desirable, relationship between structure, conduct and performance make it imperative that a search be instituted for supplementary control devices.

The case becomes even stronger when it is recognized that there is empirical evidence demonstrating that firms do not operate as efficiently as assumed in economic theory. Economists have tended to concentrate on allocative efficiency, assuming there is no problem of internal efficiency, since each output is produced at the lowest possible cost. We are not arguing that the possibility of internal misallocation of resources has never been recognized but rather that most economic reasoning has proceeded on the assumption of internal efficiency within the firm. The distinction between allocative and internal efficiency has recently been made by Leibenstein, who has also amassed an imposing amount of evidence to show the importance of internal or "X-efficiency". He argues as follows:

One idea that emerges from this study is that firms and economies do not operate on an outer-bound production possibility surface consistent with their resources. Rather they actually work on a production surface that is well within that outer-bound .... (Therefore) two general types of movements are possible. One is along a production surface towards greater allocative efficiency and the other is from a lower surface to a higher one that involves greater degrees of X-efficiency .... The data suggest that in a great many instances the amount to be gained by increased allocative efficiency is trivial while the amount to be gained by increasing X-efficiency is frequently significant.[8]

If the Leibenstein position is accepted it follows that efficiency should be viewed as a function of management rather than a function solely of the market. This is an important proposition, because it indicates that the nature of the control device we are seeking must be one that will directly affect the management process. This conclusion is further strengthened when the innovation process is examined. Carter and Williams, for example, have emphasized that research and development is a management technique that must be considered as an integral part of the total activity of the firm.[9] Similarly, the pricing policy of the firm, and thus the third objective, will be affected by a control mechanism in so far as the latter affects the motivation of management and the decision-making processes.

DECISION PROCESSES WITHIN THE FIRM

The theoretical arguments of some of the new approaches to the theory of the firm are relevant for understanding the kinds of behaviour mentioned above, and preparatory to developing a supplementary control mechanism to the traditional one of competition, we need to develop more explicitly a model of decision-making in the firm. This model is based on recent theoretical and empirical work on managerial decision-making within the firm, and its relevance increases as the market becomes less competitive.[10] The model can be described in the following terms:

1. The firm does not know its average revenue curve, its average total-unit-cost curve nor its marginal-cost curve with certainty and must make decisions on the basis of the best estimates it can get from its internal and external information systems.
2. The managerial coalition of the firm establishes a number of different goals it wishes to achieve in any decision period. These goals represent two major elements. First, the goals are the resultant of the best judgement of each of the members of the coalition as to the achievement necessary in sales, production and profit for the firm to survive and grow. Second, the goals represent the desires of the individual members of the coalition for the survival and growth of the individual sub-units they represent within the firm.
3. These goals are acceptable-level goals in the sense that they define the lower bounds of a feasible decision space. The set of decisions made on price, output, investment, production, inventories, employment and other items in the budget must be expected to achieve all the goals.
4. When available decision alternatives are not capable of achieving the vector of goals a search process is instituted by the firm. This search process is aimed at changing internal or external (or both) conditions to enable a set of decisions to be found that will achieve the goals.
5. The goals themselves are a function also of the level of achievement in the market. The achievement of the goals in one period will lead to increasing the appropriate goals in the next period. If, on the other hand, the firm is unsuccessful in achieving its goals it will institute a search process that will enable it, in prospect at least, to achieve them.

INTERNAL GROWTH AS A CONTROL MECHANISM

We are led to argue from the above analysis and the available empirical evidence that it is during the process of search that improvements in efficiency can be attained by the firm. Therefore a policy that induced firms to engage in an increased amount of search behaviour would lead to an increase in efficiency of operation of the firms. It follows from our analysis that the way to induce firms to exhibit more search behaviour is by stimulating them to raise goals to a higher level than would ordinarily be done. This line leads us to propose a growth policy of fiscal and monetary measures in particular which would stimulate firms to attempt to grow internally and to stimulate those firms already growing to increase their rate of growth.

The growth of firms has recently received much attention from economists.[11] In these studies many different measures of growth have been used, including net assets, profit, net output, sales and productive capacity. No one of these measures has a general claim to superiority, and for our purpose several different measures could be used. To be specific, however, we will measure growth by the percentage increase in the net output of the firm. By internal growth we will mean the increase in the net output of the firm when neither mergers nor acquisitions take place.

The way in which a growth policy would affect the firm can be envisaged by examining Figure 3.1. There the line G_π represents the profit goal as a function of time on the assumption that the goal of the

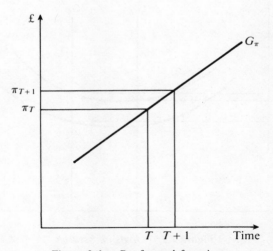

Figure 3.1: Profit goal function

previous period was attained. The form of the function will differ from firm to firm, and the goal value will be a function of a number of variables. These will include such factors as the profit of rivals, the evaluation of the market potential and the internal requirements of the firm. In drawing the profit goal function as a function of time alone we are assuming the other variables with fixed values. The function is given a positive slope in recognition of the natural drive of managers to have their firms grow. The net effect of a successful national growth policy of the kind we are discussing is to increase the slope of the goal function so that the firm is led to seek higher values for all its goals than it would have without the policy.

The relationship between goals and search can be seen from Figure 3.2. Assume that in period t the output goal of Q_t has estimated average unit costs equal to C_t and that this output at a given price of P and actual average unit costs of C_t produces the profit goal of π_τ. Estimated costs are treated as being equal to actual costs for simplifying purposes. In the next period, then, the profit goal is $\pi_{\tau+1}$ and the output goal, which is derived from a function analogous to G_π, is Q_{t+1}. Average unit costs are derived from the currently estimated average unit cost function and are estimated to be equal to C_{t+1}. When the output goal and the given price of P are used along with these costs it is determined that the profit goal will not be attained. It is at this point that the search routine is invoked by the firm. We assume that the search produces a new estimate of the average-unit-cost curve, C_2, and that the estimated costs are consistent with the profit goal. It is this criterion which provides the stop rule for

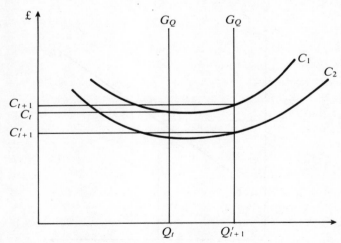

Figure 3.2:   Goals and search

the search. We would expect this kind of process to continue. If no shocks affected the system presumably the firm would closely approach the cost curve assumed in economic theory under the pressure of search to attain ever-increasing goals. However, the firm is also subject to the counter pressures of increasing costs as the result of continued attainment of goals and a relaxation of the motivation to be as efficient as possible. A further pressure for increased efficiency comes from the search activity which results from goal failure, i.e., when actual costs (or revenue) are not equal to estimated. When the firm fails to attain its goals it will search for improvements, just as it will when its estimates indicate that it cannot reach its goals.

In this context it is also interesting to use the notion of search to examine a process which establishes the familiar relationship between increases in output and efficiency as measured by output per head. Our theory would have these two variables highly correlated but could not select one as the causal variable with any consistency. On the basis of the decision process just described we should expect interaction between them, and in different circumstances either could be viewed as the causal variable in the sense of its occurring first. Assume, for example, an unexpected increase in the demand curve of the firm. The effect would be that the firm easily achieved its output goal, and its profit goal. To meet the increase in demand in the short run the firm may be forced to utilize some old equipment. In the next period the growth and profit goals would be raised and there might be more difficulty in achieving them. Eventually a search process will be needed to find a satisfactory decision set. When this is done it would be expected that the old equipment would be replaced and that other methods of improving productivity would be found, so that we go from increased output to increased efficiency. Without an increase in demand or with a fall in demand we should expect by similar reasoning to have the causal relationship reversed.[12]

We will not attempt to mass the evidence of the effectiveness of search, whether done in the face of impending goal failure or after the fact, and whether done by the firm's management directly or with the help of outside consultants. This evidence is now recorded in many places. The evidence covers a wide variety of cases. There is, for example, the report of M. W. Reder on the Ford Motor Co., which after losing about $50 million on operations during the first three quarters of 1946 announced that it had found methods of reducing operating costs (on a given volume of output) by about $20 million per year.[13]

O. E. Williamson made several detailed company studies of the search process in response to adversity. One of his descriptions is particularly appropriate to our discussion.[14]

Within nine months the number of employees had been cut by 20 per cent. This produced annual savings, before taxes, estimated at more than 10 million dollars. Further reductions have since been possible so that two years after the inception of the program, *with production unchanged*, the company reported:

1. *Return on investment: increased* by 125 per cent.
2. *Breakeven point: reduced* from 95 to 74 per cent.
3. Total *employment: decreased* by 25 per cent; salaried employees reduced by 32 per cent, hourly by 20 per cent.
4. *Payrolls: reduced* by 16 per cent or 12 million dollars.
5. *Overhead: reduced* from 14 million dollars to 12 million dollars scheduled to go to 8 million dollars.
6. *Headquarters employment: reduced* from 782 to 462 (with plans to decrease it to 362).

Results in a similar vein based on consultants' records are reported by J. Johnston. He calculated the net return on consultancy fees by dividing the net savings per annum on a job by the consultancy fee. The average return was 206%.[15]

In more general terms we should expect the search behaviour that is originated under the pressure of an internal growth goal to produce more efficient firm behaviour in three areas: (*a*) costs; (*b*) management; and (*c*) capital stock.

(*a*) The pressure which is created by higher goals which evoke search will lead to improved costs through two incentives. First, the firm will be striving to increase its capacity as a method of growing. This will mean that pressure will be exerted on existing facilities and their utilization. Efforts will be made to organize production in the way that will make the maximum utilization of existing plant and equipment possible. Secondly, there will be pressure to improve profits so that a constant retention ratio will still enable the firm to increase the dividend and increase the amount of internal finance available for expansion.[16]

(*b*) In the process of searching for solutions which will enable it to attain its goals, the firm will be forced to evaluate the managerial personnel in the various functions. Inevitably some will be viewed as inadequate and replacements sought. The firm will in this way tend to attract better managerial talent at all levels. There will be a society-wide tendency through this process to attract better people into management as opportunities increase and as restrictions decrease. The fact that an organisation is growing gives it an advantage over stable or contracting ones in attracting and holding good personnel because of the increased opportunities and resources available for members of the organization.[17]

(*c*) In a somewhat similar fashion, as the firm's management examines its productive facilities with a view towards improving its costs, the capital stock will tend to be upgraded. Old machines will be replaced where this replacement will result in lower costs. [18] As the rate of growth increases in the firm the greater will be the utilization of the capital and the more rapid will be the scrapping of non-economical equipment— usually the older capital. Therefore we would expect the age distribution of the capital stock of the growth firm to have a lower mean age and a lower variance than in firms of stable or declining size. As Meyer and Kuh have noted, "Firms that are on the downgrade as indicated by an aged capital stock typically do not reverse the trend, while the more dynamic firms continue to 'rejuvenate' their capital stock by investing at higher rates." [19]

DIVERSIFICATION

A growth policy for firms of the type envisaged in this chapter will invariably have the effect of stimulating firms to diversify. Diversification will be induced because it will often be difficult for the firm to grow at a faster rate than the rate of growth of the industry, and if a few firms are able to do so it means that other firms cannot. Therefore, as the firm searches internally for solutions which will enable it to achieve its increasing goals, it will inevitably be led to the possibility of entering other markets where the rate of growth will be greater. [20] The firm can enter new markets either by developing new products as part of the process of internal growth or by acquisitions. In this section we concentrate on diversification by internal growth, leaving the problem of growth by acquisition to be discussed in a later section.

As search activity for solutions consistent with the acceptable-level goals proceeds it is logical to expect the firm to be led towards an interest in research and development or to a policy of getting information on new developments from another company, either in the same economy or a different one. The most likely strategy to be followed is the allocation of funds to research and development activity. Not all research and development activity, of course, is for the purpose of diversification. If the original market of the firm is growing rapidly it is likely that the firm will concentrate its research and development activity on innovation in that industry. Only as the growth rate in the original market becomes insufficient to sustain the firm's growth potential will the firm become more interested in diversification. In this fashion internal growth supplements the competitive control mechanism, particularly when it provides new entry into established industries. In industries where barriers to entry are high, entry from the diversified firm may be the only kind possible, and since the diversified firm is a growing one and one which has already proved profitable, there should be few industries that are barred to it.

The diversified firm, motivated by a desire to maintain its rate of growth, has other virtues when viewed from the standpoint of control mechanisms. The strategy of such a firm is to enter a market that is growing and build its investment in that market as long as the rate of growth is increasing. When the rate of growth begins to decline the firm will be forced to move into other, faster-growing markets to maintain its rate of growth. Thus it would be possible for the large diversified firm to be small in every product market in which it sells; through internal growth such a large firm could diversify and maintain a high rate of growth, but at the same time it would not be a threat to the working of the competitive control mechanism in any market.

The most serious problem raised by diversification is the opportunity given to the firm to follow a variety of short-run strategies that will enable it to profit in the long run. The most obvious example is the possibility of gaining a market share in one market through unprofitable prices while higher profits from other markets are in effect subsidizing the loss market. This strategy, of course, is profitable in the long run only if the firm is able to acquire monopoly power in the market through the policy of unprofitable pricing and is then able to exploit the market. Such a policy, however, would probably require the firm to modify its original growth goals in favour of greater profit alone.

EMPIRICAL EVIDENCE

Our analysis leads us to expect a positive relationship between growth and efficiency. In so far as profitability or productivity can be used as a measure of efficiency, this conclusion is subject to empirical test. The statistical work that has been done in this area falls into two main groups. The first group examines the relationship between changes in output and output per head, differential changes in the latter being a measure of relative efficiency and in the former of relative growth. This index of relative efficiency is only a partial index, but the results of the analysis found by taking capital into account are not changed significantly.[21] On an industry basis the positive association between these two variables is well established.[22] On an individual-firm basis there is less evidence. However, Downie, in his book *The Competitive Process*, finds that on an individual firm basis there was "a very definite association in most industries between changes in productivity and growth"[23] for the periods 1935–48.

These statistical results do not tell us whether it is high output increases which cause high productivity gains or whether it is the latter which induce the former. But our analysis has shown either direction of causation to be consistent with the behaviour of a firm operating under a goal structure in which growth is a significant factor.[24]

The second group of empirical studies has examined the relationship between profitability and the rate of growth of firms in terms of assets. Here again, it is clear that the variation in profitability is an imperfect measure of variations in efficiency, part of the former reflecting differences in other factors, such as the degree of monopoly. However, profitability differences will on average be associated with efficiency differences in the same direction. The finding, therefore, in a number of studies, that growth and profitability are positively correlated is relevant to and consistent with our arguments relating to the relationship between growth and efficiency.[25]

Another significant point about these studies is that neither productivity nor profitability were found to be related significantly to the size of the firm. For instance, Downie found that "no association (between size of firm and productivity) can be distinguished when size is measured by employment," and the "result is in most cases not much stronger when size is measured by net output."[26] Again, in a recent study of the size, growth and profitability of United Kingdom companies between 1948 and 1960 it was found that "average profitability was on the whole (with some exceptions) lower the larger the size of the firm, but the difference in average profitability of firms between size classes was not found to be statistically significant at the 5 per cent level, by the usual tests, for most of the populations of firms considered."[27]

In addition to *average* profitability, however, there are significant differences in the *dispersion* of profit rates, the tendency being for the degree of dispersion to vary inversely with the size of the firm.[28] This finding has been explained by the fact that large firms are more diversified, and that the managements of large firms are more skilful in avoiding projects which result in losses, but at the same time are less adventurous and so lose the chances of making exceptional gains. Another important element in the explanation might be a greater capacity in the larger firm for offsetting falling profits due to adverse changes in conditions external to the firm by increasing internal efficiency. The finding, however, has no obvious implication one way or the other as far as allocative efficiency is concerned.

The statistical results relating to size and profitability do not imply that there are no economies of scale or that such economies are unimportant. Much work on economies of scale was summarised by Caleb A. Smith, who concluded that, with factor costs held constant, average costs of production decline with increasing size of plant, at least from small to medium size.[29] However, the same author concluded that:

Examination of the data that are available and that conceivably might be available shows that we cannot hope to make very satisfactory empirical studies of the long run cost function. I believe that if we asked the student of the data to tell us in detail just what cost differences exist between different types and sizes of plant and firm and what causes, if any, he could discover for those differences, the information would go farther to clarify the practical questions to which we seek answers than would studies of the relation of cost to size.[30]

This statement draws attention to two points of particular importance. First, as mentioned earlier, a great deal of evidence suggests that, between firms in the same field, there is substantial variation in output for similar amounts of capital and labour and for similar techniques.[31] This suggests the importance of such factors as differences in the quality and motivations of management. Secondly, there is the important distinction between the *potential* economies of scale which are available under "ideal" conditions and the *process of realising* these economies. The latter may be relatively easy or difficult, depending on such factors as the rate of growth of the industry and the quality of management which is available.

PRICING POLICY IN THE GROWTH FIRM

It is important to examine the implications of the growth-oriented firm for the prices paid by consumers. One argument is that the expanding firm will relate its short-run pricing policy both to the availability of finance for expansion and to the effects on future demand. The availability of finance, whether internal or external, depends on past profitability and future prospects as seen by the capital market. The firm, therefore, can increase the availability of finance by earning abnormal profits achieved both by cost reduction and price increase, with the extent of the latter depending upon the inelasticity of the demand curve in the relevant range. Price increases will, however, tend to decrease the rate of growth of the firm, and if growth is the major objective of the firm it will have to strike a balance between the effect of higher prices on the short-run availability of finance and the effect on the rate of growth of demand for the firm's products.[32]

It is not possible to predict the precise path the growth firm will take, but it is interesting to speculate on the comparative behaviour of an oligopolistic industry where growth is the main motivation of the firm, an oligopolistic industry with short-run profit as a goal and competitive industry, assuming for each one that there is a rightward shift of the demand curve.

For both the profit-maximizing industries, price policy will be based on current demand conditions, so that in Figure 3.3 the price for the competitive industry will be near to OC_1 in period 1 and the immediate response to the increase in demand to D_2 will be a price increase to OC_2, with the long-run adjustment resulting in a price of OC_1 assuming constant costs. For the profit-maximizing oligopolist the price in period 1 is OP_1 and in period 2 it is OP_2.

In the case of the oligopolistic industry with growth as the main motivating force, the firm will be concerned with the effect of the price charged in period 1 on the demand in period 2, so that price adjustments are likely to be a much less important short-run response to increases in demand. The price has to be consistent with the firm's growth aim. The firm may be assumed to have some idea as to the increase in market demand, its own goal in terms of market share, and what this implies in terms of growth, or it may simply have a goal of maximizing growth. At price OP^* the increase in demand will be AB, and this will require a certain amount of finance. This price will also be associated with a given profitability, which in turn, assuming a given dividend policy, is associated with the ability to raise finance. If profitability at price P^* is such as to enable the firm to raise the finance required to expand capacity to meet

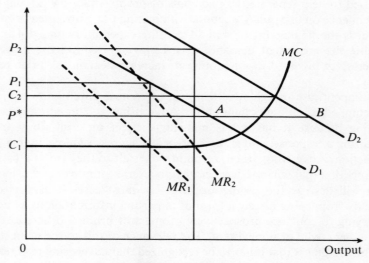

Figure 3.3: Price policy

the extra demand, then this price will be consistent with both the firm's dividend requirements and its requirements of finance for growth.

On the basis of pricing policy alone, therefore, it is likely that the relatively inflexible price of the growth-motivated firm will lie somewhere between the high and low points of the competitive industry, and it is possible that on average the prices and profits of the competitive industry and the growth motivated one will not be substantially different. Another interesting case arises where the combined need for finance to expand and low prices to foster growth can be met by inter-temporal price discrimination. Such a pricing policy might apply in particular to the introduction of a new commodity with the first lot of units sold at a high margin. The high price enables the firm to generate finance for further expansion, which is induced by allowing prices to fall more rapidly than costs over time. In this respect, the sequence of events is also similar to highly competitive situations, with high profits in the short run followed by low profits in the long run.

So far we have ignored the advertising and other sales-promotion expenditure of firms, and it is necessary to take these expenditures into account at this point. It would seem that one important aspect of advertising is that it is an attempt to separate the joint considerations of the firm's need for finance and future growth of demand.[33] If the policy weapons of the firm are restricted to price competition, then every proposed price change must be viewed with respect to its effect on short-run profitability and long-run growth of demand. Advertising can be used to help separate the two goals of profits and growth from their dependence on one policy weapon, with pricing policy oriented primarily towards the finance factor and advertising expenditure aimed at maintaining the growth of demand. This behaviour reduces the degree of uncertainty involved in attempting to increase demand by price reductions.

Competition through advertising is, of course, a well-known method of competing among oligopolists. Advertising is chosen rather than pricing because it has a less immediate effect on rivals in terms of requiring a response, and is therefore a less aggressive move than a price reduction. Advertising, then, recommends itself to the firm as a form of competition that will not degenerate into a series of moves and responses that will destroy the competing firms. In most cases it departs quite quickly from being merely a form of imparting information to a method of trying to convince prospective customers of product differences that are either trivial or nonexistent. The relevance of this to the main theme of this chapter is that it has to be recognized that advertising may tend to reduce the extent to which the policies of the growth firm will result in the passing on of gains in efficiency to the consumer.

EXTERNAL GROWTH AND GAINS IN EFFICIENCY

Our discussion so far has related to the internal growth of firms, but it is clearly important also to consider growth by acquisition and merger. Much of the debate on the desirability of a merger has focused on the problem of the tradeoff between the potential gains in efficiency and the danger of increased monopolization. We are concerned here with the question of efficiency only.

It is difficult to generalize about the efficiency gains or losses following from mergers, but our earlier discussion of growth and its association with efficiency does bring out some broad points which can be of use in developing a framework of analysis for thinking about this important issue.

First, there is need to distinguish between size and the process of attaining large size. We have argued that the most important elements of increased efficiency are associated with the process of growth rather than with size as such, so that the efficiency gains obtained simply by merging firms into larger units may be small.

Secondly, even if a merger does lead to substantial efficiency gains, account has to be taken of the time-lag between the merger and the realization of the gains. If the time-lag is of the order of, say, two or three years it must be recognized that a great deal could have been accomplished in the same period by internal growth. In this connection the nature of the market, and in particular the rate of growth of demand, is of importance. Thus in a rapidly expanding industry internal growth will be effective in increasing the size of the firm, and in particular the expansion of demand will provide the safety element, which is necessary to induce firms to undertake investment in increased capacity and in research and development. In a declining industry, on the other hand, and particularly one with a highly competitive market structure, there may be serious obstacles to the internal growth of firms, and the case for mergers can be quite strong. Such an industry may be characterized by chronic excess capacity because of the slow adjustment of capacity to the lower level of demand, a capital stock biased towards old equipment and a declining quality of management. In such a situation the major benefits from a merger are: (*a*) to encourage the scrapping of old machines and investment in new ones by reducing the degree of uncertainty associated with excess capacity, and (*b*) to increase the proportion of the industry's assets under the control of efficient managers.

Thirdly, the previous paragraph draws attention to the importance of management, and in particular to the fact that the loss of efficiency due to internal or managerial weaknesses might be large. The contention that mergers may strengthen the control mechanism in so far as they result in a change of management attitudes is a general point which in principle is applicable to all industries. However, the degree of urgency with which structural change is needed and the availability of feasible alternatives does vary according to the nature of the industry under consideration. Thus in a highly competitive market with little or no growth there may be strong arguments in favour of mergers which increase the concentration of resources controlled by the more efficient management teams, because the alternative of internal growth is likely to be slow and uncertain. Furthermore, internal growth in the growth-motivated firms may well take the form of diversification into the newer growth sectors of the economy, and while this in itself is to be desired, it does little to increase efficiency in the declining industry.

In expanding industries there will again be managements of differing degrees of efficiency, but in these cases the need to concentrate resources in firms which currently have the most efficient management is much less. The fundamental point is that in expanding sectors it is much more likely that the firms which fall behind will be able to find ways, often by the infusion of new management, of increasing their efficiency and thereby recreating favourable growth conditions. The search behaviour described in earlier sections of this chapter and also, for instance, Downie's analysis of the competitive process are consistent with the expectation that in expanding firms a setback to growth will be followed by remedial measures. The encouragement of mergers in order to concentrate resources in the hands of the management team which is currently the most efficient and growth motivated is a short-sighted policy which does not recognize the fact that the most efficient firm of today may in the future be superseded by another. Of course, a firm may be slow in improving its efficiency, but this may indicate not so much the desirability of an acquisition as the need to put pressure on management to improve performance. The same point can be made to qualify the argument that the capital market, and in particular the threat of a take-over bid, is an effective sanction against the inefficiency of management. Because in so far as a firm which currently has inefficient management is taken over, this in the long run many not in all cases be the change which results in the biggest gain in efficiency. Furthermore, a recent study of acquisitions has cast doubt on the assertion that the companies which are taken over are on balance those of relatively low profitability; "the evidence provided by our 1967 sample does not support the thesis that it is a distinct characteristic of the majority of companies being acquired to have a rate of return that is relatively low for the industry concerned."[34] An important feature of a large proportion of acquisitions is not that there is a consistent relationship between the profitability of the acquired and the acquiring company but the fact that the acquiring company is larger, and in particular has, in absolute terms, greater liquidity.

This brings us to the next point we wish to make about acquisitions and growth. The pattern of growth of the small firm indicates that there are critical points in development at which a major reorganization of management and finance has to take place in order to form a basis for sustained growth.[35] Even where management has recognized and accepted the need for organizational changes, substantial difficulties may face the firm attempting to grow by internal expansion when it is in a transitional phase; difficulties which in particular relate to recruiting new management personnel and in raising capital through outside finance. Firms in such a position are obviously susceptible to a take-over bid. There is a wide variety of methods for giving managerial and financial assistance to small companies, but there is no benefit in trying to detail the alternatives here. Suffice it to say that the long-run benefits from aid of this kind can be of real value to the economy. The growth of the small firm needs to be encouraged, and therefore a close control should be kept of take-over bids for the small growth company.

In an earlier section we drew attention to the benefits of growth by diversification. Diversification may be achieved by internal growth on the basis of the firm's own research effort, or by the acquisition of an already existing firm. It follows from the above that diversification by acquisition may not give the best long-run results.

SUMMARY AND CONCLUSIONS

In this chapter we have attempted to analyse the effects on the behaviour of the firm resulting from governmental policies designed to encourage the internal growth of firms. We have not attempted to spell out the kinds of measures necessary to achieve internal growth, since that would take us beyond the scope of this chapter. Our analysis has rather been concerned with trying to determine the benefits from a policy that was successful in stimulating firms to achieve growth. We were led to an investigation of internal growth in firms by the need for control mechanisms in the economy to supplement the traditional one of competition. Our basic argument can be summarized in the following steps:

1. Western capitalist societies have relied upon a competitive economic system to achieve the objectives of efficiency, innovation and the passing on of the resulting gains to the society.
2. There is evidence that the structure of large sectors of the United Kingdom economy is oligopolistic. In these markets we cannot assume that competition will provide an effective control mechanism.

3. Many studies have shown that internal efficiency is not at the level generally assumed in economic theory. In addition, there is evidence that much innovation is subject to managerial discretion rather than forced by the market.

4. From our knowledge of the decision-making process in firms it is evident that the efficiency of firms is improved through a search process which is invoked when firms fail to attain their goals or when it is anticipated that goals will not be attained.

5. Firms can be forced to search more frequently than usual by a policy that induces them to set higher goals.

6. In these circumstances it is highly likely that firms can be induced to utilize research and development activities in an attempt to grow more rapidly, and particularly in an attempt to grow by diversification.

In other words, we see the need for policies which will act directly upon managers rather than through the market, which has been the traditional way of attacking the problem. At the same time we are not advocating the elimination of competition but rather the supplementing of competition by the encouragement of internal growth.

We have shown that internal growth enables firms to improve efficiency by taking advantage of any economies of scale that might exist, by the more rapid application of new techniques and by the introduction of new people into management. Furthermore, the diversification element in growth which is stimulated by research and development activities is important in reducing entry barriers. The encouragement of internal growth may also have the beneficial effect of loosening collusive behaviour in tightly knit oligopolistic industries.

Finally, internal growth will not destroy itself as a control mechanism because of its inevitable tendency to force firms to diversify to gain the advantages of the growth policy. Diversification will make it difficult for individual firms to achieve positions of dominance in any particular market. Thus internal growth as a control mechanism will function as a supplementary control device to competition. The problem remaining, which is neither to be viewed as trivial nor impossible, is to devise the broad set of policies which will stimulate managers directly to seek internal growth for their firms.

NOTES

1. We are indebted to A. B. Atkinson, A. Beacham, M. Lovell, R. L. Marris, A. Silberston, O. Williamson and G. Whittington for helpful comments on an earlier version of this chapter, and to the John Simon Guggenheim Memorial Foundation for financial support.

2. In view of our later argument, the concept of efficiency, that is operating on the lowest possible average-unit-cost curve, in the competitive system should be clarified. The argument in the competitive model assumes that the most efficient size plant and the most efficient organization of resources is known. Given this assumption, then, it is always possible to demonstrate that any firm deviating from the most efficient pattern will be forced from the industry.

3. R. Evely and I. M. D. Little, *Concentration in British Industry* (Cambridge: Cambridge University Press, 1960), pp. 8–25.

4. A. G. Armstrong and A. Silberston, 'Size of Plant, Size of Enterprise and Concentration in British Manufacturing Industry, 1935–58', *Journal of the Royal Statistical Society*, Series A, Vol. 128, Part 3, 1965, p. 404.

5. This information and the data shown in Table 3.1 are taken from H. B. Rose and G. D. Newbould, 'The 1967 Take-Over Boom', *Moorgate and Wall Street*, Autumn 1967.

6. J. S. Bain, *Industrial Organization* (New York: John Wiley and Sons, 1959), p. 15.

7. *Ibid.*

8. H. Leibenstein, 'Allocative Efficiency versus X-efficiency', *American Economic Review*, Vol. 56 (1966), p. 413.

9. C. F. Carter and B. R. Williams, *Industry and Technical Progress* (London: Oxford University Press, 1957), pp. 47–60.

10. R. M. Cyert and J. G. March, *A Behavioral Theory of the Firm* (Englewood Cliffs: Prentice Hall, 1963), pp. 114–28; H. A. Simon, 'A Behavioral Model of Rational Choice', *Quarterly Journal of Economics*, Vol. 69 (1955), pp. 99–118.

11. See E. T. Penrose, *The Theory of the Growth of the Firm* (Oxford: Basil Blackwell, 1963); R. Marris, *The Economic Theory of 'Managerial' Capitalism* (London: Macmillan, 1964); W. J. Baumol, 'On the Theory of the Expansion of the Firm', *American Economic Review*, Vol. 52 (December, 1962), 1078–87; J. Williamson, 'Profit, Growth, and Sales Maximization' , *Economica*, February 1966, pp. 1–16.

12. If the fall in demand is a result of a long-run decline in the industry there is less certainty that the increase in efficiency will be followed by an increase in output.

13. M. W. Reder, 'Marginal Productivity Theory Reconsidered', *Journal of Political Economy*, Vol. LV (1947), p. 453.

14. O. E. Williamson, *The Economics of Discretionary Behavior: Managerial Objectives in a Theory of the Firm* (Englewood Cliffs, N.J.: Prentice Hall, Inc., 1964), p. 95.

15. J. Johnston, 'The Productivity of Management Consultants', *Journal of the Royal Statistical Society*, Series A, Vol. 126, Part 2, 1963, pp. 245–6.

16. Regardless of the stock-market theory subscribed to, it is clear that an increased dividend will not hurt the firm's chances of raising outside capital for expansion.

17. H. A. Simon, D. W. Smithburg and V. A. Thompson, *Public Administration* (New York: Knopf, 1950).

18. W. E. G. Salter, *Productivity and Technical Change* (Cambridge: Cambridge University Press, 1966), pp. 74–82.

19. J. Meyer and E. Kuh, *The Investment Decision* (Cambridge, Mass.: Harvard University Press, 1957), pp. 99–100.

20. Penrose, *op. cit.*, pp. 104–52, for an excellent discussion of diversification.
21. W. B. Reddaway and A. D. Smith, 'Progress in British Manufacturing Industries in the Period 1948–1954', *Economic Journal*, March 1960, p. 29.
22. Salter, *op. cit.*, pp. 106–13.
23. J. Downie, *The Competitive Process* (London: Gerald Duckworth & Co., 1958), p. 181. No. 313—Vol. LXXIX.
24. On the general interaction between output and productivity see W. B. Reddaway's Addendum to Salter, *op. cit.*, pp. 207–8.
25. See K. D. George, 'A Note on Profitability, Concentration, Barriers to Entry and Growth', *Review of Economics and Statistics*, May 1968, Vol. L, No. 2, pp. 273–5; A. Singh and G. Whittington, *Growth, Profitability and Valuation* (Cambridge: Cambridge University Press, 1968), pp. 148–90; R. L. Marris, 'Incomes Policy and the Rate of Profit in Industry', University of Cambridge, Department of Applied Economics, Reprint Series No. 238.
26. Downie, *op. cit.*, p. 182.
27. Singh and Whittington, *op. cit.*, p. 144. In a recently published article J. M. Samuels and D. J. Smyth conclude that 'profits rates and firm size are inversely related'. 'Profits, Variability of Profits and Firm Size', *Economica*, May 1968, p. 139.
28. Samuels and Smyth, *op. cit.*, p. 134.
29. C. A. Smith, 'Survey of the Empirical Evidence on Economies of Scale', in *Business Concentration and Price Policy* (Princeton: Princeton University Press, 1955), p. 229.
30. *Ibid.*, p. 223.
31. Leibenstein, *op. cit.*, p. 404.
32. See, for instance, R. J. Ball, *Inflation and the Theory of Money* (London: Allen and Unwin, 1964), pp. 109–16.
33. See W. J. Baumol, *Business Behavior, Value and Growth* (New York: Macmillan, 1959).
34. Rose and Newbould, *op. cit.*, p. 17.
35. Cf. E. A. G. Robinson, *The Structure of Competitive Industry* (Cambridge: Cambridge University Press, 1958), pp. 105–6. Professor Robinson there defines the 'pessimum' size of a firm as that size 'which combines the technical disadvantages of smallness with the managerial disadvantages of being too large for individual control'.

Part II
Theory

4 Theory of the Firm: Past, Present, and Future; An Interpretation*

with Charles L. Hedrick†

Fritz Machlup, in his 1966 presidential address to the American Economic Association [18, 1967], attempted to look at the theory of the firm in perspective. As a former combatant in the battle to defend virtue, his account was really an attempt to show how much territory was left in the hands of the marginalists.

Hence, even if the "partial equilibrium analyst" knows full well that the actual situation is not really a competitive one, he probably will still make a first try using the competitive model with good old-fashioned profit maximization. And if the results appear too odd, appropriate qualifications may still be able to take care of them more simply than if he had started with a cumbersome managerial model. (In saying this, I am showing my bias.) [18, p. 30]

More recently we have seen a survey of micro-economics through curmudgeonly eyes [25, Shubik, 1970]. This survey was essentially a look at various broad approaches that have been taken to micro-economic problems and concluded with a "plague on all your houses" pronouncement.

We have our own view of which approaches have been successful and what needs to be done now. This view will become apparent soon enough. But we think it is important that such discussions take place against a background of understanding what economists are actually doing when they do research on developing descriptive theories of the firm. This chapter will attempt to fill in some of that background. First, it will be desirable to make some comments about the theoretical context of current writing.

* Reprinted by permission of *Journal of Economic Literature*,
† Charles Hedrick was supported during this research by a National Science Foundation Graduate Fellowship. The authors wish to thank D. Cass, R. Lucas, M. Shubik, and R. Weil for their constructive criticisms.

In one sense the controversy over the theory of the firm has arisen over a non-existent entity. The crux of micro-economics is the competitive system. Within the competitive model there is a hypothetical construct called the firm. This construct consists of a single decision criterion and an ability to get information from an external world, called the "market" [8, Cyert and March, 1963, pp. 4–16]. The information received from the market enables the firm to apply its decision criterion, and the competitive system then proceeds to allocate resources and produce output. The market information determines the behaviour of the so-called firm. None of the problems of real firms can find a home within this special construct. There are no organizational problems nor is there any room for analysis of the internal decision-making process. In fact, all of the empirical content in this neo-classical model lies in the description of the environment within which the firm must operate. Even the sole objective of the firm, profit maximization, is determined by the environment because any other behaviour of the firm will lead to its extinction. The theory of the firm is *a priori* in the sense that its behaviour can be deduced from assumptions that describe the environment.

More empirical content can be given to the theory of the firm in two ways. First, the assumptions describing the environment can be made more realistic with a resulting increased complexity of firm behaviour e.g., inventory control. If no more detail is added concerning the behaviour of the firm other than by changing the assumptions describing the environment, the theory remains *a priori* as the term is used above. The second way to add empirical content is to specify some aspects of the firm's behaviour directly. These models cease to be *a priori* since the firm's behaviour is no longer deduced from the assumptions describing the environment.

The two major revisionist approaches that have been attempted so far, the behavioural and the managerial, fall into the second category. The behavioural approach concentrates on making empirical analyses of decision processes of individual firms and incorporating the results into models of the firm. The managerial approach incorporates within the objective function the results of empirical observations of individual firm behaviour. The firm is assumed to maximize the function as in the standard approach. Both approaches utilize behavioural knowledge but the models differ in form. The behavioural model contains explicit decision rules (generally excluding maximization). By proper manipulation of the objective function one can derive from managerial models some of the broad conclusions of the behavioural models.

The purpose of this chapter is to determine from current writings the extent to which neo-classical theory is being extended in an *a priori* manner and the extent to which it is being replaced by one of the revisionist approaches.

Our approach has been to survey the literature of the last two years and to categorize the articles. We have examined every article related to the theory of the firm appearing in the *American Economic Review*, the *Journal of Political Economy* and the *Quarterly Journal of Economics* for 1970 and 1971 (I–III). We have not prejudiced our results by selecting only those articles of special interest to us or viewed as important by some other criterion. We have attempted to classify those articles that showed a definite model of the firm [1] according to the degree to which that model agrees with or departs from neo-classical theory. The bulk of this chapter is concerned with explaining the resulting classifications and examining in some detail illustrative examples of each.

This survey is biased in two major ways. First, it fails to show the large amount of effort that has gone into articles that make useful comments about the theory of the firm but do not use explicit models that we could classify.[2] Second, there is bias in our use of only three journals, even though we picked three journals that are widely read by American economists. Many of the models that are most directly responsive to the behavioural challenge, particularly computer simulations, are being published in other places.[3]

UNMODIFIED NEO-CLASSICAL APPROACH

The unmodified neo-classical approach is characterized by an ideal market with firms for which profit maximization is the single determinant of behaviour. Thus predictions can readily be made by combining the description of the market with the results of maximization of the relevant Lagrangian. Constraints such as limited information processing ability of the participants are excluded from models taking the neo-classical approach. It is basically a deductive rather than inductive approach to describing the firm, in the sense that it does not use empirical observations of the behaviour of the firm as inputs for developing models.

S. R. Dittrich and R. H. Myers [9, 1971] intend their paper on Chinese agriculture in 1937–40 to answer the question of whether traditional agriculture is properly described by the neo-classical theory of the firm. Since optimal allocation of labour and capital could gain only about 6 per cent in income, they conclude that neo-classical theory approximates the actual behaviour fairly well. There are two problems with this approach. The first comes from the attempt to short-circuit the "as if" arguments and check profit maximization directly. In fact it would be convincing evidence that the neo-classical model did hold if it were shown that profit actually was maximized by a set of firms meeting the requirements placed on the theoretical firms. But a negative result is inconclusive in the light of the "as if" justification. Second, the main purpose of neo-classical theory is to predict the behaviour of major economic variables. The size of the discrepancy between the observed result and the theoretical maximum is an ambiguous measure for validating the theory since there is no way of relating the size of the profit discrepancy to the deviation of price and output from their predicted values. For example, Dittrich and Myers are unconcerned by a 6 per cent gap in income between actual and what would result from optimum allocation of resources. Other writers might conclude that a 3 per cent gap is evidence of gross misallocation [29, Thornton, 1971].

Another article fitting this classification is one by P. L. Swan [28, 1970]. It is a treatment of the influence of monopoly on the introduction of new products. Swan shows the sufficiency of certain conditions on the demand function to prove that a monopoly and a competitive market produce the same products from a range of available products, with given technology. He finds these conditions to be reasonable ones. Furthermore, he shows that a likely result of violating them is a speedup of introduction of new products by the monopoly compared to the competitive market. Machlup [18, 1967] had reservations about whether the neo-classical model was applicable to monopolies and duopolies; the number of participants is small enough so that their individual natures may become relevant. In fact this is probably more serious for duopoly than monopoly. As will be seen below, in the case of duopoly there is not even a unique neo-classical solution, and we have no choice but to talk about strategy. In the case of a monopoly, however, there is no opponent to predict, so the situation is simpler. It is true that the behaviour of a monopoly may be greatly influenced by unique policies and other attributes of that particular firm. Nevertheless, if we ignore these individual peculiarities we may get predictions that will be true of an "average" monopoly. Hopefully, the difference between the predictions of this model and a competitive model will correctly represent the difference in the real world averaged over several industries. There will be circumstances, such as policy debates, when we are interested in knowing what behaviour is a direct result of monopoly, and we will be willing to forgive efforts in prediction of any specific case due to a failure to represent idiosyncratic behaviour.

SIMPLE EXTENSIONS OF THE NEO-CLASSICAL APPROACH

Many papers are based on fairly straightforward modifications of the neo-classical method. They extend the model to deal with "real-world" issues not faced by the simple text-book models, but retain the *a priori* character, in that all of the detail added is descriptive of the environment. The firm's behaviour is still deduced from the assumption describing the environment. In fact, many of these models are motivated by the desire to show that the neo-classical model can explain events that seem on the surface to be explainable only by behavioural rules. Even assuming that these models describe correctly the reaction of real participants under the postulated conditions, there is still a major problem. To build a neo-classical model dealing with every possible complication simultaneously is an obvious absurdity. But the choice of which ones are most important can also be a difficult task, especially if the effects of different complications interact.

One of the simplest extensions was done by Y. Barzel [2, 1970]. The objective of his paper was to determine whether the existence of non-price competition had any effect on the validity of the argument that monopolistic competition leads to inefficient operation. He proceeds by considering increased quality or advertising to be utility-producing for the buyer. Thus the buyer is really getting a bundle of two goods, the basic good and a non-price component. The effect is to add another dimension to the argument, which can be carried through in the same way as without the non-price component. This approach seems to be safely within the neo-classical methodology.

W. D. C. Wright [32, 1971] makes another extension which formally is no more significant than Barzel's. Wright considers the effect of plant location on prices of inputs and outputs. Transportation costs will be a large part of the effect, but there may be additional labour costs involved in attracting workers to an out-of-the-way location. This location dependence can be added to the profit function in a fairly straight-forward way, and then conventional maximization done. The result of the approach is to develop expressions for the partial derivatives of the plant location and output with respect to transportation costs, etc. The difference between this extension and Barzel's is that this one is in an area where individual plants must be analysed. Unless the author is trying to predict an industry-wide "centre of gravity", this model must be applied directly to real-world plants. The paper runs the risk of confusing firms as theoretical constructs for building neo-classical models with real firms. The plant location decision would seem a particularly dangerous place to follow a static maximization approach since the decision involves more qualitative factors (future tax policy of city and state governments, attitudes toward pollution control, etc.) than the day-to-day decisions that are the usual subject for neo-classical models. Of course, the model also deals with the effect of changes of location-dependent costs on output, but it would seem that the unextended model could handle those costs, too.

Even further along the dimension of increasing realism in treating actual details is a model by W. H. L. Anderson [1, 1970]. It is an attempt to explain the response of employment to seasonal production variations. Inventories, both of finished goods and intermediate goods, can be used to smooth production. He views the actual production decision as a result of trading off inventory holding costs against a quadratic labour cost function. For a given time-path of sales, he uses the calculus of variations to minimize cost. Although this model takes into account more complications, and uses mathematical methods that are somewhat foreign to neo-classical models, it is probably more nearly in the neo-classical spirit than Wright's. The complications it deals with are characteristic of the entire industry, and are not entwined with individual firm policy. Even though the process they use is given more internal structure, the firms in the model remain constructs. Nevertheless, this model is not the only one that might be used for explaining seasonal labour variations. The assumptions of quadratic labour cost and no adjustment costs are not the only ones that will led to similar results. If we want to keep the model as simple as possible, we will probably want to use only one of the possible explanations. But with the "as if" philosophy prevalent in neo-classical circles, it is not clear how such a decision should be made. To be fair, we should point out that one of the main purposes of the article seemed to have been to point out that lack of uniqueness. It has been believed by some that labour-force adjustment costs were "the" explanation of the fact that the labour force varied less than sales, and this model was designed to show that the phenomenon could be explained without postulating adjustment costs.

MODIFICATIONS OF THE OBJECTIVE FUNCTION

One way to break a little more cleanly with the neo-classical approach than the models previously discussed, is to change the objective function. This modification can be made by substituting another entity (sales, for example) for profits and then proceeding to maximize the new entity. A second way is to substitute a utility function (which includes the effects of several entities) for profit and proceed to maximize utility. The latter approach enables one to introduce arguments into the utility function that have been ignored by neo-classical theory. Both of these approaches were characterized as "managerial" in the introduction. A third approach in modification is to add a constraint to the objective function.

The first approach has been taken by W. J. Baumol [3, 1959]. Since his work has received sufficient attention, it will not be discussed here. It is of interest to note that in our survey of recent journal articles we do not find any that follow the first approach.

The second approach stems from O. E. Williamson's work and although it is not in our survey, we will briefly discuss a model taken from his recent book that is a prototypical example [30, 1970]. Williamson develops a utility function, $U = U(S, p - p_0 - T)$ where S is staff, p is profit, p_0 is minimum profit, and T is lump sum taxes. He then proceeds to maximize this function. He is able to make some interesting predictions about the different effects of various kinds of taxes. This model has great formal similarity to neo-classical models, and we might be tempted to consider it just another extension. In fact, however, it is an attempt to include behavioural characteristics in the model. No longer is an objective view of the economic task sufficient to determine behaviour. Some empirical evidence will be needed about the way management perceives its task and whether it has private objectives that it tries to achieve along with the task. It does have one advantage over an entirely behavioural model, however. Only one behavioural mechanism need be chosen, the rest of the model being neo-classical. One need not try to build a detailed behavioural model that explains every action of the firm, but only find one important factor and add it to an already existing framework. That should not blind us to the fact that the results of the model really are the consequences of the behavioural content. The response of this model to various kinds of taxation is different from a purely neo-classical model's. That difference is why the model is exhibited in the first place, and it is clearly due to Williamson's changing of the objective function to fit his ideas about "slack."

J. P. Newhouse [22, 1970] takes a similar, if less formal, approach in trying to explain the behaviour of hospital management. For a non-profit organization, maximization is not a relevant goal at all, so rather than just supplement it with other goals, he replaces it. He views the objective of hospital management as being a combination of quantity and quality of services rendered, constrained by a certain maximum deficit. The addition of the quality component allows him to explain overinvestment in expensive, "prestigious" equipment, as well as differences in the type of care given by non-profit and profit-making hospitals. Again, although neo-classical machinery is used, the objective function is such as to have it used for behavioural purposes.

There are other things that one can do to the objective function (besides changing it). E. E. Zajac's article [33, 1970] deals with the Averch-Johnson model of regulated utilities. In this case rather than change the objective function, he adds a constraint: percentage return on capital cannot exceed some "fair return" set by the regulating agency. The result is that profit maximization leads to the use of more capital and less labour than is otherwise optimal for the firm. Although this model may seem to have a behavioural flavour, it probably should be viewed as neo-classical. The fair return constraint, after all, is imposed from the outside and is part of the objective economic situation for the management. Given that situation and profit maximization, this model follows, with no need for consideration of the actual nature of the firm. The field of public utilities is, of course, an appropriate place for a behavioural approach, and Zajac mentions several alternatives to the Averch-Johnson model. These must all depend upon some alternative to profit maximization, however, and so are clearly on a different plane.

GENERALIZED MAXIMIZATION TECHNIQUES

Having considered extensions within a strictly neo-classical structure, and then changes in the objective function, we now consider models that do not use the ordinary maximization methods, although their intent is still the same. These methods arise in an attempt to extend neo-classical models to cases where there is uncertainty. In general these models maximize expected profit. Such an approach is not the only course that could be followed, even by an organization whose sole concern was profit, so in a sense it is a behavioural assumption, and any model using it lacks the *a priori* character of the usual neo-classical models. However, writers generally tend to view maximization of expected profit as the rational alternative under uncertainty, and any other hypothesis as having a behavioural colour.

Even if the firm's attitude towards profit is not adequately represented by its expected value, as long as the attitude is self-consistent in the sense described by the von Neumann-Morgenstern axioms, it can still be handled relatively easily. An article by A. Sandmo [24,1971] is one example. In fact, a firm whose attitudes meet these conditions will maximize the expected value of some increasing function of the profit. This device allows some general statements to be made. However, to get any interesting results it is necessary to make an assumption about the shape of the function of profit. Sandmo assumes it is convex, which corresponds to an attitude of risk aversion. An example of the kind of result obtained is the prediction that output decreases as fixed costs increase. Of course this result is critically dependent upon the convexity of the utility function. This must be called a behavioural assumption in the same sense as the addition of staff to the objective function by Williamson. It has the same disadvantage of requiring empirical evaluation and the same advantage of attaching only a single behavioural assumption to an otherwise *a priori* model.

The other two papers in this section deal with the duopoly problem. As is well known, the difficulty with the duopoly situation is that there is no solution that can deserve to be called the neo-classical solution. The optimum strategy depends upon the reactions of the other duopolist, and there is no obvious optimum way to predict that. D. K. Osborne [23, 1971] summarizes the situation from the point of view of game theory. There is a set of widely known strategies, and if one knows that the other duopolist is using one of these strategies, there is an optimum strategy to use against it. There is also a maximum solution, but in many cases the opponent will not be acting to minimize one's gain, since it is a co-operative game. There are also Pareto optimal solutions, which Osborne seems to think are the most relevant. In fact he draws policy implications from them, recommending policies which prevent the occurrence of conditions that make one particularly socially inefficient set of strategies Pareto optimal. Although one would certainly not call this a neo-classical paper, it is in a sense trying to use game theory to maximize profits. No other behavioural rules are invoked than ones relevant to game theory.

It turns out that much of the difficulty of duopoly is due to the usual assumption that decisions must be made simultaneously by the two participants, neither knowing the other's decision until he has made his. By assuming that the participants make their decisions at the beginning of alternating periods, and follow the same decision for two periods, Cyert and M. H. DeGroot [6, 1970] were able to come up with a single explicit solution. Although this solution is certainly closer to being derived from *a priori* assumptions than is, say, the Cournot solution, it should be emphasized that it is based upon a particular behavioural assumption. Each participant is assumed to make the decision that maximizes his total long-run profit if the other participant also makes his decision this way. This seems generally consistent with the neo-classical attitude, but the assumption that each participant expects the other to maximize profits is not imposed by the environment. With these provisions, dynamic programming allows an explicit solution to be derived by working back from the final period. Fortunately the solution approaches an asymptote as it gets away from the final period, so that the horizon can be allowed to go to infinity. Another indication that this is not really a unique neo-classical solution is the fact that neither firm is as well off as it could be with explicit or implicit collusion. The authors [7, Cyert and De-Groot, 1971] showed how this co-operative situation could develop from the dynamic programming solution mentioned here by a process of Bayesian learning. This model represents to some extent a merging of behavioural assumptions into a model in such a way that mathematical methods can still be used for the analysis.

NON-MAXIMIZING MODELS

Finally, we come to two papers that are explicitly non-maximizing. This is not to say that they postulate irrational behaviour or behaviour resulting from altruism or other non-profit motives. Some effort is spent in both papers to justify the *ad hoc* rules used, from the point of view of a firm trying to maximize its profits. Nevertheless, the authors apparently feel, for one reason or another, that they cannot account for the full range of behaviour by explicit maximizing models.

The first such model to be considered here is in a paper by R. L. Miller [20, 1971]. It is an attempt to account for seasonal employment in the textile industry. The author views firms as holding "inventories" of unused labour during the off-peak periods. The reason for holding the inventory is the avoidance of costs involved in adjusting the labour force. To some extent there is also a trade-off between labour inventory and goods inventory, since if the holding and adjustment costs of the latter were negligible it would be possible to have completely smooth production, hence no need for labour inventories. The model takes the form of two sets of simultaneous equations: one for peak periods, the other for off-peak periods. Goods inventories are set by a theoretically-motivated inventory equation. Employment and hours during the peak are determined by minimizing a quadratic cost function. During off-peak periods an *ad hoc* demand for reserve labour equation is used, a function of anticipated future sales, product inventories, wages, product inventory adjustment cost, and a trend term. The model does not assume instantaneous adjustment, but involves a partial adjustment towards desired employment.

This model was compared against actual industry data, quarterly from 1960 to 1967. The predicted signs of the regression coefficients are all substantiated, and the T-statistics appear acceptable, but it is still not clear that this model would do any better than an equivalent neo-classical model, say along the lines of Anderson's model mentioned above. Although the standard deviation of the model is half that of a model without the demand for reserve labour, there is still a considerable component of seasonal variation left in the error. Unfortunately, the r-statistic was not given, so it is difficult to know how much of the total variation was explained by the model.

The other model is G. A. Hay's [16, 1970]. At first glance it appears to be a maximizing model, since the solution is derived by maximizing revenue minus cost. However, the cost includes terms that would seem quite strange in a neo-classical model. For example, the desired level of inventory is defined by $a + b$ (production). Then an inventory cost of $c + d$ (actual − desired)^2 is included. There is also an explicit cost for changing production and price. The latter involves ($\Delta[P$-factor cost]).[2] The justification is that changing prices, when there has been no change in factor prices, will be considered an aggressive action by fellow oligopolists, while prices that only keep pace with factor cost are considered allowable. The result of the maximization of revenue minus cost over N periods with a discount is a set of linear decision rules for production, price, and inventory. These were checked against the paper and lumber industry, 1953–66, with reasonably good results. Again, since there is no alternative model applied to that data for comparison, it is difficult to evaluate success.

The classification of this model as non-maximizing may seem strange, since it seems to be merely a neo-classical model extended to include types of cost not normally considered. However, it is unlikely that such costs as ($\Delta[P$-factor cost])[2] are real monetary costs. The actual costs of price change will be the same whether factor price has changed or not. Rather, what is being looked at is a generalized utility function in equivalent monetary units, and "costs" are costs in a broader sense than just monetary. In this case the cost of raising price is a subjective matter related to a particular oligopolistic strategy. One could consider classing this as another example of additions to the objective function but that is not really right either. In the case of Williamson, the objective function represents the real final objectives of the firm, and maximization takes place over every possible policy. However, in Hay's model the policies are all given and are represented by the cost functions. The utility function represents how close the firm is to its policies, not how close it is to its goal. The policies are *ad hoc* and are not entirely consistent with each other. Maximization of the utility function represents a tradeoff between them.

ASSESSMENT OF CURRENT STATE

As is obvious, it is difficult to draw definitive conclusions from the small survey we have made. In fact, the economic literature is now so large that it is difficult to make anything resembling a complete survey. Nevertheless, we feel that some conclusions can be made, and we will also attempt to speculate about future directions.

Any model in any science must ultimately be justified on the basis of the knowledge about the real world that is generated by the model. This new knowledge may come from empirical work resulting from hypotheses derived from the model or from theoretical results that lead to other models and eventually to increased knowledge about the real world. As a first step in our evaluation, it is useful to examine current work from the standpoint of the generation of new knowledge.

In Part I of this chapter (the unmodified neo-classical approach) we see two types of articles. The first is an attempt to apply the maximization model directly to an economy and draw conclusions about the efficiency of resource allocation. The model as applied represents a theoretical optimum and the attempt is to measure empirically how close an actual economy comes to the theoretical maximum efficiency point. This use of the model is an interesting and time-honoured one. The real question is whether the results have any meaning since the model itself has never been in actual practice. Given a gap, which implies inefficiency, how should the system be changed? Too many empirical questions about a competitive system remain unsolved to use it prescriptively. The second type of article is oriented toward drawing further inferences from the theory. The approach is to take a particular problem, usually one from the literature, and attempt to analyse the problem through the use of standard models. This exercise is useful for helping economists to understand the implications of the models in existence. Unfortunately the analysis makes no attempt to connect with the real world. Thus it is difficult to argue that this approach leads to new knowledge about the real world.

Anderson's model in Part II (simple extension of the neo-classical approach) demonstrates another difficulty of the neo-classical model in deriving new knowledge. The model used can be justified solely on an "as if" basis. The underlying implicit firm decision models have no proven relationship to reality. Their justification comes from putting together a "package" which in the aggregate is not inconsistent with some data. Anderson shows that his story is as good as a previous story, labour adjustment costs. One method for choosing among alternatives might be the actual decision processes used at the firm level.

In Part III (modifications of the objective function) we are closer to gaining new knowledge than in I and II. The modification of the objective function represents an attempt to utilize empirical knowledge about the goals of the micro-economic units. The Williamson and Newhouse works are particularly good examples of the fruitfulness of this approach. The power of the approach comes from utilizing empirical behaviour and building the observations into the objective function. The question that arises is whether the individual arguments are best treated by combining them into a single objective function. We suspect that better results might be obtained by treating each argument as a separate goal and analysing the processes of the firm in achieving the individual goals.

In Part IV (generalized maximization techniques) the approaches taken represent an attempt to develop models that will improve the description of reality by dealing with uncertainty. The papers in this category are almost all theoretical and can be justified by the possibility that they may eventually lead to models with more empirical content. The importance of developing models that are dynamic and incorporate uncertainty is obvious if economics is to explain reality. The major question again is whether or not by sacrificing maximization and some elegance, models with empirical content can be developed more quickly. Progress in finance is clearly being made in the analysis of firm behaviour under conditions of uncertainty. The concept of maximization is retained, but the progress comes from the fact that the objective function has a measurable counterpart in the real world [19, Mao, 1969 and 11, Fama and Miller, 1972].

The articles in Part V (non-maximizing models) are an attempt to develop models that incorporate decision rules that have some empirical validity. Some of the rules are *ad hoc* rules of thumb, some come from the management science literature, and some from the empirically descriptive economic literature. The models are still, however, aimed at explaining the world at a gross level—the industry. No attempt is made to test individual decision rules separately against the decision processes of individual firms. The advantages of a behavioural approach are not apparent until there is an attempt to test at the individual firm level.

Thus it seems difficult from this review of our survey to justify the neo-classical model on the basis of leading either to new knowledge about the world or interesting theoretical results. The need for the simple maximization approach functions as a barrier to reaching the world. The most interesting results seem to us to stem from the enrichment of the objective function (in Part III). Work in this area moves the model closer to giving more detailed explanations of the real world. More specifically, the inclusion within the objective function of variables actually used in the decision process increases the explanatory power of the model. The latter conclusion is true even if the actual process of decision-making is not utilized but is approximated by a maximization process. We do not wish to leave the impression, however, that we believe behavioural and managerial models to be automatically superior to maximizing ones. For example, P. A. Frost [13, 1971] gives a maximizing model to explain banks' demand for excess reserves. The model is specifically designed to explain apparently anomalous behaviour in certain rapidly changing situations, and does so quite well, better in fact than a behavioural rule that was previously suggested as an explanation. The major theoretical accomplishment of that article was the derivation of a stable curve of demand for excess reserves as a function of interest rate. We suspect that the model was successful largely because so much information was able to be summarized by a single curve. Inevitably this curve represents a somewhat gross optimum, various detailed information having been suppressed or averaged over in its derivation. In fact these are just the sort of characteristics we would expect in a behavioural rule.

The crucial problem of finding a substitute process for maximization and maintaining rigour is not easily solved. Nevertheless, it is necessary for more effort to be exerted in this direction, especially when we recognize the ambiguity of the meaning of profit maximization under uncertainty. A further difficulty that arises from the maximization process is the difficulty of rejecting a model when the "as if" philosophy negates looking at actual decision processes. This difficulty is made even more severe by the recognition that some maximand can be found to explain any series.

In addition to the difficulties already discussed, there is a great diversity of views about the proper objectives of a theory of the firm. (The closest element to a common thread is the use of the maximization process.) Stemming from the original introduction of the firm as a hypothetical construct, there has been a prevailing opinion that economists ought to be interested only in propositions that were true for a large group of firms (an industry, for example). Taking this point of view eliminates any interest on the part of the researcher in making observations on the way individual firms operate. The economist is then free to make up a story, in the form of a model, about the way in which decisions on some variable of interest (prices, output, investment, advertizing, etc.) are made. The story that is viewed as best is the one that fits the aggregate data best.

This concentration on group behaviour is not peculiar to economics. The social sciences as a whole have been characterized by the idea that the behaviour of individual organisms, whether men or firms, is unpredictable, hence uninteresting. That this view is overly pessimistic may be suggested by the recent success in explaining human problem solving on a minute-by-minute level [21, Newell and Simon, 1972]. The contrast in attitudes between the authors of this study and the micro-economic tradition is quite interesting. Newell and Simon, together with many other psychologists of similar bent, seem to be constantly looking for ways of collecting larger and larger amounts of data per unit time. Thus we see the utilization, first of the thinking-aloud protocol, and then the eye-movement camera. The object is to build theories with the highest possible "density" of explained data.

One possible path out of the dilemma faced by micro-economics is the route of simulation. Simulation allows the model builder to embed the variables that are deemed relevant on the basis of his empirical observations. He can, as well, incorporate the actual process of decision-making and is not bound by conventional mathematics to assuming that the economic units maximize. There are many examples of interesting and successful simulations of firms and industries [10, Dutton and Starbuck, 1971 and 17, Hoggatt and Balderston, 1963]. Simulation models can be made for individual units, markets, or economic systems. The models are not elegant and there are problems in testing the validity of the models.

Nevertheless, these rather trivial esthetic problems do not explain why this particular methodology and the behavioural approach to theory have remained relatively infrequently used in economics. Reasons spring to mind—the status of mathematical models, the training of economists, the difficulties in obtaining the data inherent in the behavioural approach, the concern that special models must be developed for each firm, and so on.[4] All of these are reasons that we believe account in part for the relative ignoring of an important approach at the micro-economic level. (Simulation has been accepted as an important tool at the macro-economic level.)

Equally important, however, has been the lack of agreement on the crucial questions to which the theory of the firm should address itself. The fundamental difference centres on the question of whether the theory should explain actual decision-making in the firm. The prevailing position, and the major rationale for neo-classical theory, is that the actual process is irrelevant. The critical test is prediction and any process that produces predictions valid in the aggregate is adequate. This position is justified on the "as if" rationale.

On the basis of our brief survey we conclude that there is growing uneasiness with the neo-classical approach (Parts III, IV, V) but that the above rationale is still held by most economists. This position plus the other virtues of mathematical models (prestige as well as rigour) maintain the importance of the role of maximization. We see no evidence at this time for a substantial change despite the restricted progress being made by current approaches. The real world still escapes our models; our explanations remain at an aggregate level. The problem is clearly difficult, but we wonder whether economics can remain an empirical science and continue to ignore the actual decision-making process of real firms.

NOTES

1. The 42 articles found to be relevant to this study are listed as Appendix I. We are aware that classification is often somewhat arbitrary and apologize in advance to those authors who may be perplexed by the inclusion or exclusion of their articles from our list.

2. The Proceedings issue of the *American Economic Review* is particularly rich in these articles. We would like to call particular attention to the comments of E. T. Grether and others in the Industrial Organization section of the 1970 Proceedings [15, Grether, 1970; 26, Singer, 1970 and 14, Grabowski and Mueller, 1970]. Their comments also indicate the need for more detail in models of firms. When considering the virtues of the competitive model, articles like those of O. E. Williamson [31, 1971] and J. L. Bower [5, 1970] are also interesting. They are representative of a growing suspicion that a large, horizontally integrated corporation may actually be more efficient than a competitive market in allocating resources (particularly capital).

3. A quick check of the extensive bibliography assembled by W. H. Starbuck and J. M. Dutton [27, 1971] shows that the computer simulation articles published in *Management Science* alone outnumber those in all economics journals, 44 to 43. When macro-economic and purely methodological articles are not counted, the ratio increases to 30 to 18.

4. For some particularly cogent critiques of the behavioural approach, see the article by W. J. Baumol and M. Stewart [4, 1971].

APPENDIX I: ARTICLES REVIEWED

Anderson, W. H. L. 'Production Scheduling, Intermediate Goods, and Labor Productivity', *American Economic Review*, March 1970, *60*(1), pp. 153–62.

Auerbach, R. 'The Effects of Price supports on Output and Factor Prices in Agriculture', *Journal Political Economics*, Nov. 1970, *78*(6), pp. 1355–61.

Bardhan, P. K. and Srinivasan, T. N. 'Cropsharing Tenancy in Agriculture: A Theoretical and Empirical Analysis', *American Economic Review*, March 1971, *61*(1), pp. 48–64.

Barzel, Y. 'Excess Capacity in Monopolistic Competition', *Journal Political Economics*, Sept. 1970, *78*(3), pp. 1142–9.

Belli, P. 'Farmer's Response to Price in Underdeveloped Areas: The Nicaraguan Case', *American Economic Review*, May 1970, *60*(2), pp. 385–92.

Berhold, M. 'A Theory of Linear Profit-Sharing Incentives', *Quarterly Journal of Economics*, August 1971, *85*(3), pp 460–82.

Bischoff, C. W. 'A Model of Nonresidential Construction in the United States', *American Economic Review*, May 1970, *60*(2), pp. 10–17.

Brittain, J. A. 'The Incidence of Social Security Payroll Taxes', *American Economic Review*, March 1971, *61*(1), pp. 110–25.

Chipman, J. S. 'External Economies of Scale and Competitive Equilibrium', *Quarterly Journal of Economics*, August 1970, *84*(3), pp. 347–85.

Cyert, R. M. and DeGroot, M. H. 'Multi-period Decision Models with Alternating Choice as a Solution to the Duopoly Problem', *Quarterly Journal of Economics*, August 1970, *84*(3), pp. 410–29.

———, 'Bayesian Analysis and Duopoly', *Journal Political Economics*, Sept. 1970, *78*(5), pp. 1168–84.

Dittrich, S. R. and Myers, R. H. 'Resource Allocation in Traditional Agriculture: Republican China, 1937–1940', *Journal Political Economics*, July 1971, *79*(4), pp. 887–96.

Ehrenberg, R. G., 'Absenteeism and the Overtime Decision', *American Economic Review*, June 1970, *60*(3), pp. 352–8.

Frost, P. A. 'Banks' Demand for Excess Reserves', *Journal Political Economics*, July 1971, *79*(4), pp. 805–25.

Grabowski, H. G. 'Demand Shifting, Optimal Firm Growth, and Rule-Of-Thumb Decision Making', *Quarterly Journal of Economics*, May 1970, *84*(2), pp. 217–35.

Gross, J. G. 'Incentive Pricing and Utility Regulation', *Quarterly Journal of Economics*, May 1970, *84*(2), pp. 236–53.

Hay, G. A. 'Production, Price, and Inventory', *American Economic Review*, Sept. 1970, *60*(4), pp. 531–45.

Hayami, Y. and Ruttan, V. W. 'Factor Prices and Technical Change in Agricultural Development: The United States and Japan, 1880–1960', *Journal Political Economics*, Sept. 1970, *78*(5), pp. 1115–41.

Lucas, R. E. 'Capacity, Overtime, and Empirical Production Functions', *American Economic Review*, May 1970, *60*(2), pp. 23–7.

McCall, J. J. 'The Simple Economics of Incentive Contracting', *American Economic Review*, Dec. 1970, *60*(5), pp. 837–46.

McClure, C. E., Jr. 'Taxation, Substitution, and Industrial Location', *Journal Political Economics*, Jan. 1970, *78*(1), pp. 112–32.

Miller, R. L. 'A Short-Term Econometric Model of Textile Industries', *American Economic Review*, June 1971, *61*(3 : I), pp. 279–89.

Newhouse, J. P. 'Toward a Theory of Non-profit Institutions: An Economic Model of a Hospital', *American Economic Review*, March 1970, *60*(1), pp. 64–74.

Oi, W. Y. 'A Disneyland Dilemma: Two-Part Tariffs for a Mickey-Mouse Monopoly', *Quarterly Journal of Economics*, Feb. 1971, *85*(1), pp. 77–96.

Osborne, D. K. 'The Duopoly Game: Output Variations', *American Economic Review*, Sept. 1971, *61*(4), pp. 538–60.

Pashigian, B. P. 'Rational Expectations and the Cobweb Theory', *Journal Political Economics*, March 1970, *78*(2), pp. 338–52.

Peltzman, S. 'Capital Investment in Commercial Banking and its Relationship to Portfolio Regulation', *Journal Political Economics*, Jan. 1970, *78*(1), pp. 1–26.

Quirk, J. P. 'Complementarity and Stability of Equilibrium', *American Economic Review*, June 1970, *60*(3), pp. 358–63.

Radner, R. and Miller, L. S. 'Demand and Supply in U.S. Higher Education: A Progress Report', *American Economic Review*, May 1970, *60*(2), pp. 326–34.

Rafferty, J. A. 'Patterns of Hospital Use: An Analysis of Short-Run Variations', *Journal Political Economics*, Jan. 1971, *79*(1), pp. 154–65.

Rao, C. H. H. 'Uncertainty, Entrepreneurship and Sharecroppng in India', *Journal Political Economics*, May 1971, *79*(3), pp. 578–95.

Rothenberg, T. J. and Smith, K. R. 'The Effect of Uncertainty on Resource Allocation in a General Equilibrium Model', *Quarterly Journal of Economics*, August 1971, *85*(3), pp. 440–59.

Sandmo, A. 'On the Theory of the Competitive Firm Under Price Uncertainty', *American Economic Review*, March 1971, *61*(1), pp. 65–73.

Sengupta, S. S. 'Capacity and Market Structure', *Journal Political Economics*, Jan. 1971, *79*(1), pp. 97–113.

Shen, T. Y. 'Economies of Scale, Penrose Effect, Growth of Plants and Their Size Distribution', *Journal Political Economics*, July 1970, *78*(4:I), pp. 702–16.

Swan, P. L. 'Market Structure and Technological Progress: The Influence of

Monopoly on Product Innovation', *Quarterly Journal of Economics*, Nov. 1970, *84*(4), pp. 627–38.

Thornton, J. 'Differential Capital Charges and Resource Allocation in Soviet Industry', *Journal Political Economics*, May 1971, *79*(3), pp. 545–61.

Weintraub, E. R. 'Stochastic Stability of a General Equilibrium Model', *American Economic Review*, May 1970, *60*(2), pp. 380–4.

Wellisz, S.; Munk, B.; Mayhew, T. P. and Hemmer, C. 'Resource Allocation in Traditional Agriculture: A Study of Andhra Pradesh', *Journal Political Economics*, July 1970, *78*(4 : I), pp. 655–84.

Westfield, F. M. 'Methodology of Evaluating Economic Regulation', *American Economic Review*, May 1971, *61*(2), pp. 211–17.

Wright, W. D. C. 'Some Substitution Effects in the Location of a Firm', *Journal Political Economics*, July 1971, *79*(4), pp. 903–8.

Zajac, E. E. 'A Geometric Treatment of Averch-Johnson's Behavior of the Firm Model', *American Economic Review*, March 1970, *60*(1), pp. 117–25.

REFERENCES

1. Anderson, W. H. L. 'Production Scheduling Intermediate Goods, and Labor Productivity', *American Economic Review*, March 1970, *60*(1), pp. 153–62.

2. Barzel, Y. 'Excess Capacity in Monopolistic Competition', *Journal Political Economics*, Sept. 1970, *78*(5), pp. 1142–9.

3. Baumol, W. J. *Business Behavior, Value and Growth*. New York: Macmillan, 1959.

4. —— and Stewart, M. 'On the Behavioral Theory of the Firm', in R. Marris and A. Wood, (eds), *The Corporate Economy: Growth, Competition, and Innovation Potential*. New York: Macmillan, 1971.

5. Bower, J. L. 'Planning Within the "Firm"', *American Economic Review*, May 1970, *60*(2), pp. 186–94.

6. Cyert, R. M. and DeGroot, M. H. 'Bayesian Analysis and Duopoly Theory', *Journal Political Economics*, Sept. 1970, *78*(5), pp. 1168–84.

7. —— 'An Analysis of Cooperation and Learning in a Duopoly Context', *American Economic Review*, March, 1973.

8. Cyert, R. M. and March, J. G. *A Behavioral Theory of the Firm*. Englewood Cliffs, N. J.: Prentice Hall, 1963.

9. Dittrich, S. R. and Myers, R. H. 'Resource Allocation in Traditional Agriculture: Republican China, 1937–1940', *Journal Political Economics*, July 1971, *79*(4), pp. 887–96.

10. Dutton, J. M. and Starbuck, W. H., (eds). *Computer Simulation of Human Behavior*. New York: John Wiley & Sons, 1971.

11. Fama, E. F. and Miller, M. H. *The Theory of Finance*. New York: Holt, Rinehart and Winston, 1972.

12. Friedman, M. *Essays in Positive Economics*. Chicago: University of Chicago Press, 1953.

13. Frost, P. A. 'Banks' Demand for Excess Reserves', *Journal Political Economics*, July 1971, *79*(4), pp. 805–25.

14. Grabowski, H. and Mueller, D. 'Industrial Organization: The Role and

Contribution of Econometrics', *American Economic Review*, May 1970, *60*(2), pp. 100–4.

15. Grether, E. T. 'Industrial Organization: Past History and Future Problems', *American Economic Review*, May 1970, *60*(2), pp. 83–9.
16. Hay, G. A. 'Production, Price, and Inventory', *American Economic Review*, Sept. 1970. *60*(4), pp. 531–45.
17. Hoggatt, A. C. and Balderston, F. E. (eds). *Symposium on Simulation Models: Methodology and Applications to the Behavioral Sciences.* Cincinnati, Ohio: South-Western, 1963.
18. Machlup, F. 'Theories of the Firm: Marginalist, Behavioural, Managerial', *American Economic Review*, March 1967, *57*(1), pp. 1–33.
19. Mao, J. C. T. *Quantitative Analysis of Financial Decisions.* New York: Macmillan, 1969.
20. Miller, R. L. 'A Short-Term Econometric Model of Textile Industries', *American Economic Review*, June 1971, *61*(3 : I), pp. 279–89.
21. Newell, A. and Simon, H. A. *Human Problem Solving.* Englewood Cliffs, N.J.: Prentice Hall, 1972.
22. Newhouse, J. P. 'Toward a Theory of Nonprofit Institutions: An Economic Model of a Hospital', *American Economic Review*, March 1970, *60*(1), pp. 64–74.
23. Osborne, D. K. 'The Duopoly Game: Output Variation', *American Economic Review*, Sept, 1971, *61*(4), pp. 538–60.
24. Sandmo, A. 'On the Theory of the Competitive Firm Under Price Uncertainty', *American Economic Review*, March 1971, *61*(1), pp. 65–73.
25. Shubik, M. 'A Curmudgeon's Guide to Microeconomics', *Journal of Economic Literature*, June 1970, *8*(2), pp. 405–34.
26. Singer, E. M. 'Industrial Organization: Price Models and Public Policy', *American Economic Review*, May 1970, *60*(2), pp. 90–9.
27. Starbuck, W. H. and Dutton, J. M. 'Simulation Model Construction' in J. M. Dutton ad W. H. Starbuck, (eds), *Computer Simulation of Human Behavior.* New York: John Wiley & Sons, 1971, pp. 9–102.
28. Swan, P. L. 'Market Structure and Technological Progress: The Influence of Monopoly on Product Innovation', *Quarterly Journal of Economics*, Nov. 1970, *84*(4), pp. 887–96.
19. Thornton, J. 'Differential Capital Charges and Resource Allocation in Soviet Industry', *Journal Political Economics*, May 1971, *79*(3), pp. 545–61.
30. Williamson, O. E. *Corporate Control and Business Behavior.* Englewood Cliffs, N. J.: Prentice-Hall, 1970.
31. —— 'The Vertical Integration of Production Market Failure Considerations', *American Economic Review*, May 1971, *61*(2), pp. 112–23.
32. Wright, W. D. C. 'Some Substitution Effects in the Location Decision of a Firm', *Journal Political Economics*, July 1971, *79*(4), pp. 903–8.
33. Zajac, E. E. 'A Geometric Treatment of Averch-Johnson's Behavior of the Firm Model', *American Economic Review*, March 1970, *60*(1), pp. 117–25.

5 Towards a Control Theory of the Firm*[1]

INTRODUCTION

The theory of the firm in neo-classical theory is simple and clear. The firm is assumed to be maximizing profits and, therefore, follows a single decision rule. That rule tells the firm's management to operate at the point where marginal cost equals marginal revenue. By moving to the demand curve at that point the firm can determine the appropriate price and output. This general rule lies in back of all micro theory relating to the firm. New models consist of making a behavioural assumption and then showing how the marginal revenue curve can be determined. Once the marginal revenue curve is found a "solution" is immediately forthcoming. The dominant firm model and the kinked-demand curve model are obvious examples (see Cohen and Cyert). There has been little empirical testing of any of the propositions from the theory of the firm and, where there has, the testing casts doubt on the theory.

Nevertheless, the theory has played a useful role in increasing the understanding, in a general sense, of the way the price system operates. By assuming competitive markets and utilizing the decision rule described above, economists have gained insight into the resource allocation problem within an economy. Little insight, however, is gained about the actual decision-making process of individual firms. This chapter is motivated by a desire to develop a theory of the firm that corresponds more closely to the behaviour of firms I have observed. My observations have been made as a member of the board of directors of some ten firms for various periods of time over ten years. Firms in the real world do function under conditions of uncertainty and the theory we will develop will assume uncertainty. The relationship between the

* Reprinted by permission of College of Business Administration, Oklahoma State University.

approach that we will take in this chapter and neo-classical theory will be explored after the theory is developed.

THE FIRM

In neo-classical theory, the firm is viewed as consisting of a single person, an entrepreneur, who makes decisions in accordance with the decision rule. In fact, all firms have more elaborate organizational structures, and most of these structures are of a decentralized form. The basic unit in each firm is typically a division. Each division is a profit centre and is usually managed as though it were an independent firm. The firm will sell a number of different products and through its divisions, will operate in a number of different market structures in which it will have different market shares.

The manager of each division will usually be a vice-president, although this person's title may range from manager to president depending on the size of the firm. The division vice-president will have the power to make pricing and output decisions as well as some capital expenditure decisions. Furthermore, the division vice-president, along with the chief executive officer of the firm, will constitute the management coalition of the firm, although this coalition may also contain other executives depending on the nature of the business and the characteristics of the individuals involved (see Cyert and March).

The firm in our theory operates under conditions of uncertainty. Thus the chief executive officer and his managers must make decisions about events whose occurrence is uncertain. Uncertainty as we use it might be described by a stochastic model in which the probability distribution of the observable random variables depends on the unknown values of various parameters (see DeGroot). Under these conditions, the true values of the parameters cannot usually be learned with certainty. Thus there will always be uncertainty facing the firm as it makes decisions because of both the stochastic nature of the variables to be observed and the unknown values of the parameters.

The description of the firm that we have presented is appropriate for most corporations regardless of size and, therefore, our theory is meant to be general.

DEVELOPING THE PLAN

Since the concept of maximizing profits has no unique meaning under conditions of uncertainty, the firm cannot derive any operational guidance from the simple desire to maximize profits. Therefore, the management of a firm attempts to develop a plan from which some specific operational steps will follow. The form of the plan consists of a series of target values for certain critical variables. These target values are developed on a monthly as well as annual basis. They are specified for the firm as a whole as well as for the divisions. The targets together with the initial positions of the firm and its divisions enable the firm to develop some specific strategies and tactics to attain the targets. The plan essentially gives structure to an unstructured situation characterized by uncertainty. The firm in neo-classical theory in a perfectly competitive market does not suffer from such a lack of structure and hence does not need a plan. In fact, the situation for the firm in perfect competition is so structured that it does not need a manager.

In order to develop such a plan, the management must be concerned with three sets of conditions: (1) conditions in the economy as a whole, (2) conditions in the industry and, in particular, in competitive firms, and (3) conditions inside the firm.

The initial step in the process of developing target values is to forecast the first set of conditions specified above. The management is particularly interested in the growth expected in the economy as a whole in each of the countries in which it is operating. The aim is the development of the growth factors that can be applied to the specific markets in which the firm sells—the second set of conditions. Out of a more complex framework than that given here, the firm's planners arrive at a specific estimate of the total sales expected in the industry, essentially based on estimated growth rates.

The third step is to take account of the set of conditions inside the firm. The planners must determine the firm's capability of expanding production over the previous period. They must look at such variables as labour negotiations, capital expenditures, and similar items related to the firm's productive capacity. The next step is the establishment of the targets.

ESTABLISHING TARGETS

In the planning process management selects certain key variables, which we shall call target variables, whose actual values during the year reflect the progress of the firm. The firm's management selects specific target values for these variables for the firm as a whole and for each of the divisions. The plan consists of these target values specified for the firm and each division on a monthly basis and for the year. The target values are the goals for the firm. These goals are believed by management to have a reasonable probability of being attained and thus, the plan is a prediction. This predictive process does not lead to unique values for the plan. Predictive probabilities are established for a range of values of the variables, and management, with the approval of the board, must select the values that will constitute the plan.

The target values established are a compromise generated by an interactive process between the board and the management. Management wants to have high prior probabilities of achieving any targets that it selects. The board of directors wants target values that show a significant rate of growth for the firm. Thus, the management tries to establish lower targets and the board tries to establish higher targets.

The target variables will vary somewhat from firm to firm. We will specify some targets that are generally used in order to illustrate our theory. We shall consider six targets for the firm as a whole: (1) net earnings per share, (2) net dollar sales, (3) cash flow, (4) return on investment, (5) return on stockholders' equity, and (6) new orders received.

1. *Net earnings per share (EPS)* is equal to the net profit divided by the number of shares outstanding, and represents the profit target for the firm. This variable is important because management will be evaluated on the attainment or non-attainment of its target values, and executive compensation plans are frequently tied to the degree of attainment.
2. *Net dollar sales* are important because of their relationship to market share. The firm in our theory does not know its demand curve with certainty and gains information about it through the trend of net sales. Net earnings in the future are a function of this trend as is the long-run survival of the firm. In a period of inflation, the sales figure is examined closely to see if the number of physical units sold has increased or decreased.
3. *Cash flow* is equal to net profit plus depreciation plus deferred taxes, and is crucial to the firm since the ultimate measure of the success of the firm is the amount of cash the firm generates. The flow of cash gives the firm information about the need for short- and long-term borrowing and, thus, becomes another indicator of the firm's overall well-being in the face of uncertainty.
4. *Return on investment* represents the proportion of the money invested in the firm by owners and lenders that is being returned as profit. It gives information to the firm that is important as a measure of quality of performance, and in addition, its value is one criterion of whether the firm should stay in business or not.
5. *Return on stockholders' equity* has many of the same characteristics as return on investment. By focusing on the return on stockholders'

equity the firm's management recognizes its responsibilities to the owners.

6. *New orders received* give a measure that, like net sales, enables the firm to determine how well it is doing with respect to the future. It is a significant variable because it gives the firm information about changes in its demand curve.

The monthly target values for variables 1 through 6 are important because they are related to the targets for the year. If the target value for a variable is attained each month, the firm will reach its target for the year. Thus, whenever the actual value for a variable is less than its target value in any month, the firm is concerned.

The division targets are essentially the same as those for the firm as a whole. However, the return on stockholders' equity does not make as much sense for the division as for the firm and is replaced by a target variable representing the ratio of net profit to sales. This variable gives the division a measure of the effectiveness of its pricing policy in producing profit since it shows the amount of profit per dollar of sales revenue.

Thus, from a situation of uncertainty, the firm and its divisions establish a set of target values. Once the plan is completed the firm must choose specific strategies to attain the target values and then wait for feedback to see if changes in strategy are necessary.

COMPARISON OF ACTUAL AND TARGET

This feedback is obtained from the monthly financial statements for the divisions and the firm as a whole. Each month the financial system generates actual values of the target variables. When these are printed the division managers meet with the CEO and analyse their positions. They examine the actual values for each of the target variables. Each division manager assesses his situation in the light of the three sets of conditions utilized to determine the plan. The objective of the meeting is to develop explanations for discrepancies between the actual values and the target values. The explanations are desired whether the actual values are less than, greater than, or equal to the target values.

If the actual value is less than the target value for one or more of the target variables an explanation must be found. This part of the process is known as the analysis phase.

An explanation must be found for the deficiency of an actual value from its target whether the target relates to a particular division or to the firm. This explanation must be presented in terms of the present and recent past values of the variables involved in the three sets of conditions on which the plan is based. The search for an explanation depends on the relationship between the particular target variables being considered and the variables in these three sets. If no satisfactory explanation is found, then, as in other sequential decision processes, the firm takes no new actions but rather waits for more information during the following month. The process of searching for an explanation is essentially a process of making inferences from the body of data consisting of the three sets of conditions and continues until an explanation is found with a high enough probability to warrant acceptance. Once an explanation is accepted the firm enters the next phase of the process, namely, the control phase.

CONTROL ACTIONS

If the explanation indicates that the deficiency in the actual values is due to random factors that are essentially transient in nature, no action will be taken. Frequently, however, even when the explanation lies in the variables relating to the economy as a whole the firm may be able to take internal actions designed to bring the actual values into control, that is, make the actual values equal to or greater than the target values for future months.

The various control actions that might be used by the firm are many and varied. Some actions affect the firm's interactions with the market, such as price changes, marketing policy changes, and mergers and acquisitions. Others relate to the contraction of the firm's operation such as closing a plant, selling a division, or reducing the labour force. Basically, the first set is designed to increase revenue and the second to reduce cost.

In the usual control models, a cost function drives the model, but the cost function is usually chosen to have a canonical form, more for its mathematical convenience than its relationship to reality (see DeGroot). The specification of the cost function for the control process in the theory of the firm has the same difficulties. Consider, for example, the total earnings-per-share target. Management sets the target it desires to achieve for a variety of reasons. Some of these may be personal relating to executive compensation plans. Others may be professional, since the achievement of the goal is a measure of the quality of the management. Still others may involve the concept of responsibility to the shareholders. It is difficult, therefore, to give meaning to the notion of the cost of falling short of the target.

On the basis of the explanation the management must decide what actions to take in order to make the actual values meet the targets in future periods. Two aspects of each action that must be considered by management are the length of time required to take the action and the length of time for the effects of the action to become apparent. As examples, we will describe five commonly used control actions: (1) price changes, (2) mergers and acquisitions, (3) contraction, (4) selling some parts of the business, and (5) changing management.

1. *Price change* is, of course, the primary action that has generally been considered in economic theory. The firm that is considering this action goes through the kind of reasoning that has generally been portrayed in oligopoly theory. The reaction of competitors is of major concern. Of equal importance, however, is a judgement about the position of the demand curve based on the information flowing from net sales and new orders. The advantage of a successful price change is that it takes effect quickly and the firm, therefore, can be brought into control relatively soon.

2. *Mergers and acquisitions* are part of a longer-run set of actions designed to make actual values equal to or greater than target values. This form of control action is used when the explanation indicates a structural deficiency that results in the firm's inability to attain its targets.

3. *Contraction* as a control action includes such activities as closing plants, reducing the labour force and, hence, the output, eliminating certain products completely, and similar actions. These actions are taken, generally, when the firm believes it cannot affect the market and must respond by internal changes. The aim of the control is to reduce expenses proportionally more than revenues.

4. *Selling parts of the firm* that are losing money is a common, longer-run type of control. Again this method tends to be used when the explanation indicates that fundamental problems in the structure of the firm are preventing it from attaining control. Frequently, these segments of the business have been retained for a period of time while they are losing money because the future prospects are bright. At some point the firm makes a decision to sell. That decision will be made when one or more of the actual values has been less than its target value for a number of months and the explanation leaves the firm with no other action that can be taken to bring the firm into control.

5. *Changing management* tends to be a last resort. Such action, obviously, follows an explanation that leads to the inference that management is at fault. Generally, this action can take place immediately and usually a replacement from within the organization is available. The effects of the change will likely be fast. Thus, this action can have immediate effects in bringing the firm into control. The management

changes might be at any level in the firm where the unit involved could have a significant effect on the target variables of the firm.

These control actions are only a subset of the total number of actions that might be taken, but they are the most important, we believe, and the ones most frequently taken. The objective of management is to select a control action that will be effective in bringing the firm into control. It must select that action among all the possible actions that will achieve this objective with the least cost over the entire planning period.

We have discussed being out of control only in terms of some of the actual values being less than the corresponding target values, but there are some control actions that may be taken when the actual is greater than the target. In particular, the firm is sensitive to the amount by which the actual EPS exceeds the target. The primary reason for this caution is that the management wants to show steady growth. This objective is desired because steady growth of a given percentage is an indication of good management and, because it is believed that the stock market places a high value on steady growth. All other things being equal, management would prefer two years of steady growth rather than one of great growth and one of relatively low growth. The firm tries to reduce profits that will push it far beyond its EPS target by putting more funds into contingency reserves of various kinds. A general contingency reserve is not allowed but it is frequently possible to reserve for plant damage or to develop reserves for unemployment insurance or workmen's compensation. Thus rather than allow the actual EPS to be significantly in excess of the target, the firm will increase its reserves and reduce profits in a particular period.

METHODOLOGICAL IMPLICATIONS

The control approach to the firm is obviously a significant departure from conventional theory. The new approach was developed because of dissatisfaction with the empirical content of the neo-classical approach, and it therefore seems important to air some of the methodological issues involved.

The basis for arguing that standard micro-economic theory provides a good account of market behaviour is weak. It consists chiefly of remarks that refer in a general way to a limited variety of situations where there is a qualitative agreement between what orthodox micro-economic models predict and what goes on in markets. Furthermore, the cases chosen for exhibiting this kind of agreement between theory and reality typically are picked out in the light of careful hindsight. Awkward disagreements between theory and reality tend to be swept under the convenient rug provided by the *ceteris paribus* clause which is a pervasive feature of the theory of the firm.[2]

According to the methodological position we hold neo-classical microeconomic theory must be replaced by a different theory because its account of the behaviour of individual firms is at odds with the facts about how firms behave. As we indicated above, the firm develops its plan as a way of making decisions under uncertainty. Profit maximization offers no operational clues to the management. The plan is a specific form of adaption to the uncertainty facing the firm.

There are a variety of ways in which economic theory can deal with uncertainty. One of these is to retreat from the analysis of the individual units and rely on an analysis of market forces (see Alchian). This approach is related to the use of the environment by the biologists to explain adaptation of species. It has merit and might be used to provide an explanation for certain kinds of behaviour in the long run and at an aggregate level. The approach in question, is however, bound to lead to theories which are deficient in one important respect—such theories will not give an account of the behaviour of the individual firms. This deficiency is important for two reasons. First, one must have an account of the behaviour of individual firms in order to deal with monopoly and oligopoly. Second, although we are concerned with micro-economics as a positive science, it must be remembered that micro-economic theories are intended to have normative uses and that one of these is to help in the making of public policy decisions. Theories which do not give an account of the behaviour of individual firms will not be helpful in policy discussion.

A second method of handling the problem of decision-making under uncertainty, which brings to bear the existing techniques of mathematical analysis, is to assume that the firm can develop subjective probability distributions of profit for decision alternatives. In addition it is necessary to assume that the firm has a utility function that enables it to convert probability distributions of profit into utilities and that the firm makes decisions so as to maximize the utility function. This may well be a useful approach if by empirical work the process by which businessmen establish probability distributions can be determined and if the form of the utility functions used by businessmen can be discovered (see Cyert and DeGroot, 1970).

A third method is to study empirically the way that businessmen make decisions in the face of uncertainty, to embed the decision process into a theory of the firm, and then to construct a theory of market behaviour based on the resulting theory of the firm (see Cyert and March). This approach is the behavioural approach. The first problem to be considered is that of constructing the desired theory of the firm. The construction of such a theory will require the making of many observations. "Observation" can be viewed as a process in which a trained scientist watches and records the actual process of making a decision. The observations will include being present at meetings, interviewing relevant participants, analysing written documents, and any other steps designed to lead to understanding of the criteria being used to make the decision and the goals these criteria are intended to serve. Such an approach requires the co-operation of the firm and the co-operation of the participants in the decision-making process. There are difficulties (e.g., the problem of getting an accurate picture of the process rather than a formalized, polished one developed for external purposes), but it is possible to make such observations (see Cyert, DeGroot, and Holt).

The critical problem involved in constructing the theory of the firm required by the behavioural approach is to determine the goals of the firm and to understand the process by which decision rules are learned and modified in the face of feedback from the environment in the interest of serving these goals. This problem is critical because one of the main ideas behind the approach is that the way to get a better theory of the firm is by viewing it as an adaptive mechanism that can learn from its environment, and it seems clear that the features of this sort of learning which will lend themselves to theoretical treatment are the decision rules used in the firms.

As an adaptive mechanism the firm is able to learn about its environment by taking actions and analysing the results. The actions it takes—raising price, increasing output, etc.—are selected from a limited number of alternatives. The actions are designed to achieve a goal—a particular level of profit, a certain market share—and the results of the actions are analysed in terms of achieving the goal. The results of the analysis are then stored within the organization's memory and the demand curve or the cost curve begin to take on certain characteristics as a result. Thus, if price is increased on a number of different occasions and demand does not slacken, it is likely that the demand curve will be characterized as highly inelastic. This example is a simple one and is designed to illustrate what we mean by the firm as an adaptive mechanism. The firm is capable of learning under far more complex conditions and adapting appropriately.

We note there is reason to think that the goals which drive this process are pretty much the same from firm to firm, when considered in general terms, though different firms will consider these goals to have been achieved by quite different levels of performance and a given firm will alter the desired levels of performance over time. This similarity of goals should make it easier to do the job we are projecting, but we also note that we do not intend to rule out the possibility that a firm may acquire new goals and discard old ones in the course of time. If this process of acquiring and discarding goals is found to be an important aspect of the working of firms, then it will have to be studied in detail.

In treating the processes to be studied, careful attention must be given to the fact that the firm (even with computers) has a limited capability to process information and, therefore, may not reach the position that hindsight analysis demonstrates to have been optimum.

We call the decision rules to be studied behavioural rules. The firm develops these rules of thumb as guides for making decisions in a complex environment with uncertainty and incomplete information. Behavioural rules incorporate the decision-makers' assumptions about the nature of the environment and the nature of the firm itself which suffice to allow a decision to be reached in such circumstances. The aim of the behavioural approach to the theory of the firm is to make business judgement susceptible of rational, theoretical treatment by analysing what is essential to the process of judgment in terms of sets of behavioural rules.

Turning from the theory of the firm to the problem of constructing a micro-economic theory based on the theory of the firm, we note that we are not recommending that the baby be thrown out with the bath water. Indeed, we lay it down as a requirement both for the theory of the firm and for the theory of market behaviour that as the behavioural theory is applied to situations in which uncertainty gives way to certainty and knowledge increases without limit, the results derived from the behavioural theory should approximate more and more closely those derived by *a priori* reasoning about the simplified situation treated by the orthodox theory.

A scientific theory is supposed to provide an account of what will happen in a variety of possible worlds, and we acknowledge that the orthodox theory works admirably for an extensive set of worlds which differ from the one that we live in chiefly by not involving decisions made under uncertainty and incomplete information. Clearly, in such a world the firm operating in the framework of the competitive system with market prices, the marginal cost curve, and the average variable cost curve known has no need for behavioural rules other than those derived by the usual marginalist reasoning. In these circumstances the firm must determine prices and output by the intersection of the price and marginal cost curve. It is the firm operating under conditions of ignorance of its demand and cost curves which must find other methods of decision-making. We are aiming at a theory which, both with respect to the behaviour of individual firms and with respect to the behaviour of markets, will explain what is going on in the latter situation and establish clearly the relations between this and the existing account of what is going on in the former.

The concept of behavioural rules is not new to economics. Every determinate model developed under conditions of some uncertainty utilizes a behavioural rule. In the cobweb model, suppliers are assumed to determine the current period's supply on the basis of the last period's price, $s(t) = f[p(t-1)]$. In the Cournot duopoly model, each firm assumes that it is independent of its rival, in particular, that a change in its output will have no effect on its rival. In the kinked demand curve model, each firm assumes its rival will always behave in the way that will hurt it the most. Thus a price increase will not be followed by rivals but a price decrease will. For other models where uncertainty exists in the situation being modelled but is eliminated in the model, some form of behavioural rule can be shown to be present.

IMPLICATIONS OF THE CONTROL APPROACH

This chapter has been an attempt to apply some of these methodological considerations. The firm establishes targets and then uses a control approach to attain the targets. In one sense the selection of optimal control techniques replaces profit maximization as the objective of the firm.

We begin by assuming that uncertainty is important and that behaviour will be different under uncertainty from that exhibited under certainty. Specifically, we argue that under conditions of uncertainty, the firm proceeds by setting a target profit figure. This figure stretches the management but has some probability of attainment that seems reasonable to management. The firm's behaviour then, we argue, can be better explained by control theory than by the assumption of profit maximization. We are not interested in whether the targets approximate maximization values or satisfying values (see Simon). We argue that the firm regards the targets as critical and selects its actions to attain its targets.

The model is based on empirical observations but we are not prepared to argue that the extent of the observations is so great that the model should be immediately accepted as valid. The observations have been used as a stimulus for theorizing, and we argue that the current model, if followed, has a better potential for yielding explanations about firm behaviour than the neo-classical model. It should also be remembered that the latter is based on certainty.

Any attempt to develop a theory, as we have done, that emphasizes process and does not explicitly use profit maximization immediately raises the "so what" question. In other words, it is incumbent on the proponents of a new approach to demonstrate that the new approach makes a difference. On that question we make the following propositions:

1. Our approach can explain when a firm will take an economically significant action. The conventional approach cannot.
2. Our approach encompasses within it actions such as price changes, mergers, acquisitions, and sell-offs. The conventional approach deals only with price changes. All other behaviours are explained separately.
3. Within our approach it is also possible to encompass the capital investment decision.
4. Marginal analysis when the data are available are not ruled out by our approach. In fact, the selection of control techniques explicitly uses a marginal approach.
5. Our approach attempts to explain behaviour for a firm explicitly organized like the firms responsible for the majority of assets in the economy.
6. Our approach deals directly with decision-making under uncertainty which is the condition under which most firms must operate.

These are a few of the reasons why we recommend our approach or variants of it that may be developed. It is true that our approach puts a heavy emphasis on the individual firm but there is no difficulty in dealing with markets as we hope to show in a subsequent chapter.

SUMMARY

We are suggesting in this chapter that the economists look at control theory as an alternative form of describing the firm to the conventional marginal analysis. The processes within the firm, we believe, can be better described by control theory. The usual cycle that conventional theory describes can also be described by control theory. The control theory of the firm describes the firm as it makes decisions under uncertainty. Critical aspects of behaviour involve the control actions that the firm takes when the actual results are below the target. It is these actions which result in price changes, output changes, inventory changes, layoffs, mergers, and acquisition. It is our belief that it is only through understanding the development of the plans, the setting of targets, and the control actions that the decision-making behaviour of the firm can be understood. We have tried to make a start on a descriptive theory of decision-making: As Simon has said "We have now lived through three centuries or more of vigorous and highly successful inquiry into the laws of nature. Much of that inquiry has been driven by the simple urge to understand, to find the beauty of order hidden in complexity. Time and again, we have found the 'idle' truths arrived at through the process of inquiry to be of the greatest moment for practical human affairs. I need not take time here to argue the point. Scientists know it, engineers and physicians know it, congressmen and members of parliaments know it, the man on the street knows it.

"But I am not sure that this truth is as widely known in economics as it ought to be. I cannot otherwise explain the rather weak and backward development of the descriptive theory of decision-making including the theory of the firm, the sparse and scattered settlement of its terrain, and the fact that many, if not most, of its investigators are drawn from outside economics—from sociology, from psychology, and from political science" (Simon, 1979).

NOTES

1. This chapter borrows significantly from a mathematical version of an unpublished paper, 'A Behavioural and Control Theory of the Firm' by R. M. Cyert and M. H. DeGroot.
2. Some of this material is taken from Richard M. Cyert and Garrel Pottinger, 'Towards a Better Microeconomic Theory', *Philosophy of Science*, Vol. 46, No. 2, June, 1979.

REFERENCES

1. A. Alchian, 'Uncertainty, Evolution, and Economic Theory', Journal of Political Economy, Vol. 58, 1950.
2. K. J. Cohen and R. M. Cyert, *Theory of the Firm: Resource Allocation in a Market Economy* (Englewood Cliffs, N. J.: Prentice Hall, 1975).
3. R. M. Cyert and M. H. DeGroot, 'Bayesian Analysis and Duopoly Theory', *Journal of Political Economy*, Vol. 78, 1970.
4. R. M. Cyert, M. H. DeGroot, and C. Holt, 'Capital Allocation within a Firm', *Behavioral Science*, Vol. 24, 1979.
5. R. M. Cyert and J. G. March, *A Behavioral Theory of the Firm* (Englewood Cliffs, N.J.: Prentice Hall, 1963).
6. Morris H. DeGroot, *Optimal Statistical Decision* (New York: McGraw Hill, 1970).
7. H. A. Simon, 'A Behavioral Model of Rational Choice', *Quarterly Journal of Economics*, Vol. 69, 1955.
8. H. A Simon, 'Rational Decision Making in Business Organization', *The American Economic Review*, Vol. 69, No. 4, 1979.

6 Collusion, Conflict, and Economics*

with Lester B. Lave†

INTRODUCTION

Economic thinking about oligopoly seems to take one of three lines: one group, perhaps the majority of economists, proceeds on the assumption that, "...under all plausible conditions, what they (rational businessmen) would do is to form a monopoly" (Henderson, 1954, p. 565). A second group builds models that seem to have no relation to the world since they involve extremely implausible assumptions about behaviour (see Bertrand; 1883; Cournot, 1897; Worcester, 1958). A third group is concerned with working out concepts of workable competition and describing individual cases of collusion (see Oxenfeld, 1951; Papandreou and Wheeler, 1954; Stigler, 1952).

The first group has a plausible argument if we assume a rational man will act without inflicting needless damage on himself. Under this assumption, the obvious solution is for the oligopolists to maximize joint profits. Which particular point on the contract curve the firms choose (which division of profits) is of no importance since we are concerned only with the theorem that oligopolists maximize joint profits.

Little need be said about the second group. The Cournot assumption or some variant of it has been typically used in these models. Even as a first approximation, it is difficult to believe that a duopolist will act on the assumption that his rival will pay no attention to his moves.

* This research was supported by grants of the Graduate School of Industrial Administration from the School's research funds and from funds provided by the Ford Foundation for the study of organizational behaviour. The authors are indebted to their colleagues at the Graduate School of Industrial Administration for comments, in particular Trenery Dolbear and Martin Bronfenbrenner. Judy Rice and James March contributed many useful suggestions.
† On leave to Northwestern University.

Economic relevance has generally been sacrificed to mathematical elegance.

The third group is characterized by a preoccupation with empirical data. Lengthy polemics about individual cases substitute for an attempt to develop general principles of collusion. The specific case presents only one observed point on each of many variables that influence collusion. In going from one case to another, many, if not most, of the parameters take on new values and so the new case seems to have little to do with the previous one.

Since these three groups have dominated the study of oligopoly, it is not surprising that the formal study of collusion is virtually absent from the economic literature.

However, neither the amount known about collusion nor even the amount of research in the area is a measure of the importance of a theory of collusion to economics. The possibility of profitable collusion exists for nearly every firm of any size in the economy. Virtually all prices are set at least indirectly by a process other than pure competition. Notice that neither of these two arguments denies the existence of evolutionary forces in the economy, that would tend to drive inefficient firms out of business or lower collusive prices. However, in the short run and before all adjustments have been made, imperfect competition rules the economy.

We have argued above that the traditional approaches of economics are not suited to the task of developing a theory of collusion. It is necessary, therefore, to turn to new methods. One approach we view as promising is the controlled experiment. There are already a number of results from the rapidly developing field of experimental economics relevant to the study of collusion. In this paper we attempt to develop the foundation of a theory that will explain the existence and form of collusion and predict its appearance.[1]

We begin with a description of the form of past experiments relevant to this discussion. Then we develop a framework within which to analyse collusion. Finally, we utilize the experimental results to measure the importance of the variables affecting collusion according to our theory.

THE FORM OF THE EXPERIMENTS

The experiments relevant to collusion have utilized a number of situations. The situations have a common element: they are all of mixed-motive structure. Subjects have to collude in order to enjoy a high payoff, but each subject can enjoy an even higher payoff (at least temporarily) by being alone in refusing to collude. One such situation, used by Deutsch and Krauss (1962), involves a game between two trucking firms. Payoffs depend upon the speed with which deliveries are made. Each firm has two routes. The route giving the quickest time of delivery is held in common. The firms have to use the common road to gain a positive payoff. Since only one firm can be on the road at one time, the firms have to co-operate to make money. The experimental treatments include giving subjects the possibility of communication and giving subjects a "gate" which they might close and thereby prevent the other subject from ever using the main road.

A second situation involves a market that contains two or more firms which have to negotiate an agreement with either a group of buyers or a competitive group of sellers. Within this framework Siegel and Fouraker (1960) gave each subject a schedule showing the relation of his profits to price (or quantity) (see also Fouraker and Siegel, 1963 and Siegal and Harnett, 1964). One experimental treatment involves information: knowing the profit table of the other subjects. Subjects exchange bids until an agreement is reached. In the hands of Smith (1962, 1964) a number of buyers and a number of sellers are present in the same room. In one treatment each seller individually offers his unit at some price. Any buyer can accept the offer or wait for a better one; the market goes on for a given amount of time. Each participant is given a reservation price and his earnings depend on the difference between the price of the transaction and the reservation price. In other treatments Smith has the buyer quote price, or has both parties quoting price.

The situation most generally treated in the experimental literature is the prisoners' dilemma (see Deutsch 1949, 1960a, 1960b; Lave, 1962, 1964, 1965; Rapaport and Orwant, 1962). This situation is illustrated in Figure 6.1. Here Firm A must decide whether to chose a high (collusive) price or a low (competitive) price; Firm B must also choose between these alternatives. The consequences of these actions are noted in the matrix. If both firms choose a high price (collude), both win 3. If one firm

		Firm B	
		High Price	Low Price
Firm A	High Price	3, 3	− 50, 4
	Low Price	4, − 50	− 3, − 3

The first payoff in each square goes to Firm A, the second to Firm B.

Figure 6.1: The prisoners' dilemma

Green Player

	1	2
I	2, 5	− 5, 10
II	10, − 5	− 3, − 3

Blue Player

The first payoff in each square goes to Blue Player, the second to Green Player.

Figure 6.2: A prisoners' dilemma with asymmetric profits

decides to cut price (low price) while the other maintains a high price, the former firm will make 4 while the latter firm loses 50. Finally, if both decide to cut price, both lose 3.

In one experimental treatment the matrix is present as in Figure 6.2 in a setting where the subjects cannot see each other. They are told the game will involve a number of trials, which may be specified, and that rewards depend directly on their winnings in the game. Some of the other matrices are shown in Figure 6.3. There are many different treatments, but generally subjects choose simultaneously and know the results of the last trial before proceeding.

Player B

	1	2
1	a, a′	b, c′
2	c, b′	d, d′

Player A

Again, the first payoff in each square goes to Player A, the second to Player B.

Matrix: Payoffs:	a	b	c	d
1	3	− 100	4	− 3
2	3	− 75	4	− 3
3	3	− 50	4	− 3
4	3	− 5	4	− 3
5	3	− 5	10	− 3
6	2,5*	− 5	10	− 3

* If both players choose strategy 1 in Matrix 6, Player A receives a payoff of 2 while Player B receives a payoff of 5 (illustrated in Figure 6.2).

Figure 6.3: Some matrices used in experiments

All of these experiments show that collusion is an extremely delicate phenomenon where apparently subtle changes in the experimental conditions give rise to wide differences in the amount of collusion or competition found. We now go on to define collusion, present the factors influencing it, and show the implications of the experimental evidence.

NATURE OF COLLUSION

Economists generally think of collusion as occurring when the firms in an industry behave so as to achieve the monopoly solution, i.e., maximize joint profit. This behaviour may be implicit or explicit. The firms may explicitly negotiate a division of markets and profits or they may achieve a similar result without direct communication as in the case of price leadership.

This definition is too narrow for our purposes. In an uncertain, evolving world, "approach the monopoly solution" should be substituted for "achieve the monopoly solution". Neither we nor the firm know the relevant demand and cost curves and so we cannot know when the monopoly solution is actually achieved. However, as long as a group of firms is significantly far from the solution that would be achieved under pure competition, we will look on it as collusion. Along with the usual price collusion, we include non-price collusion in such forms as quality stabilization, agreements on markets, extent of advertising, etc. These cases are generally harder to discover and analyse.

THEORETICAL FRAMEWORK

As Marshall has argued and Friedman (1953, p. 7) has further emphasized, one important function of economic theory is to provide "systematic and organized methods of reasoning". The need is for organizing concepts; concepts which will determine the relevant variables, and which will reflect changes in the relevant parameters.

To find these organizing concepts, we have examined the process of collusion. The framework we have developed incorporates three functions—the perception function, the communication function, and the bargaining function.

These functions are defined over a range where zero indicates conditions completely unfavourable to collusion and one indicates favourable conditions. If the value of any one function is zero (or, in general, very small), the process of determining a collusive agreement immediately stops. These functions are viewed as sequential in time. The steps toward collusion are never started if the perception function has a value of zero. If it has a high value, the bargaining function is relevant. Only if all three functions have taken on values close to unity does collusion emerge.

The product of the three values might be interpreted as either (a) an index of the value of collusion given the difficulty of attainment, or (b) the probability of collusion occurring. There are tradeoffs between the functions, and a high value of one function can compensate for the low value of another. However, collusion is likely only when the product of the three is close to one. Thus, we view collusion as sensitive and tenuous; marked resistance (a low value of any of the functions) will choke it off and make it extremely unlikely to occur.

The perception function is defined as the demand function for collusion. It is a function of those variables which tend to make a firm seek collusion as a solution to its problems. The theory of the firm underlying this analysis envisions a firm with a complex set of goals. When the firm fails to achieve these goals, it searches for alternative solutions that will enable it to achieve its goals. Collusion, implicit or explicit, is one of the alternatives. The value of the perception function (between 0 and 1) summarizes the net effect of the variables affecting the demand for collusion.

If the value of the perception function is high, the second stage, communication, becomes relevant. The communication function takes on a high value when it is easy to communicate with rivals. This function represents the communicative ability of the firms in the industry, the ability of firms to discuss the possibility of collusion with each other once the value of the perception function is satisfactorily high. This discussion might take the form of direct confrontation by rivals or the form of market behaviour designed to signal intentions.

The bargaining function summarizes the ability of the firms to reach an actual agreement, implicitly or explicitly. A value of one means that an agreement can be reached. Thus the value of the bargaining function depends on those variables which determine the ability of each of the firms to achieve a satisfactory collusive agreement.

FACTORS AFFECTING PERCEPTION

Every management develops rules of thumb to evaluate its performance in relation to a complex set of goals. These rules of thumb probably include comparison of the firm's profit, sales, and market-share with those of competitors. If the firm is not fulfilling its goals, it will begin to search for solution alternatives. The reasons for deficiency in performance might include structural changes such as new entrants into the industry, new competing products, a drop in demand, overcapacity in the industry, etc. The net effect of such structural changes is to reduce the expected return resulting from independent market behaviour of the firm. Thus collusion becomes relatively more attractive.

The perception of the attractiveness of collusion in experimental situations closely parallels this description; when the subject is not achieving his goals independently of other subjects, he will search for alternative actions such as collusion. Lave (1965) has attempted to develop a theory to predict when subjects in a prisoners' dilemma will perceive collusion as worth the cost of possible loss. In brief, the argument is that the greater the difference between "a" and "d" (in Figure 6.3), the greater will be the incentive to collude. This difference might be interpreted as the profit resulting from collusion. The greater is the absolute value of "b" relative to the other entries, the greater will be the barrier to collusion initially.[2]

The second factor influencing the value of the perception function is the perceived danger from antitrust enforcement. Unfortunately, antitrust law has tended to be general and the laws (e.g., the Sherman Act) have conveyed little operational guidance (see Papandreou and Wheeler, 1954). The courts have decided specific cases and provided limited guidelines for the businessman's behaviour. Even today there is evidence that businessmen have neither a good idea of what is illegal nor completely satisfactory criteria for judging their own acts.[3] Each Attorney General has had much influence in speeding up or slowing down the gathering of evidence on cases; the court has interpreted the law differently at different times. There is no direct experimental evidence related to the threat of law enforcement, but it seems clear that a vigorous Justice Department increases the threat value of the law. Prospective law suits diminish the expected value of collusion by increasing expected costs, thereby moving the value of the perception function toward zero.

A third factor influencing the demand for collusion is the amount of opportunity presented to the firm by the environment. When demand expands faster than capacity, the firm is likely to be achieving its goals and should have no need for collusion. Even if some goals are not achieved, these conditions will make other actions more attractive than collusion. Thus an environment presenting many desirable alternatives to the firm will tend to move the value of the perception function toward zero.

Some experimental evidence bearing on this point is found in a round-robin experiment run with businessmen where alternatives are provided in the form of an opportunity to exploit each new rival. In this case players were informed that they would play a one trial game with each of the other players in the room, although in each trial the specific rival was unknown. Although each player was involved in a fourteen-trial game with men whom he knew and liked, the result was virtually no collusion. In interviews subjects explained that each new player represented an opportunity to achieve the highest payoff.[4] Thus the collusive strategy was viewed as an unattractive alternative and rarely played. A similar group of businessmen immediately came to collusion when the environment was stabilized keeping the same rival (see Lave, 1964).

A special case of the third factor relates to the organizational structure of the firm. The amount of available opportunity might be limited within the firm since a manager in a decentralized organization will have fewer alternatives open to him than one in a centralized organization. If a division is not achieving its goals, a centralized management can shift resources to more successful divisions. A semi-independent division may have no choice other than failure or collusion.[5]

Colluding firms cannot approach the monopoly solution unless all relevant firms are in the agreement. Therefore, the perceived amount of interdependency among firms affects the demand for collusion (cf. Chamberlain). If, for example, domestic firms in a particular industry take no account of their foreign competitors, attempted collusion will result only in increased imports: the perception function in effect then is zero.[6]

In the experimental context, the prisoners' dilemma is usually presented in such a way that subjects see that they are interdependent, but nevertheless, do not realize the nature of the interdependence until a trial or trials have taken place. By the end of the experiment, almost all subjects have seen the nature of the problem and may have succeeded in collusion.

The factors affecting the value of the perception function are summarized in Table 6.1.

Table 6.1: Factors influencing the perception function

a. The degree to which the firm is fulfilling its goals (non-fulfilment might result from gradual or sudden shifts in the structure such as new entrants, new products, a drop in demand, overcapacity, etc.
b. The degree to which antitrust enforcement is perceived as a threat (extent of laws, extent of present enforcement).
c. The extent of opportunities in the industry or the firm.
d. Amount of recognized interdependence among firms. For example, unless domestic firms take account of foreign competitors, no collusion can result.

THE COMMUNICATION FUNCTION

Given a demand for collusion, the communication function describes the ability of firms to learn that collusion is a feasible alternative. It is a function of the capacity to learn the demand of other firms for collusion (determining the value of the perception function of each of the rival firms). This process will be a complex one involving direct and indirect means of determining each rival's position.

The ability to communicate effectively and co-ordinate the acts of firms will first of all be a function of the number of firms and of their size distribution. The larger the number of firms, the more difficult it will be to get them together at any one time and to get them to agree in principle on collusion. This logic also suggests that the more unequal the size distribution of firms, the easier it will be to achieve communication and agreement. After all, a dominant firm has a strong claim to leadership.[7] Equal firms may have such a habit of competition that even communication is difficult. Also, perceived equality will led to direct insistence on continued equality, a difficult outcome to achieve. A dominant firm might gain or lose a few percentage points on industry share without undue concern.

The experimental literature shows that agreements between *two* firms are quite likely to occur (see Deutsch, 1949, 1960a; Fouraker and Siegel, 1963; Lave, 1962, 1965). However, under experimental conditions allowing no communication between subjects, Fouraker and Siegel (1963) found no collusion for experiments involving more than two subjects. The failure to find collusion with more than two subjects is not directly relevant to the economy since firms do have ways to communicate. Nevertheless, this result demonstrates the significance of the effect of increasing the number of firms when no communication is possible.

A second factor influencing the value of the communication function is the extent to which the management of the firms in the industry identify with each other. For example, they might be physically located in the same city, might belong to the same social clubs, and might regard each other as friends. We would expect such a set of facts to move the communication function toward one. On the other hand, if there are new entrants in the industry, if the managements are geographically separated, and if the new firms gained entry with the help of government, we would expect the communication function to tend toward zero.[8]

The influence of the social milieu cannot be overstated. Minz (1951) describes a panic experiment where subjects were able to perform the task only when interdependence and co-operation were stressed. These orientations tend to develop, for example, when communication is allowed (Loomis, 1959 and Deutsch 1960a). Deutsch also found collusion rose in a prisoners' dilemma when subjects were allowed to reverse their choices until a satisfactory outcome developed. A slight variation on procedure illustrates how tenuous this orientation can be: a prisoners' dilemma was run under conditions of sequential choice. Here the temptation to double-cross and underlying suspicion rose in importance until collusion almost disappeared.

In general the social environment should tend to promote collusion: we would expect a feeling of identification to exist among the presidents of firms in an industry. After all, they are professional managers running firms which have similar problems, including problems with stockholders: why should they compete against one another in addition.[9]

In some of Lave's experiments the subjects couched their reasons for following the collusive strategy in terms of "I would expect any fellow (Harvard) student to..." or "I believe this game is rigged since no (Reed) student would..." In three schools (Reed, MIT, and Harvard) where such sentiments were expressed, the proportion of experiments ending in collusion was significantly greater than in another school (Northeastern) where such expressions were absent (see Lave, 1962, 1965).

The last factor influencing the communication function is the existence and form of historical channels of communication. If an industry begins with a format for collusion, there is a much greater chance of achieving it.

Direct communication is not always required; collusion may come from tacit communication. After all, "talk is cheap; actions count." Firms may agree on quality standards and on manufacturing costs. It is easier to agree on standard markups if there is agreement on the costs they are marking up. One example of this occurs in certain areas of retailing. Over time some groups have managed to standardize their methods of costing and their markups. Now prices may change and new goods may be introduced, but all sellers are able to preserve uniform retail prices.[10]

This standardization might occur by any number of means: there may be patents, some buyer of the industry's products that sets the standard, some seller of raw materials to the industry, the salesmen in the industry, trade associations, or a single CPA for the large firms in the industry (as happens in a number of cases). One final way is that the firms may be linked in an international cartel agreement, although it is illegal for them to collude domestically. This association will tend to force standardization and so indirectly aid domestic collusion.

Let us look at some of these factors in more detail. Patents, for example, enable the company holding them to insist on a "quality standard" as a pre-requisite for licensing. Once a standard product is being sold and being produced at standard costs determined by the fees, uniform retail prices are only to be expected.

In many industries there are so many possibilities for diverse products that any standardization seems unlikely. However, if one buyer sets a standard, advertises it heavily, and sets a price, the rest of the industry is likely to go along or make small variations on this theme. Similarly, the sellers of raw materials might tend to regulate behaviour by imposing standard costs on the industry.

Trade associations have much to do with standardizing procedures.[11] Their journals tend to provide information about what other firms are doing and so promote followership. Certainly new procedures which are the result of a firm not being aware of "standard practice" will never occur with a strong trade association in existence. In the same vein, those industries that use a single accountant throughout most of the industry will tend to have the same costing procedures. Although accountants differ in their treatment of items, they try to adhere to an industry standard if one exists. As argued before, standard costs combined with a standard markup satisfy the conditions necessary for tacit communication. There is no formal experimental evidence on tacit communication but Schelling (1960) has gathered some evidence which is of interest.

The communication among firms may be explicit: there may be direct discussion in the industry. In such a situation a leader must emerge to introduce the collusion and help carry it through. Since even the initial sounding out is illegal, the leader must be trusted. A dominant firm, a coalition of middle-sized firms, or a firm that enjoys special information or prestige may provide the leadership. The last case might happen if this firm had special cost or marketing information, was the oldest firm, or the quality setter.

The economist generally sees direct communication as promising collusion. There is some experimental evidence to support this (see Deutsch, 1960 and Deutsch and Krauss 1962). The possibility of direct communication does not guarantee a value of 1 for the communication function. There must be a demand for collusion (a value of 1 for the perception function) as is shown in the experiments of Deutsch and Krauss (1962, p. 75):

> The mere existence of channels of communication is no guarantee that communication will indeed take place; and the greater the competitive orientation of the parties *vis-à-vis* each other, the less likely will they be to use such channels as do exist.

If firms demand collusion and find communication possible, the bargaining function becomes relevant. The factors affecting the value of the communication function are summarized in Table 6.2.

Table 6.2: Factors affecting the communication function:

a. The number and size of firms in industry.
b. The extend of feelings of identity with other firms (including professionalism in managers).
c. The existence of historical channels of communication, the development of a language of collusion, metacollusion (tacit versus explicit, trade associations, journals, unions sellers, international cartels, buyers, existence of leader or potential leader).

THE BARGAINING FUNCTION

Given that the values of the perception function and communication function are high, there are still substantial difficulties in the way of consummating a collusive agreement. The bargaining function encompasses the activities involved in achieving the actual agreement. (The most important factor determining the division of payoffs is the existence of an objective criterion upon which the parties can agree.) While bargaining may be explicit or tacit, it is interesting only in the case of explicit collusion. But direct communication is not an unmixed blessing as is shown in the experiments of Deutsch and Krauss (1962, p. 75):

The results...justify a reconsideration of the role of communication in the bargaining process. Typically, communication is perceived as a means whereby the bargainers coordinate effort (e.g., exchange bids, indicate positions, etc.). Usually, little emphasis is given to interaction of communication with motivational orientation. Certainly the coordination function of communication is important. However, as Siegel and Fouraker point out, free communication may also be used to convey information (e.g., threats, insults, etc.) which may intensify the competitive aspects of the situation.

Communicating by actions, as in the case of tacit collusion, necessitates simple solutions. In particular, the lack of explicit communication eliminates the possibility of a redivision of profits. Even within these limits, bargaining by action can give rise to complex solutions.

Experimental evidence from the asymmetrical prisoners' dilemma experiments (see Figure 6.2) bears upon this point (Lave 1965). Subjects were not satisfied with the simple collusion solution (payoffs of 2 and 5 respectively giving the highest joint profit) because of the lack of equality (expressed in written comments). A significant number of subjects negotiated by action patterns giving equal positive payoffs. For example, one common pattern which emerged was to alternate between strategies I, 2 and II, 1. Other more complicated patterns were also observed. In this case it seems clear that equality was the only objective criterion on which there could be agreement.

The problem of finding an objective criterion is no less difficult under explicit collusion. The existence of easy communication increases the number of possible solutions. The problem is complicated by the host of plausible possibilities: output, capacity, equal rate of return on invested capital, stable market shares, etc.

The problem is to agree on one of these. Frequently, an industry has a tradition of paying attention to one such measure. If this is so, the bargaining process will be more quickly concluded; that is, the value of the bargaining function will tend toward one.

Even if firms have some criteria for division of profits, there may still be severe disagreement. For example, disagreements on the optimal strategy for the present or future course of the industry may cause the breakdown of collusion. Stigler cites the example of Henry Ford believing that low priced, standard cars would be desired in America while members of the Selden patent pool believed that expensive, individually designed cars were the wave of the future. With such a basic disagreement, it is unlikely that a group of firms could collude (see Stigler, 1952).

This factor will move the bargaining function toward zero. However, since it is likely that a wrong act made in collusion will prove more profitable than the correct act made in competition, it pays a firm to smooth over disagreements in favour of collusion. [12]

The final point influencing the bargaining function is the necessity for unanimity of collusion if it is to be effective. Even a small firm can disrupt a collusive agreement by expanding capacity and shading price. However, the industry can use moral and economic sanctions to force collusion. They can exclude the deviating firm from the industry association, try to poison his line of credit, stir his customers and suppliers against him, and generally make it uncomfortable enough for deviants to coerce them to collude.

There is also a tendency toward conformity among the members of a group that will aid in achieving the unanimity. Experiments by Asch

Table 6.3: Factors affecting the bargaining function

a. Search for some just division of profits (easiest if there is some recognized objective criterion, e.g., capacity).
b. Different perceptions of present and future (e.g., Henry Ford versus Selden patent pool).
c. Unanimity is required and may be achieved through moral and economic sanctions and through tendency toward conformity.

(1958) show that subjects will go to incredible lengths to conform with group opinion. The factors affecting the value of the bargaining function are summarized in Table 6.3.

THE STABILITY OF COLLUSION

Our theory bears primarily on the process by which collusion is achieved. However, our approach leads directly to another important question: Once an agreement has been reached, how stable will it be? One factor affecting stability is the extent of structural changes in the industry. New products and processes, new entrants, or shifts in demand may swamp collusive agreements. We expect collusive agreements to be maintained only in industries whose structures are relatively constant. The downturn phase of the business cycle is commonly thought to destroy collusive agreements. There is evidence that casts doubt on this point, however (see Cyert, 1955).

Another factor is the extent to which cheating is effective and can be detected. Price shading is both effective and difficult to detect. Thus, we would argue that agreements which use some easily enforceable criteria tend to be stable. Thus, a collusive agreement that relies on a geographical division of markets would tend to be more stable than one based on price fixing.

Occasionally, one firm will conclude that the structure of the industry is going to change so radically that the agreement must break down. At such a point it is to his advantage to violate the agreement, take the extra profits, and never have to fear sanctions. This phenomenon is investigated experimentally by specifying the end of the game. Subjects tend to change to a competitive strategy on the last or next to last trial. Rarely is that change made earlier, although most subjects do change when an end of the game is explicitly stated in advance (see Lave, 1965).

The last factor influencing the stability of collusion is related to increases in the level of aspiration of a firm. If this rise occurs, we might expect to see management attempting to shade the agreement since small increases become quite important. On the other hand, this firm will react strongly to even minor setbacks since the level of aspiration has become stable and sensitive. Thus, the argument can be paraphrased as saying that stable agreement is liable to lead to its own downfall. The experimental evidence cited above indicates that subjects are always ready to compete even in the most stable situations. Thus it can be said that there is always latent competition in collusion. These factors are summarized in Table 6.4.

Table 6.4: Factors affecting the stability of collusion:

---

a. Structural changes in industry.
b. Imperfect knowledge on violations of collusion.
c. End point effects from structural change.
d. Stability will cause a rise in aspiration levels and so small increases will become important and firms will tend to shade price and nibble away at the agreement.

SUMMARY AND CONCLUSION

The study of collusion has not been fruitful in economics since the right tools have not been used. Economic treatments of collusion have been characterized by the lack of good data: these treatments have tended either to ignore reality or to get bogged down in it. The data for fruitful exploration must hold most factors constant so that the investigation can find the influence of each factor, the tradeoff between factors and the interaction effects, *ceteris paribus*. The controlled experiment is the best tool for such investigations, although it brings with it the difficult problem of transferring results from the laboratory to the world.

Three functions are assumed to be the principal influence on collusion: the perception of the value of collusion, the extent and kind of communication between firms, and the bargaining over the division of payoffs. All three functions must take on satisfactory values if collusion is to be achieved.

The factors influencing the perception of the value of collusion include the degree to which the firm is fulfilling its goals, the degree to which antitrust enforcement is perceived as a threat, the number of alternatives open to the firm, and the amount of recognized interdependence between firms.

More experimental work is required to find how firms react to the threat of the discovery of collusion. The current knowledge of risk taking is a start here, but we do not know how the threat of the law is perceived. Experimental treatment of collusion under changing structures, e.g., entrants and new products, is quite important. Some partial results suggest this is an extremely important influence about which we have little knowledge.

Factors influencing the communication function include the number and size distribution of firms, the feeling of identity between managers of different firms, the problem of getting others to see the value of collusion, and the historical means of communication.

The number and size of firms is probably the factor where investigation has been most intensive. Social psychologists have been concerned with the realized collusion under conditions of strong positive or negative feelings (affect). In general, this area contains the greatest amount of experimental work, although much remains to be done.

The bargaining function is tied to a search for a "just" division of profits, of different perceptions of the present and future market, and of the fact that unanimity is required for agreement. Unanimity might be impossible without the moral and economic sanctions open to the colluding firms against deviates. There is also a strong tendency toward conformity with group norms.

Future research might explore the objective criterion firms have actually used to guide the division of profits. How does one develop and how strictly are they used? It would also be helpful to get a further idea of the kinds and strength of the economic sanctions available.

A last factor affecting collusion is the stability of agreement. Whatever position a firm takes, from insider to deviant, it is more profitable for the collusion to be stable. The important influences here are the structural stability of the industry, the ability to detect cheating, the tendency to disrupt collusion if it appears that the agreement might end in the future, and the pressures toward gaining at the expense of others within the agreement.

The two most promising areas for experimental work are the second and last ones. How will firms behave if they know cheating is not easily detected? How will they punish a cheater who is caught? How strong is the pressure for a rise in the aspiration level of a firm under conditions of stable collusion? When will a firm irrationally risk dissolution of collusion for a small gain? We intend to pursue a few of these experiments.

NOTES

1. One of the notable treatments of collusion in economics literature is Fellner (1949). Some of his arguments parallel our treatment.
2. In addition to the relative values of the entries in the matrix, the number of trials influences the perception of collusion in the prisoners' dilemma. The larger the number of trials the greater is the incentive to collude. The theory predicts that collusion will result if the number of trials is such that:

$$n < 3 \frac{b - d}{a - d}$$

If the number of trials fulfils this condition, subjects will perceive collusion as worth attaining.
3. In speaking of the reactions of businessmen to antitrust legislation, one prominent businessman characterized their feeling as: "Businessmen move at

their peril while the law waits in ambush" (Hazard, 1961, p. 61). It must be emphasized that it is the perceived, not actual, law that influences the function. In a rational, informed society, ambiguous laws would do more to inhibit collusion than specific ones: until the issue was clarified, businessmen would avoid questionable acts. However, if businessmen perceive the attorney general or society to be friendly, only a specific prohibition would inhibit collusion.

4. The amount of money involved in these experiments was always significant. In this case if players had colluded on all trials, earnings could have been $120 for a 90 minute experiment; in fact some earnings reached $60.

5. This division manager is squeezed from the top since, to all businessmen (especially to his boss), "...profit is the reward for good management, and loss is the unpardonable business sin" (Hazard, 1961, p. 61).

This factor might be used to comment on the GE-Westinghouse case where the high officials in each company claimed to have known nothing of the collusion. Such testimony was generally ridiculed by economists. The argument above makes it plausible that the divisional executives were faced with the need to raise their division's profitability. There was no alternative to collusion if they wanted promotion out of this division. It was incumbent upon them to keep the collusive agreements unknown to top management since few executives would think of describing their merits for promotion in terms of having achieved collusion in their previous job.

6. Some experimental results to the contrary involve the 'minimal social situation' (Sidowski, *et al.* 1956). Here subjects learned to co-operate even though they had no idea they were interacting with another person. However, this result is quite special as can be seen by examining results of Suppes and Atkinson(1950).

7. See the literature on price leadership, in particular Oxenfeld (1951, pp. 292–302).

8. Experimental evidence on the effect of motivation and communication is provided by Deutsch (1960a). He found that collusion declined significantly if the motivation of subjects was changed from cooperation to an individual orientation, to a competitive orientation. The possibility of communication, even though agreement was not binding, increased collusion.

9. When businessmen interact, socially, the conversation naturally tends to gravitate toward business problems. As the President of US Steel testified before the TNEC (Temporary National Economic Committee), "I find steel men ... are very much like professional men and men in other lines of business. Whenever they meet they talk about the steel business. I always find myself talking about the steel business when I meet a steel man" (Oxenfeld, 1951, p. 289). See also note 11.

10. Notice this standardization tends to force collusion one level back on the manufacturers of retail goods. If all sellers have standard costs, manufacturers know what their prices will be. With fixed prices and the model of markups of their retail customers in mind, manufacturers tend to plan the costs and implicitly collude.

11. 'People of the same trade seldom meet together, even for merriment and diversion, but the conversation ends in a conspiracy against the public, or in some contrivance to raise prices. It is impossible indeed to prevent such meetings, by any law which either could be executed, or would be consistent with liberty and justice. But though the law cannot hinder people of the same

trade from sometimes assembling together, it ought to do nothing to facilitate such assemblies; much less to render them necessary' (Smith, 1776, p. 128).

12. To paraphrase Stigler's (1939) conclusion on the kinked demand curve: Disagreement on strategy is a barrier to increasing profits, 'and business is the collection of devices for circumventing barriers to profits'.

REFERENCES

Asch, S. 'Effects of Group Pressure Upon the Modification and Distortion of Judgements', in Maccoby, E. *et al.* (eds), *Readings in Social Psychology*, New York: Holt, Rinehart and Winston, 1958.

Bain, J., Industrial Organization, New York, Wiley, 1959.

Bertrand, J., 'Recherches', *Journal des Savants*, 1883.

Bishop, R., 'Duopoly: Collusion or Warfare?' *American Economic Review*, 50, 1960.

Chamberlin, E., *The Theory of Monopolistic Competition*, Cambridge: Harvard University Press, 1933.

Cournot, A., *Researchers in the Mathematical Principles of The Theory of Wealth*, New York: Macmillan, 1897.

Cyert, R., 'Oligopoly Price Behavior in the Business Cycle', *Journal of Political Economy*, 63, 1955.

—————— and March, J., 'Behavioral Theory of the Firm', Englewood Cliffs: Prentice Hall, 1964.

Deutsch, M., 'An Experimental Study of the Effects of Cooperation and Competition Upon Group Progress', *Human Relations*, 2, 1949.

—————— 'The Effect of Motivational Orientation Upon Trust and Suspicion', *Human Relations*, 13, 1960a.

—————— 'Trust, Trustworthiness, and the F. Scale', *Journal of Abnormal and Social Psychology*, 61, 1960.

—————— and Krause, R., 'Studies of Interpersonal Bargaining', *Journal of Conflict Resolution*, 6, 1962.

Fellner, W., *Competition Among the Few*, New York: Knopf, 1949.

Fouraker, L. and Siegel, S., *Bargaining Behavior*, New York: McGraw-Hill, 1963.

Friedman, M., *Essays in Positive Economics*, Chicago: University of Chicago Press, 1953.

Hazard, L., 'Are Big Businessmen Crooks?', *The Atlantic Monthly*, 1961.

Henderson, A., 'The Theory of Duopoly', *Quarterly Journal of Economics*, LXVIII, 1954.

Lave, L., 'An Empirical Approach to the Prisoners' Dilemma', *Quarterly Journal of Economics*, LXXVI, 1962.

—————— 'The Behavior of Executives in the Prisoners' Dilemma', *Quarterly Journal of Economics*, 1964.

—————— 'Factors Affecting Cooperation in the Prisoners' Dilemma', *Behavioral Science*, 9, 1965.

Loomis, J., 'Communication, The Development of Trust, and Cooperative Behavior', *Human Relations*, 12, 1959.

Mintz, A., 'Non-adaptive Group Behavior', *Journal of Abnormal and Social Psychology*, 46, 1951.

Oxenfeldt, A., *Industrial Pricing and Market Practices*, Englewood Cliffs: Prentice Hall, 1951.

Papandreou, A. and Wheeler, J., *Competition and its Regulation*, Englewood Cliffs: Prentice Hall, 1954.

Rapoport, A. and Orwant, C., 'Experimental Games: A Review', *Behavioral Science*, 7, 1962.

Schelling, T., *The Strategy of Conflict*, Cambridge: Harvard University Press, 1960.

Scodel, A., Ratoosh, P., Minas, J. and Lipetz, M., 'Some Descriptive Aspects of Two-Person Non Zero Sum Games', *Journal of Conflict Resolution*, 3, 1959.

———, Minas, J., Marlow, D. and Rawson, H., 'Some Descriptive Aspects of Two-Person Non Zero Sum Games, II', *Journal of Conflict Resolution*, 4, 1960.

Sidowski, J., Wyckoff, L. and Tabory, L., 'The Influence of Reinforcement and Punishment in a Minimal Situation', *Journal of Abnormal and Social Psychology*, 57, 1956.

Siegel, S. and Fouraker, L., *Bargaining and Group Decision Making*, New York: McGraw-Hill, 1960.

——— and Harnett, D., 'Bargaining Behavior: A Comparison Between Mature Industrial Personnel and College Students', *Operations Research*, 12, 1964.

Smith, A., *The Wealth of Nations*, New York: The Modern Library, 1937.

Smith, V., 'An Experimental Study of Competitive Market Behavior', *Journal of Political Economy*, LXX, 1962.

——— 'Effect of Market Organization on Competitive Equilibrium', *Quarterly Journal of Economics*, LXXVIII, 1964.

Smithies, A. and Savage, L., 'A Dynamic Problem in Duopoly', *Econometrica*, 8, 1940.

Stackleberg, H., *Markform und Gleichgewicht*, Berlin: J. Springer, 1934

Stigler, G., 'The Kinky Demand Curve and Rigid Prices', *Journal of Political Economy*, XLVII, 1939.

——— *The Theory of Price*, New York: Macmillan, 1952.

Suppes, P. and Atkinson, R., *Markov Learning Models for Multiperson Interactions*, Stanford: Stanford University Press, 1960.

Worcester, D., 'A Partial Theory of Collusion', *American Economic Review*, 48, 1958.

7 Behavioural Rules and the Theory of the Firm*

with M. I. Kamien

The neo-classical theory of the firm as synthesized by Samuelson is an example of the use of deductive arguments to arrive at meaningful theorems in economics.[1] Starting with only a few explicit assumptions, a number of interesting theorems and corollaries are derived. The theorems describe a set of optimal-decision rules which a profit-maximizing firm should follow to determine its levels of outputs and inputs given market price. Failure to follow these rules will not only diminish profit but will make it impossible for the firms to survive under the free entry market conditions assumed. If it does follow them, the firm has no problem of dealing with uncertainty because nothing is uncertain in the model posited.

The received theory of the firm is a useful and significant intellectual contribution. It has enabled economists to explain many kinds of behaviour in the world and has, in general, served as a framework for both scientific work and policy recommendations.

Our aim in this chapter is to nurture a growing body of work which aims at developing a theory of the firm that will lead to confirmable propositions explaining the behaviour of the firm in noncompetitive markets. At the heart of our chapter is the judgement that the firm is an adaptive mechanism operated by human beings with limited information-processing capabilities. We propose to look at the firm under conditions which are less restrictive than those of the neo-classical theory. We will relax the assumption of certain knowledge of market environment and the internal technological conditions. In the process we hope to provide an explanation for use of behavioural rules (rules of thumb) by firms for pricing and output decisions.

We begin with the proposition that profit is, at the very least, a major

---

* Reprinted by permission from *Prices: Issues in Theory, Practice and Public Policy* A. Phillips and O. E. Williamson (eds), University of Pennsylvania Press, 1967.

objective of the firm. The task is to devise an analytic model which explains how the firm makes its decisions in the face of uncertainty so as to earn profits enabling it to survive and grow. Herbert Simon's work on satisficing and R. A. Gordon's references to satisfactory profits are attempts to develop decision criteria in an environment that more closely resembles the real world than does the classical model.[2]

BEHAVIOURAL RULES

Without going into the other objectives of the firm and the other obstacles to profit-maximization, it is reasonable to suppose that the firm devises approximate solutions for the attainment of its goals. The approximating procedures are often referred to as behavioural rules. These rules presumably evolve through confrontation with similar situations over time and some experimentation. The firm may discover some simple relationships between the price it sets and sales volume, market share, and profit by trying several different price levels. Or the behavioural rules may be based on customary procedure in the given industry. An example of this might be the markup above cost.[3]

Behavioural rules not only serve to approximate the optimal procedure for achieving certain objectives but also help preserve internal stability within the firm. Recognition of the separation of ownership and control in a modern corporation requires that the managers of such a firm be viewed collectively as an organization. We know from organization theory that the internal stability of a decision-making organization is enhanced by the ability to transform decision processes into programmed behaviour. Behavioural rules are a form of programmed decision-making.

RELATIONSHIP OF BEHAVIOURAL THEORY AND DYNAMICS

While the behavioural approach to the theory of the firm appears promising, its achievements to date have been limited. For the most part, this can be attributed to the infancy of the approach. The tools required for better exploitation of the method have not yet been fully developed. Moreover, an economist venturing into this area must acquaint himself with the rudiments of organization theory, while the organization theorist must learn some basic economics.

These difficulties aside, the behavioural theory of the firm lacks most, in terms of completeness, a dynamics (although this may be interpreted as an overstatement, since in the behavioural approach no clear delineation between statics and dynamics has yet been made). Again, if we reflect on the development of classical economic theory, this is not too surprising. Even now the definition of economic dynamics is a somewhat elusive concept. In particular, the accepted definition appears to be "a system is dynamical if its behaviour over time is determined by functional equations in which *variables at different points in time* are involved in an *essential* way."[4]

But what of dynamics in the behavioural approach? How does time enter in an essential way in the decision-making processes of the firm as conceived in the behavioural theory. We believe it does this in two ways. In the first place, recognition of the future compounds the uncertainties that the firm must presently face. Not only does the firm often lack knowledge of the shape of its present cost and demand functions but it must also contemplate the possibility that these functions might change over time.

Secondly, time enters in an essential way into the behavioural theory approach to the firm through the evolution of its decision rules. The behavioural decision rules ordinarily use past values of the relevant variables for determining the current values of these variables. The rules are altered in the sense of their functional form or exclusion of certain variables and the inclusion of other variables in their stead on the basis of how well these rules perform in meeting the desired objectives. The time element imposes a need for flexibility in the formation of behavioural rules, or, in other words, to allow learning to take place. This is not the case, for example, with regard to behaviour posited for the suppliers in the naïve cobweb model. The supplier always determines his production level on the basis of last period's prices despite the fact that he may often be ruined by following this rule. The same type of stereotyped behaviour is displayed by the competitors in the Cournot duopoly model.

We should in fact expect the firm not only to revise its behavioural rules on the basis of past experience but also to do this at an increasing rate. The learning process itself has to be learned, and we might assume that it improves with experience. This point has not as yet, it seems, been incorporated into the study of behavioural rules. Baumol and Quandt, for example, rely on initially short reaction time or certain values of elasticities of demand and cost in order to obtain stable learning behavioural rules.[5] A more complete analysis would incorporate the notion that the reaction time itself changes over time, presumably getting shorter.

Time enters into the behavioural approach, as the medium through which complete adjustments to the environment take place. This is the distinction in adjustment which necessitates the definitions of a short run and a long run. In the classical theory the short run differs from the long run in that in the latter case the firm is capable of altering all its factors of production, whereas in the former case it cannot. It seems to us, in the light of what has been said above, that the analogous concept in the behavioural approach should be that in the short run the firm cannot cause all decision processes to be of the programmed variety, whereas in the long run it can. An immediate consequence of this definition is that the firm's reaction time to an exogenous change in its environment would be more rapid in the long run than in the short run. Of course, as long as some uncertainty exists, and the future will assure this, reaction time will not become zero but rather approach this limit asymptotically.

Focusing our attention on the definitions of long run and short run proposed above should also enable us to understand and explain economic phenomena which have not been satisfactorily explained by the classical theory. The most prominent of these is the behaviour of oligopolistic firms and price movements in such markets. Several attempts have been made to explain the constancy of prices over long periods of time despite changes in technology and input costs. Also, when price changes do take place they are typically initiated by one firm and almost immediately followed by the other firms. The common explanation offered is collusion among these firms. Sometimes, of course, this is the case. However, at other times evidence to support the collusion hypothesis cannot be found, and we must suppose that the goings on are an inherent feature of this type of market organization.

Among the other better-known explanations of the behaviour of firms in oligopolistic markets are the kinked demand curve model, the dominant-firm model, and the game theoretic approach. Unfortunately none of these provides a commonly accepted explanation of oligopoly behaviour. While the notion of the kinked demand curve is appealing at first glance, it fails to explain the simultaneous increase in prices often observed in actual oligopolistic markets, e.g., the recent advances in steel prices and automobile prices. The firms in the model behave asymmetrically with regard to a change in the price initiated by one of the firms. If any firm lowers prices, the rest will all follow. This is basically a defensive act. On the other hand, firms will not follow a price increase. This behaviour appears to be more of an aggressive nature. Putting it another way, the firms appear to regard their relationship to the market as a zero-sum game. They always fail to recognize that higher profits might be obtained by co-operating.

In terms of the dynamics described above, the explanation of the same phenomena might go something like this. At the inception of the industry in which there are many small firms a great deal of learning and formation of behavioural rules has to take place. As the industry progresses through time behavioural rules are developed and refined.

Some firms leave the industry because they cannot compete successfully. Consolidations may be the result of learning that economies of scale exist. Over time the remaining firms develop more refined rules. The amount of information shared in common by these firms becomes large. Each can anticipate to a great extent the actions of his competitors and recognize the basis on which a competitor makes a move. Response time decreases. The end result is seemingly simultaneous, since each firm over time becomes like the other firms and is affected in the same way by external changes (e.g., increases in prices of raw materials).

AN ILLUSTRATIVE MODEL[6]

We now return to the main focus of our paper, namely the evolution of behavioural rules.

Some of the arguments set forth above can best be clarified with a simple price-setting model exhibiting the way in which behavioural rules, learning, and time enter into the description of firm behaviour. The model we present below is meant to convey the spirit of the methodology we think appropriate for the study of the firm rather than a description of actual behaviour.

We posit a firm which sells a single product in a market consisting of many firms selling products of varying degrees of substitutability. In other words, some of the firms are lesser competitors to the firm in question than others. The important feature of this market situation is that the relevant firm does not regard only one or a few rivals directly responsive to its pricing decisions. The responses are instead diffused among its several competitors.

Let us suppose further that the firm's cost function is of the form

$$(1) \qquad C(q) = cq$$

where c is a positive constant, and that its demand curve is describable by the equation

$$(2) \qquad q = a - bp$$

where $a, b > 0$, providing that its rivals maintain current prices. Consequently, the firm's profit as a function of price is

$$(3) \qquad \pi(p) = (a + bc)p - bp^2 - ca,$$

or lettering $\alpha = -b$, $\beta = (a + bc)$, and $\gamma = -ca$ we can rewrite (3) as

$$(4) \qquad \pi(p) = \alpha p^2 + \beta p + \gamma$$

Now

(5) $$\pi'(p) = 2\alpha p - \beta$$

and

(6) $$\pi''(p) = 2\alpha < 0$$

which indicates that $\pi(p)$ is concave. If the firm knows the values of the parameters α, β, γ, it can determine the optimal price directly by setting $\pi'(p) = 0$. If we designate the optimal price by p^*, then in this instance, $p^* = -\beta/2\alpha$. If the firm knows only that the profit function $\pi(p)$ is unimodal, it can arrive at the optimal price in a series of steps by means of a sequential search procedure. A simple rule such as that to increase (decrease) price by 10 per cent as long as the resulting increment to profit is positive and to stop the first time incremental profit is zero or negative will achieve the desired objective or at least come very close.

Suppose, however, the true increment in profits stemming from a change in price is confounded by extraneous events as, for instance, income fluctuations, price changes in related products not in the given market, and price movements within the industry which are exogenous to the firm under consideration. In this case, neither of the above procedures will necessarily yield p^*. Formally, this situation can be described by incorporating an error term into expression (2), thereby altering (4). Thus (2) becomes

(2') $$q = a - bp + \epsilon$$

where ϵ represents an error term, and (4) becomes

(4') $$\pi(p) = \alpha p^2 + \beta p + \gamma + \epsilon p.$$

Then

(5') $$\pi'(p) = 2\alpha p + \beta + \epsilon$$

wherein, we implicitly assume that $d\epsilon/dp = 0$. In other words, changes in the error term ϵ are independent of changes in price p.

We also assume that the firm has a point estimate of the parameter α from past experience and that this estimate is considered to be fairly reliable. Moreover, we assume that α remains fixed so that changes in ϵ serve merely to shift expression (5') up and down. The firm now seeks to locate the "optimal" price. We purposely leave "optimal" undefined at this point to emphasize, for reasons that will become apparent below, the multiplicity of meanings that can be associated with the term. Finally, we suppose that the firm has no knowledge of the expected value of ϵ. Instead, $E[\epsilon]$ is a random variable. The firm does, however, believe that $E[\epsilon]$ is distributed according to some distribution function $g(\xi)$. By setting price at different levels and observing the outcome, the firm revises its prior distribution function $g(\xi)$ to conform with the new information obtained. In this manner the firm learns and adapts itself to the environment.

To be more specific, let us assume that the firm structures this problem in terms of two decisions, viz.,

(7) $$D_1 : p_t = (1 + r)p_{t-1}$$
$$D_2 : p_t = (1 - r)p_{t-1}$$

where $0 \leqslant r \leqslant 1$.

The firm may raise price by r per cent above last period's price, decision D_1, or lower price by r per cent from last period's price, D_2. We let u_1 denote the probability that decision D_1 will result in a positive increment to profit, and consequently $(1 - u_1)$ is the probability that decision D_1 will result in a decrease in profit. Similarly, we let u_2 denote the probability that decision D_2 will lead to an increase in profit, and therefore that $(1 - u_2)$ is the probability that decision D_2 reduces profit. We further designate an increase in profit, regardless of its magnitude, by 1 and a reduction in profit by -1. It should be noted that the probabilities u_1 and u_2 are taken to be independent of the current price level. The firm does not know these probabilities but does believe that they are generated by the distribution functions $g_1(\xi)$ and $g_2(\xi)$ respectively.

We may envision the firm under these circumstances as, say, making decision D_1, observing the outcome and then updating its prior beliefs regarding $g_1(\xi)$ and $g_2(\xi)$. This behaviour could be described by Bayes's formula. In particular, suppose that after τ decisions have been made, k have been on the D_1 type and that the number of times profit increased thereafter was l. On the basis of this information the firm's revised distribution should be according to Bayes's formula.

(8) $$f_1(\xi|k,l) = K_1 \xi^l (1 - \xi)^{k-l} g_1(\xi)$$

where $f_1(\xi|k,l)$ is defined as the probability that u_1 lies between ξ and $\xi + d\xi$ given k and l and where K_1 is a normalizing factor chosen so that

$$\int_0^1 f_1(\xi|k, l)d\xi = 1.$$

Now, given that τ decisions have been made, net profits have increased j times in all, and decision D_1 has been chosen k times before with l subsequent successes, we can deduce that decision D_2 must have been chosen $(\tau - k)$ times before and yielded $1/2 (\tau + j) - l$ successes. Thus, defining $f_2(\xi|\tau, j, k, l)$ as the probability that u_2 lies between ξ and $d\xi$ it follows that

(9) $\qquad f_2(\xi|\tau, j, k, l) = K_2\xi^{1/2(\tau+j)-l}(1 - \xi)^{i-k-1/2(\tau+j)+l}g_2(\xi)$

where K_2 has a similar interpretation as K_1.

If we further suppose that the firm chooses as its initial distributions the uniform distributions

$$g_1(\xi) = 1 \qquad g_2(\xi) = 1 \qquad 0 \leqslant \xi \leqslant 1$$

then expressions (8) and (9) simplify to

(8') $\qquad\qquad f_1(\xi \mid k, l) = K_1\xi^l(1 - \xi)^{k-l}$

and

(9') $\qquad f_2(\xi \mid \tau, j, k, l) = K_2\xi^{1/2(\tau+j)-1}(1 - \xi)^{i-k-1/2(\tau+j)+l}$

Let us now turn to the question of what might constitute an optimal method of selecting between D_1 and D_2 at each stage of the process. The first criterion might be to select the decisions in such a way as to maximize the increment to profits over the entire duration of the process. The process terminates when a price has been found such that deviations from this price can only result in a decrease in profit.

In the language of dynamic programming as applied to adaptive control processes we define the optimal value function $V(\tau, j, k, l)$ to be the expected value of the process starting at stage τ (time τ), in the course of which profits have increased j times and where k previous choices of decision D_1 have been followed by l increases in profit. It should be noted that the function V is the firm's subjective expected value rather than the ordinary expected value which would be calculated if the probabilities u_1 and u_2 were known. We also note that t will designate the stage of the process and j the state of our process.

Suppose now that the firm chooses D_1 and that u_1 equals a particular number ξ.[6] Then with probability ξ the result will be 1 (profits will rise) and the process advances to state $(\tau + 1, j + 1, k + 1, l + 1)$. On the other hand, the probability that profits decrease is $(1 - \xi)$ and in this case the process advances to state $(\tau + 1, j - 1, k + 1, l)$. Thus, if $u_1 = \xi$ the future expected value of the process is given by

(10) $\xi(1 + V(\tau + 1, j + 1, k + 1, l + 1)$
$\qquad\qquad\qquad + (1 - \xi)[-1 + V(\tau + 1, j - 1, k + 1, l)]$

But, since the hypothesis that $u_1 = \xi$ is based only on our best information to date, expression (10) must be weighted by the probability that $\xi \leqslant u_1 \leqslant \xi + d\xi$, namely $f_1(\xi|k,l)$ and integrated over all ξ. We thereby obtain

(11) $\int_0^1 \{1 + V(\tau + 1, j + 1, k + 1, L + 1)$
$\qquad\qquad + (1 - \xi)[-1 + V(\tau + 1, j - 1, k + 1, l)]\}$
$\qquad\qquad f_1(\xi | k, l) d\xi$

But under the special assumptions made regarding the prior distribution $g_1 (\xi)$ it turns out that

(12) $\qquad\qquad \int_0^1 \xi f_1(\xi | k, l) = \dfrac{l + 1}{k + 2}$

By employing arguments analogous to those used in obtaining (11) to the selection of decision D_2 we conclude that

(13)

$$V(\tau, j, k, l) = \max \begin{cases} D_1 : \left(\dfrac{l + 1}{k + 2}\right)[1 + V(\tau + 1, j + 1, k + 1, l + 1)] \\[2mm] \quad + \left(1 - \dfrac{l + 1}{k + 2}\right)[-1 + V(\tau + 1, j - 1, k + 1, l)] \\[2mm] D_2 : \left(\dfrac{1/2(i + j) - l + 1}{i - k + 2}\right)[1 + V(\tau + 1, j + 1, k, l)] \\[2mm] \quad + \left(1 - \dfrac{1/2(i + j) - l + 1}{i - k + 2}\right)[-1 + V(\tau + 1, j - l, k, l)] \end{cases}$$

The natural terminus of the process is the stage T at which $V(T, j, k, l) = -1$. That is, the optimal price will have been reached when the expected value of any further change in price is -1. The immediate question that comes to mind is whether a stage T exists for which $V(T, j, k, l) = -1$. We shall not attempt to establish the existence of such a T rigorously here; intuitively it would seem that by virtue of the learning process employed that this stage will exist at least as a limit in probabilities.

Yet, even if this stage exists it will be in the distant future. This natural termination point might, therefore, be undesirable for two reasons. First, the future brings with it additional uncertainty, such as the possibility that the firm's demand function may undergo a drastic change. Second, the required information-storage processing ability for the execution of this process will almost certainly exceed the capability of the firm. Consequently, the firm might instead settle for the achievement of some profit level deemed acceptable for termination of the process. In this case the firm would look not only at the direction of change in profits but at the actual magnitudes. Having achieved the desired profit level it would stop adjusting prices.

While the above model is admittedly a member of the simplest variety of adaptive control processes, it does serve to point up several of the points made before. In particular, a firm seeking to maximize profit under uncertainty may pursue short-run behavioural rules which would be construed in the light of a neo-classical interpretation as nonoptimal and yet may in fact be optimal when viewed from the behavioural standpoint. Moreover, our model helps to explain how the distant future, which brings with it greater uncertainties and the inherent computational difficulties in the pursuit of even the simplest optimal adaptive control process, causes the firm to adopt more modest goals than profit-maximization.

A more complete model would incorporate the firm's pursuit of several objectives and the firm's use of variables in addition to profits, such as market share and sales, as measures of its performance. The cost of changing price, which in this case would be the cost of searching for an optimum, would also be introduced into an expanded model. Explicit consideration of this cost should serve to reinforce the conclusion that the firm will stop changing price short of the conventional optimum.

SUMMARY OF OUR APPROACH

We see the firm as operating in an environment of uncertainty without the knowledge of its demand and cost curves, which are necessary to select an optimum strategy for maximum profits. Since it is forced to make price, output, advertising, and investment decisions under this set of circumstances, it proceeds in a particular way. The firm gauges its ability to cope with the environment and then sets consistent profit and sales objectives for itself for a limited period in the future. It then utilizes its decision rules and the best internal and environmental information it can get to make price and output decisions.

These decisions result in an interaction with the environment which eventually returns imperfect information to the firm on the quality of its decisions. The firm must then transform this information, and any other it may get through salesmen, industry publications, consultants, etc., into a new set of decisions and actions. These actions may require adaptation of the internal structure of the firm or a modification of decisions (e.g., price changes) that directly affect its interaction with the environment.

The evaluation of the results in a particular instance is made by using the specified goals as a criterion. If these goals are reached or surpassed, the firm views the past decisions as successful and then must decide whether the goals should be raised in the next period.

NOTES

1. P. A. Samuelson, *Foundations of Economic Analysis* (Cambridge, Mass.: 1947), pp. 57–89.
2. R. A. Gordon, *Business Leadership in the Large Corporation* (Berkeley, Calif.: 1961) and H. A. Simon, 'A Behavioral Model of Rational Choice', *Quarterly Journal of Economics*, Vol. 64 (1955), pp. 99–118, reprinted in H. A. Simon, *Models of Man: Social and Rational* (New York: 1957).
3. See, for example, R. M. Cyert and J. G. March, *A Behavioral Theory of the Firm* (Englewood Cliffs, N.J.: 1963). Chapter 7.
4. Samuelson, *op. cit.*, p. 314.
5. W. J. Baumol and R. E. Quandt, 'Rules of Thumb and Optimally Imperfect Decisions', *American Economic Review*, Vol. 54 (March 1964), pp. 23–46.
6. This model is taken from Stuart E. Dreyfus, *Dynamic Programming and the Calculus of Variation* (New York and London: 1965) pp. 228–32.

Part III
Behavioural Economics and Organizational Theory

8 A Behavioural Theory of Organizational Objectives*

with J. G. March

Organizations make decisions. They make decisions in the same sense in which individuals make decisions: The organization as a whole behaves as though there existed a central co-ordination and control system capable of directing the behaviour of the members of the organization sufficiently to allow the meaningful imputation of purpose to the total system. Because the central nervous system of most organizations appears to be somewhat different from that of the individual system, we are understandably cautious about viewing organization decision-making in quite the same terms as those applied to individual choice. Nevertheless, organizational choice is a legitimate and important focus of research attention.

As in theories of individual choice, theories of organizational decision-making fall into two broad classes. Normative theorists—particularly economic theorists of the firm—have been dedicated to the improvement of the rationality of organizational choice. Recent developments in the application of mathematics to the solution of economic decision-problems are fully and effectively in such a tradition (Cooper, Hitch, Baumol, Shubik, Schelling, Valavanis, and Ellsberg, 1958). The empirical theory of organizational decision-making has a much more chequered tradition and is considerably less well-developed (March and Simon, 1958).

The present efforts to develop a behavioural theory of organizational decision-making represent attempts to overcome the disparity between the importance of decision-making in organizations and our understanding of how, in fact, such decisions are made. The research as a whole, as well as that part of it discussed below, is based on three initial commitments. The first of these is to develop an explicitly empirical

* Reprinted from *Modern Organization Theory*, M. Haire (ed.), John Wiley & Sons, Inc., 1959.

theory rather than a normative one. Our interest is in understanding how complex organizations make decisions, not how they ought to do so. Without denying the importance of normative theory, we are convinced that the major current needs are for empirical knowledge.

The second commitment is to focus on the classic problems long explored in economic theory—pricing, resource allocation, and capital investment. This commitment is intended to overcome some difficulties with existing organization theory. By introducing organizational propositions into models of rather complex systems, we are driven to increase the precision of the propositions considerably. At present, anyone taking existing organization theory as a base for predicting behaviour within organizations finds that he can make a number of rather important predictions of the general form: If x varies, y will vary. Only rarely will he find either the parameters of the functions, or more elaborate predictions for situations, in which the *ceteris paribus* assumptions are not met.

The third commitment is to approximate in the theory the process by which decisions are made by organizations. This commitment to a process-oriented theory is not new. It has typified many organization theorists in the past (Marshall, 1919; Weber, 1947). The sentiment that one should substitute observation for assumption whenever possible seems, *a priori*, reasonable. Traditionally, the major dilemma in organization theory has been between putting into the theory all the features of organizations we think are relevant and thereby making the theory unmanageable, or pruning the model down to a simple system, thereby making it unrealistic. So long as we had to deal primarily with classical mathematics, there was, in fact, little we could do. With the advent of the computer and the use of simulation, we have a methodology that will permit us to expand considerably the emphasis on actual process without losing the predictive precision essential to testing (Cyert and March, 1959).

In models currently being developed there are four major subsystems. Since they operate more or less independently, it is possible to conceive them as the four basic sub-theories required for a behavioural theory of organizational decision-making: first, the theory of organizational objectives; second, the theory of organizational expectations; third, the theory of organizational choice; fourth, the theory of organizational implementation. In this chapter we discuss the first of these only, the theory of organizational objectives.

THE ORGANIZATION AS A COALITION

Let us conceive the organization as a coalition. It is a coalition of individuals, some of them organized into sub-coalitions. In the business organization, one immediately thinks of such coalition members as managers, workers, stockholders, suppliers, customers, lawyers, tax collectors, etc. In the governmental organization, one thinks of such members as administrators, workers, appointive officials, elective officials, legislators, judges, clientele, etc. In the voluntary charitable organization, one thinks of paid functionaries, volunteers, donors, donees, etc.

This view of an organization as a coalition suggests, of course, several different recent treatments of organization theory in which a similar basic position is adopted. In particular, inducements-contributions theory (Barnard, 1938; Simon, 1947), theory of games (von Neumann and Morgenstern, 1947), and theory of teams (Marschak). Each of these theories is substantially equivalent on this score. Each specifies:

1. That organizations include individual participants with (at least potentially) widely varying preference orderings.
2. That through bargaining and side payments the participants in the organization enter into a coalition agreement for purposes of the game. This agreement specifies a joint preference-ordering (or organizational objective) for the coalition.
3. That thereafter the coalition can be treated as a single strategist, entrepreneur, or what have you.

Such a formulation permits us to move immediately to modern decision theory, which has been an important part of recent developments in normative organization theory. In our view, however, a joint preference ordering is not a particularly good description of actual organization goals. Studies of organizational objectives suggest that to the extent to which there is agreement on objectives, it is agreement on highly ambiguous goals (Truman, 1951; Kaplan, Dirlam, and Lanzillotti, 1958). Such agreement is undoubtedly important to choice within the organization, but it is a far cry from a clear preference ordering. The studies suggest further that behind this agreement on rather vague objectives there is considerable disagreement and uncertainty about subgoals; that organizations appear to be pursuing one goal at one time and another (partially inconsistent) goal at another; and that different parts of the organization appear to be pursuing different goals at the same time (Kaplan, Dirlam, and Lanzillotti, 1958; Selznick, 1949). Finally, the studies suggest that most organization objectives take the form of an aspiration level rather than an imperative to "maximize" or "minimize", and that the aspiration level changes in response to experience (Blau, 1955; Alt, 1949).

In the theory to be outlined here, we consider three major ways in which the objectives of a coalition are determined. The first of these is the bargaining process by which the composition and general terms of the coalition are fixed. The second is the internal organizational process of control by which objectives are stabilized and elaborated. The third is the process of adjustment to experience, by which coalition agreements are altered in response to environmental changes. Each of these processes is considered, in turn, in the next three sections of the chapter.

FORMATION OF COALITION OBJECTIVES THROUGH BARGAINING

A basic problem in developing a theory of coalition formation is the problem of handling side payments. No matter how we try, we simply cannot imagine that the side payments by which organizational coalitions are formed even remotely satisfy the requirements of unrestricted transferability of utility. Side payments are made in many forms: money, personal treatment, authority, organization policy, etc. A winning coalition does not have a fixed booty which it then divides among its members. Quite to the contrary, the total value of side payments available for division among coalition members is a function of the composition of the coalition; and the total utility of the actual side payments depends on the distribution made within the coalition. There is no conservation of utility.

For example, if we can imagine a situation in which any dyad is a viable coalition (e.g., a partnership to exploit the proposition that two can live more cheaply in coalition than separately), we would predict a greater total utility for those dyads in which needs were complementary than for those in which they were competitive. Generally speaking, therefore, the partitioning of the adult population into male-female dyads is probably more efficient from the point of view of total utility accruing to the coalition than is a partition into sexually homogeneous pairs.

Such a situation makes game theory as it currently exists virtually irrelevant for a treatment of organizational side payments (Luce and Raiffa, 1957). But the problem is in part even deeper than that. The second requirement of such theories as game theory, theory of teams, and inducements-contributions theory, is that after the side payments are made, a joint preference ordering is defined. All conflict is settled by the side-payment bargaining. The employment-contract form of these theories, for example, assumes that the entrepreneur has an objective. He then purchases whatever services he needs to achieve the objective. In return for such payments, employees contract to perform whatever is required of them—at least within the range of permissible requirements. For a price, the employee adopts the "organization" goal.

One strange feature of such a conception is that it describes a coalition asymmetrically. To what extent is it arbitrary that we call wage payments "costs" and dividend payments "profits"—rather than the other way around? Why is it that in our quasi-genetic moments we are inclined to say that in the beginning there was a manager and he recruited workers and capital? For the development of our own theory we make two major arguments. First, the emphasis on the asymmetry has seriously confused our understanding of organizational goals. The confusion arises because ultimately it makes only slightly more sense to say that the goal of a business organization is to maximize profit than it does to say that its goal is to maximize the salary of Sam Smith, Assistant to the Janitor.

Second, despite this there are important reasons for viewing some coalition members as quite different from others. For example, it is clear that employees and management make somewhat different demands on the organization. In their bargaining, side payments appear traditionally to have performed the classical function of specifying a joint preference ordering. In addition, some coalition members (e.g. many stockholders) devote substantially less time to the particular coalition under consideration than do others. It is this characteristic that has usually been used to draw organizational boundaries between "external" and "internal" members of the coalition. Thus, there are important classes of coalition members who are passive most of the time. A condition of such passivity must be that the payment demands they make are of such a character that most of the time they can be met rather easily.

Although we thereby reduce substantially the sized and complexity of the coalition relevant for most goal-setting, we are still left with something more complicated than an individual entrepreneur. It is primarily through bargaining within this active group that what we call organizational objectives arise. Side payments, far from being incidental distribution of a fixed, transferable booty, represent the central process of goal specification. That is, a significant number of these payments are in the form of policy commitments.

The distinction between demands for monetary side payments and demands for policy commitments seems to underlie management-oriented treatments of organizations. It is clear that in many organizations this distinction has important ideological and therefore affective connotations. Indeed, the breakdown of the distinction in our generation has been quite consistently violent. Political party-machines in this country have changed drastically the ratio of direct monetary side payments (e.g., patronage, charity) to policy commitments (e.g., economic legislation). Labour unions are conspicuously entering into what has been viewed traditionally as the management prerogatives of policy-making, and demanding payments in that area. Military forces have long since given up the substance—if not entirely the pretence—of being simply hired agents of the regime. The phenomenon is especially obvious in public (Dahl and Lindblom, 1953; Simon, Smithburg, and Thompson, 1950) and voluntary (Sills, 1957; Messinger, 1955) organizations; but all organizations use policy side payments. The marginal cost to other coalition members is typically quite small.

This trend toward policy side payments is particularly observable in contemporary organizations, but the important point is that we have never come close to maintenance of a sharp distinction in the kinds of payments made and demanded. Policy commitments have (one is tempted to say always) been an important part of the method by which coalitions are formed. In fact, an organization that does not use such devices can exist in only a rather special environment.

To illustrate coalition formation under conditions where the problem is not scarce resources for side payments, but varying complementarities of policy demands, imagine a nine-man committee appointed to commission a painting for the village hall. The nine members make individually the following demands:

Committeeman A: The painting must be an abstract monotone.
Committeeman B: The painting must be an impressionistic oil.
Committeeman C: The painting must be small and oval in shape.
Committeeman D: The painting must be small and in oil.
Committeeman E: The painting must be square in shape and multi-coloured.
Committeeman F: The painting must be an impressionistic square.
Committeeman G: The painting must be a monotone and in oil.
Committeeman H: The painting must be multicoloured and impressionistic.
Committeeman I: The painting must be small and oval.

In this case, each potential coalition member makes two simple demands. Assuming that five members are all that are required to make the decision, there are three feasible coalitions. A, C, D, G, and I can form a coalition and commission a small, oval, monotone, oil abstract. B, C, D, H, and I can form a coalition and commission a small, oval, multi-coloured, impressionistic oil. B, D, E, F, and H can form a coalition and commission a small, square, multicoloured, impressionistic oil.

Committeeman D, it will be noted, is in the admirable position of being included in every possible coalition. The reason is clear; his demands are completely consistent with the demands of everyone else.

Obviously at some level of generality the distinction between money and policy payments disappears because any side payment can be viewed as a policy constraint. When we agree to pay someone $35,000 a year, we are constrained to that set of policy decisions that will allow such a payment. Any allocation of scarce resources (such as money) limits the alternatives for the organization. But the scarcity of resources is not the only kind of problem. Some policy demands are strictly inconsistent with other demands. Others are completely complementary. If I demand of the organization that John Jones be shot and you demand that he be sainted, it will be difficult for us both to stay in the organization. This is not because either bullets or haloes are in short supply or because we don't have enough money for both.

To be sure, the problems of policy consistency are *in principle* amenable to explicit optimizing behaviour. But they add to the computational difficulties facing the coalition members and make it even more obvious why the bargaining leading to side payment and policy agreements is only slightly related to the bargaining anticipated in a theory of omniscient rationality. The tests of short-run feasibility that they represent lead to the familiar complications of conflict, disagreement, and rebargaining.

In the process of bargaining over side payments many of the organizational objectives are defined. Because of the form the bargaining takes, the objectives tend to have several important attributes. First, they are imperfectly rationalized. Depending on the skill of the leaders involved, the sequence of demands leading to the new bargaining, the aggressiveness of various parts of the organization, and the scarcity of resources, the new demands will be tested for consistency with existing policy. But this testing is normally far from complete. Second, some objectives are stated in the form of aspiration-level constraints. Objectives arise in this form when demands which are consistent with the coalition are stated in this form. For example, the demand, "We must allocate 10 per cent of our total budget to research." Third, some objectives are stated in a non-operational form. In our formulation such objectives arise when potential coalition members have demands which are non-operational or demands which can be made non-operational. The prevalence of objectives in this form can be explained by the fact that non-operational objectives are consistent with virtually any set of objectives.

STABILIZATION AND ELABORATION OF OBJECTIVES

The bargaining process goes on more or less continuously, turning out a long series of commitments. But a description of goal formation simply in such terms is not adequate. Organizational objectives are, first of all, much more stable than would be suggested by such a model, and secondly, such a model does not handle very well the elaboration and clarification of goals through day-to-day bargaining.

Central to an understanding of these phenomena is again an appreciation for the limitations of human capacities and time to devote to any particular aspect of the organizational system. Let us return to our conception of a coalition having monetary and policy side payments. These side-payment agreements are incomplete. They do not anticipate effectively all possible future situations, and they do not identify all considerations that might be viewed as important by the coalition members at some future time. Nevertheless, the coalition members are motivated to operate under the agreements and to develop some mutual control-systems for enforcing them.

One such mutual control-system in many organizations is the budget. A budget is a highly explicit elaboration of previous commitments. Although it is usually viewed as an asymmetric control device (i.e., a means for superiors to control subordinates), it is clear that it represents a form of mutual control. Just as there are usually severe costs to the department in exceeding the budget, so also are there severe costs to other members of the coalition if the budget is not paid in full. As a result, budgets in every organization tend to be self-confirming.

A second major, mutual control-system is the allocation of functions. Division of labour and specialization are commonly treated in management textbooks simply as techniques of rational organization. If, however, we consider the allocation of functions in much the way we would normally view the allocation of resources during budgeting, a somewhat different picture emerges. When we define the limits of discretion, we constrain the individual or sub-group from action outside those limits. But at the same time, we constrain any other members of the coalition from prohibiting action within those limits. Like the allocation of resources in a budget, the allocation of discretion in an organization chart is largely self-confirming.

The secondary bargaining involved in such mutual control-systems serves to elaborate and revise the coalition agreements made on entry (Thompson and McEwen, 1958). In the early life of an organization, or after some exceptionally drastic organizational upheaval, this elaboration occurs in a context where very little is taken as given. Relatively deliberate action must be taken on everything from pricing policy to paper-clip policy. Reports from individuals who have lived through such early stages emphasize the lack of structure that typifies settings for day-to-day decisions (Simon, 1953).

In most organizations most of the time, however, the elaboration of objectives occurs within much tighter constraints. Much of the situation is taken as given. This is true primarily because organizations have memories in the form of precedents, and individuals in the coalition are strongly motivated to accept the precedents as binding. Whether precedents are formalized in the shape of an official standard-operating-procedure or are less formally stored, they remove from conscious consideration many agreements, decisions, and commitments that might well be subject to renegotiation in an organization without a memory (Cyert and March, 1960). Past bargains become precedents for present situations. A budget becomes a precedent for future budgets. An allocation of functions becomes a precedent for future allocations. Through all the well-known mechanisms, the coalition agreements of today are institutionalized into semi-permanent arrangements. A number of administrative aphorisms come to mind: an unfilled position disappears; see an empty office and fill it up; there is nothing temporary under the sun. As a result of organizational precedents, objectives exhibit much greater stability than would typify a pure bargaining situation. The "accidents" of organizational genealogy tend to be perpetuated.

CHANGES IN OBJECTIVES THROUGH EXPERIENCE

Although considerably stabilized by memory and institutionalization-phenomena, the demands made on the coalition by individual members do change with experience. Both the nature of the demands and their quantitative level vary over time.

Since many of the requirements specified by individual participants are in the form of attainable goals rather than general maximizing constraints, objectives are subject to the usual phenomena associated with aspiration levels. As an approximation to the aspiration-level model, we can take the following set of propositions:

1. In the steady state, aspiration level exceeds achievement by a small amount.
2. Where achievement increases at an increasing rate, aspiration level will exhibit short-run lags behind achievement.
3. Where achievement decreases, aspiration level will be substantially above achievement.

These propositions derive from simpler assumptions requiring that current aspiration be an optimistic extrapolation of past achievement and past aspiration. Although such assumptions are sometimes inappropriate, the model seems to be consistent with a wide range of human goal-setting behaviour (Lewin, Dembo, Festinger, and Sears, 1944). Two kinds of achievement are, of course, important. The first is the achievement of the participant himself. The second is the achievement of others in his reference group (Festinger, 1954).

Because of these phenomena, our theory of organizational objectives must allow for drift in the demands of members of the organization. No one doubts that aspirations with respect to monetary compensation vary substantially as a function of payments received. So also do aspirations regarding advertising budget, quality of product, volume of sales, product mix, and capital investment. Obviously, until we know a great deal more than we do about the parameters of the relation between achievement and aspiration we can make only relatively weak predictions. But some of these predictions are quite useful, particularly in conjunction with search theory (Cyert, Dill, and March, 1958).

For example, two situations are particularly intriguing. What happens when the rate of improvement in the environment is great enough so that it outruns the upward adjustment of aspiration? Second, what happens when the environment becomes less favourable? The general answer to both of these questions involves the concept of organizational slack (Cyert and March, 1956). When the environment outruns aspiration-level adjustment, the organization secures, or at least has the potentiality of securing, resources in excess of its demands. Some of these resources are simply not obtained—although they are available. Others are used to meet the revised demands of those members of the coalition whose demands adjust most rapidly—usually those most deeply involved in the organization. The excess resources would not be subject to very general bargaining because they do not involve allocation in the face of scarcity. Coincidentally perhaps, the absorption of excess resources also serves to delay aspiration-level adjustment by passive members of the coalition.

When the environment becomes less favourable, organizational slack represents a cushion. Resource scarcity brings on renewed bargaining and tends to cut heavily into the excess payments introduced during plusher times. It does not necessarily mean that precisely those demands that grew abnormally during better days are pruned abnormally during poorer ones; but in general we would expect this to be approximately the case.

Some attempts have been made to use these very simple propositions to generate some meaningful empirical predictions. Thus, we predict that, discounting for the economies of scale, relatively successful firms will have higher unit-costs than relatively unsuccessful ones. We predict that advertising expenditures will be a function of sales in the previous time period at least as much as the reverse will be true.

The nature of the demands also changes with experience in another way. We do not conceive that individual members of the coalition will have a simple listing of demands, with only the quantitative values changing over time. Instead we imagine each member as having a rather disorganized file case full of demands. At any point in time, the member attends to only a rather small subset of his demands, the number and variety depending again on the extent of his involvement in the organization and on the demands of his other commitments on his attention.

Since not all demands are attended to at the same time, one important part of the theory of organizational objectives is to predict when particular units in the organization will attend to particular goals. Consider the safety goal in a large corporation. For the safety engineers, this is a very important goal most of the time. Other parts of the organization rarely even consider it. If, however, the organization has some drastic experience (e.g., a multiple fatality), attention to a safety goal is much more widespread and safety action quite probable.

Whatever the experience, it shifts the attention-focus. In some (as in the safety example), adverse experience suggests a problem area to be attacked. In others, solutions to problems stimulate attention to a particular goal. An organization with an active personnel-research department will devote substantial attention to personnel goals not because it is necessarily a particularly pressing problem but because the sub-unit keeps generating solutions that remind other members of the organization of a particular set of objectives they profess.

The notion of attention-focus suggests one reason why organizations are successful in surviving with a large set of unrationalized goals. They rarely see the conflicting objectives simultaneously. For example, let us reconsider the case of the pair of demands that John Jones be either (*a*) shot or (*b*) sainted. Quite naturally, these were described as inconsistent demands. Jones cannot be simultaneously shot and sainted. But the emphasis should be on *simultaneously*. It is quite feasible for him to be first shot and then sainted, or vice versa. It is logically feasible because a halo can be attached as firmly to a dead man as to a live one and a saint is as susceptible to bullets as a sinner. It is organizationally feasible because the probability is low that both of these demands will be attended to simultaneously.

The sequential attention to goals is a simple mechanism. A consequence of the mechanism is that organizations ignore many conditions that outside observers see as direct contradictions. They are contradictions only if we imagine a well-established, joint preference ordering or omniscient bargaining. Neither condition exists in an organization. If we assume that attention to goals is limited, we can explain the absence of any strong pressure to resolve apparent internal inconsistencies. This is not to argue that all conflicts involving objectives can be resolved in this way, but it is one important mechanism that deserves much more intensive study.

CONSTRUCTING A PREDICTIVE THEORY

Before the general considerations outlined above can be transformed into a useful predictive theory, a considerable amount of precision must be added. The introduction of precision depends, in turn, on the future success of research into the process of coalition formation. Nevertheless, some steps can be taken now to develop the theory. In particular, we can specify a general framework for a theory and indicate its needs for further development.

We assume a set of coalition members, actual or potential. Whether these members are individuals or groups of individuals is unimportant. Some of the possible subsets drawn from this set are viable coalitions. That is, we will identify a class of combinations of members such that any of these combinations meet the minimal standards imposed by the external environment on the organization. Patently, therefore, the composition of the viable set of coalitions will depend on environmental conditions.

For each of the potential coalition members we require a set of demands. Each such individual set is partitioned into an active part currently attended to and an inactive part currently ignored. Each demand can be characterized by two factors: first, its marginal resource requirements, given the demands of all possible other combinations of demands from potential coalition members; second, its marginal consistency with all possible combinations of demands from potential coalition members.

For each potential coalition member we also require a set of problems, partitioned similarly into an active and an inactive part.

This provides us with the framework of the theory. In addition, we need five basic mechanisms. First, we need a mechanism that changes the quantitative value of the demands over time. In our formulation, this becomes a version of the basic aspiration-level and mutual control theory outlined earlier.

Second, we need an attention-focus mechanism that transfers demands among the three possible states: active set, inactive set, not-considered set. We have said that some organizational participants will attend to more demands than other participants and that for all participants some demands will be considered at one time and others at other times. But we know rather little about the actual mechanisms that control this attention factor.

Third, we need a similar attention-focus mechanism for problems. As we have noted, there is a major interaction between what problems are attended to and what demands are attended to, but research is also badly needed in this area.

Fourth, we need a demand-evaluation procedure that is consistent with the limited capacities of human beings. Such a procedure must specify how demands are checked for consistency and for their resource demands. Presumably, such a mechanism will depend heavily on a rule that much of the problem is taken as given and only incremental changes are considered.

Fifth, we need a mechanism for choosing among the potentially viable coalitions. In our judgement, this mechanism will probably look much like the recent suggestions of game theorists that only small changes are evaluated at a time (Luce and Raiffa, 1957).

Given these five mechanisms and some way of expressing environmental resources, we can describe a process for the determination of objectives in an organization that will exhibit the important attributes of organizational goal-determination. At the moment, we can approximate some of the required functions. For example, it has been possible to introduce into a complete model a substantial part of the first mechanism, and some elements of the second, third, and fourth (Cyert, Feigenbaum, and March, 1959). Before the theory can develop further, however, and particularly before it can focus intensively on the formation of objectives through bargaining and coalition formation (rather than on the revision of such objectives and the selective attention to them), we require greater empirical clarification of the phenomena involved.

REFERENCES

Alt, R. M., 'The Internal Organization of the Firm and Price Formation: an Illustrative Case'. *Quarterly Journal of Economics*. 63, pp. 92–110, 1949.

Barnard, C. I., *The Functions of the Executive*. Harvard University Press, Cambridge, 1938.

Blau, P. M., *The Dynamics of Bureaucracy*. University of Chicago Press, Chicago, 1955.

Cooper, W. W., Hitch, C., Baumol, W. J., Shubik, M., Schelling, T. C., Valavanis, S. and Ellsberg, D., 'Economics and Operations Research: a Symposium'. *The Review of Economics and Statistics*. 40, pp. 195–229, 1958.

Cyert, R. M. and March, J. G., 'Organizational Factors in the Theory of Oligopoly'. *Quarterly Journal of Economics*. 70, pp. 44–64, 1956.

Cyert, R. M., Dill, W. R. and March J. G., 'The Role of Expectations in Business Decision Making'. *Adm. Science Quarterly*. 3, pp. 307–40, 1958.

Cyert, R. M. and March, J. G., 'Research on a Behavioral Theory of the Firm'. *Management Review*, 1959.

Cyert, R. M., Feigenbaum, E. A. and March, J. G., 'Models in a behavioral theory of the firm'. *Behavioral Science*, 4, pp. 81–95, 1959.

Cyert, R. M. and March, J. G., 'Business Operating Procedures'. In B. von H. Gilmer (ed.), *Industrial psychology*. McGraw-Hill, New York, 1960.

Dahl, R. A., and Lindblom, C. E., *Politics, Economics, and Welfare*. Harper, New York, 1953.

Festinger, L., 'A Theory of Social Comparison Processes'. *Human Relations*. 7, pp. 117–40, 1954.

Kaplan, A. D. H., Dirlam, J. B. and Lanzillotti, R. F., *Pricing in Big Business*. Brookings Institution, Washington, 1958.

Lewin, L., Dembo, T., Festinger, L. and Sears, P., 'Level of Aspiration'. In J. M. Hunt (ed.), *Personality and the Behavior Disorders*. Vol. I. Ronald, New York, 1944.

Luce, R. D. and Raiffa, H., *Games and decisions*. Wiley, New York. Chapters 7 and 10, 1957.

March, J. G. and Simon, H. A., *Organizations*. Wiley, New York, 1958.

Marschak, J., 'Efficient and Viable Organization Forms'.

Marshall, A., *Industry and Trade*. Macmillan, London, 1919.

Messinger, S. L., 'Organizational Transformation: a Case Study of a Declining Social Movement'. *American Sociological Review*, 20, pp. 3–10, 1955.

Selznick, P., *TVA and the Grass Roots*. University of California Press, Berkeley, 1949.

Sills, D. L., *The Volunteers*. Free Press, Glencoe, Ill., 1957.

Simon, H. A., *Administrative Behavior*. Macmillan, New York, 1947.

Simon, H. A., Smithburg, D. W. and Thompson, V. A., *Public Administration*. Knopf, New York. Chapters 18 and 19, 1950.

Simon, H. A., 'Birth of an organization: the Economic Cooperation Administration'. *Public Adm. Rev.* 13, 227–36, 1953.

Thompson, J. D. and McEwen, W. J., 'Organizational Goals and Environment: Goal Setting as an Interaction Process'. *American Sociological Review*, 23, pp. 23–31, 1958.

Truman, D. B., *The Governmental Process*. Knopf, New York. pp. 282–7, 1951.

von Neumann, J. and Morgenstern, O., *Theory of Games and Economic Behavior*. Second edition. Princeton University Press, Princeton, 1947.

Weber, M., *The Theory of Social and Economic Organization*. Translated by A. M. Henderson and T. Parsons. Oxford University Press, New York, 1947.

9   Research on a Behavioural Theory of the Firm*

with J. G. March

This is a report on a problem and methodology. The problem is that of constructing a predictive theory of firm behaviour. The methodology is computer simulation. We, as well as others, have suggested that computer simulation is both a feasible and desirable methodology by which to approach a rebuilding of the theory of the firm. Whether this judgement is good or bad can only be determined later. Whether it is sensible can be evaluated to a certain extent now.

At the outset let us concede that the use of a computer to simulate behaviour and computer programs to replace more classical models bears the onus of glamour. Everybody is doing it. A leading professional journal has inaugurated a special section on the use of the computer in model building and related activities. A major professional society has scheduled two panels and six papers on "The Use of Computers in the Simulation of Social Processes". An influential foundation has sponsored a summer institute on "The Simulation of Cognitive Processes".

Nevertheless, it would be premature to reject the methodology. Anyone who has attempted to use simulation is impressed with the pitfalls that exist. But in a handful of cases, model building through simulation appears to be paying off. In another handful, it looks hopeful.

The primary interest here is not in entangling ourselves in a general methodological discussion. Surely the answer to the question "Is simulation useful in the construction of theory?" is "Sometimes, but not always." There is no necessary virtue in a specific methodology. Because of these considerations, we start with an examination of a specific problem in theory—the needs of a revised theory of the firm—and

* Reprinted by permission from *Contributions to Scientific Research in Management*, University of California, 1960.

explore simulation as a technique in that specific context. Generalizations beyond this limited area are not intended.

QUESTIONS IN A BEHAVIOURAL THEORY OF THE FIRM

Decisions are made in organizations. Business decisions are made in business firms. To be sure, not all human decisions are made in organizations and not all business decisions are made in firms. But many of the most important decisions for social and economic theory are made in the context of large-scale organizations. In particular, pricing behaviour, product line choices, production level determination. resource allocation, capital expenditure—represent "organizational decisions". Moreover, such decisions comprise some of the most conspicuous outputs of one of the most conspicuous organizational institutions in contemporary western society. If these propositions are, as we believe, obvious, the motivation for a behavioural theory of the firm is also obvious. We propose to investigate the ways in which the characteristics of business firms as organizations affect important business decisions.

In a sense, therefore, what we propose is an integration of existing theories of organization and existing theories of the firm into a theory of business decision-making. A few economists have been urging such an integration for at least twenty years, and various important efforts in this direction can be cited. Despite such efforts it is still fair to say that propositions about organizational behaviour play an insignificant role in contemporary economic theory and that treatises on organizations give very little attention indeed to the theory of the firm.

One reason why the "integration" of organization and economic theory has not taken place to any significant extent is that the two theories and the research on them appear to be directed toward quite radically different questions. Those who would bring about the integration of two such disparate fields of study face a task of very substantial proportions. By the same token, it is our judgment that the focus should not be primarily one of integration. Much of what has usually been considered organization theory appears to us to have only marginal relevance to major business policy formation. At the same time, other areas of the behavioural sciences appear to have important implications for such phenomena as organizational forecasting and communication.

Our conception of the task we face is that of constructing a theory that takes the firm as its unit of study and the prediction of firm behaviour with respect to such decisions as price, output, and resource allocation as its objective. We feel no need to show necessarily how we have related a particular concept of Barnard, Weber, or Simon to firm behaviour. Nor do we particularly care whether we do or do not take explicit note of the theorems of price theory. We will try to indicate very briefly our reasons for taking this position and the implications we think it has for research.

The Theory of the Firm

The theory of the firm in economics is a logical starting place for a study of the business organization. Economists in their study of price behaviour in the market use the firm as the basic unit. The economist, working with the cost curves of the individual firms in the market and relating these curves to the market demand and supply curves, developed a theory which indicated how the firm would react to certain changes in market variables. Specifically, the theory predicts how the firm will react to changes in price, to changes in costs, and to changes in demand. In addition, the theory predicts how a firm will behave under differing tax structures.

What is called the theory of the firm has been worked out in detail, however, only for a perfectly competitive market and a monopolistic market. The theory in both cases consists of a set of decision rules which relate internal costs to market variables. A number of important assumptions are made. The crucial ones are (1) that the firm is attempting to maximize profits, (2) that the firm operates under an optimum cost structure, and (3) that the firm has U-shaped cost curves. The latter assumption is necessary in order to have the model give a unique answer.

It should be noted that the theory says nothing about the organizational structure of the firm. The implicit assumption is that regardless of the internal structure, the firm will be forced to react as the theory predicts to changes in the market parameters. The only place that the internal structure of the firm has been brought into the theory is in relation to the long-run average cost curve. There it is argued that long-run average costs must increase as the firm gets larger and larger. The primary reason given for this decreasing return to scale is that the problems of coordination in the very large firm must eventually mean that the costs would go up.

The heart of the theory is the decision rule. This rule determines the price and the output that the firm must select. It is generated mathematically from the maximization of the profit function. Verbally the rule is, of course, that an addition to cost must be balanced by an equal addition to revenue. As long as the additions to revenue are greater than the additions to cost the firm should continue to produce. When the additions to revenue are less than the additions to cost, the firm must cease producing. Thus a marginal cost curve, which shows the additional cost generated by each additional unit of output, can be drawn for the firm. A summation of these marginal curves then becomes the supply curve for the industry and, in conjunction with the demand curve of the industry, determines price for the market.

It should be understood that the theory of the firm does not pretend to be an exact replication of empirical behaviour. It is an abstraction. In effect it tells us what the businessman is trying to do and provides, thereby, a framework for empirical observation and analysis.

As we move away from the conditions assumed by this rather elementary model, the theory of the firm seems to have less relevance in explaining empirical behaviour. Specifically, as we study models of markets such as oligopolies, where the firms themselves can influence market conditions, we argue that it is necessary to study the organizational structure of the firm in order to understand how the firm makes decisions.

For our purposes there are three characteristics of the theory of the firm that we would emphasize. First, it attempts to predict a particular set of decisions (e.g., price, production) that are viewed as functions of a few "catch-all" variables (e.g., demand, costs). Second, the theory uses aggregation as a tactic; it attempts to specify total market supply and demand curves. Third, there is no attention to, or interest in, the actual process by which individual firms reach decisions.

Organization Theory

Like the theory of the firm, organization theory means different things to different people. Those meanings of the term that are relevant to our present purpose are those that emphasize the empirical study of behaviour in organizations. If we thus limit the focus, there are (as we view it) three major branches of what might be called organization theory. The first of these can best be described as "sociological", lists its founding fathers as Weber, Durkheim, Pareto, and Michels, and centres on phenomena of bureaucracy. The second is "social psychological" and has been built primarily on an experimental base with an emphasis on an "efficiency" criterion. The third is "administrative" in the sense that it focuses on the problems of the executive in dealing with an organization and is in reaction to grand organizational theories.

The early sociological theories of organization (e.g., Weber, Durkheim) emphasized the phenomena of division of labour and specialization as broad social trends and the importance of large scale organizations in utilizing specialized competences. Weber, for example, placed a considerable emphasis on the rationality of bureaucratic organization. The tendency of such theorists was to compare the depersonalized professionalization of bureaucracies with a (probably overdrawn) view of earlier personal and unspecialized systems of social organization. To a certain extent in the early theorists and to a much greater extent in modern sociological students of organizations, there is an emphasis on what Merton has labelled the "unanticipated consequences of purposive social action". Thus, the major variables considered tend to be such things as subgoal differentiation and conflict, individual personality changes, and organizational life-cycle.

Social psychological considerations of organizational phenomena have tended to be much less grandiose in scope. In general they have taken a relatively obvious criterion of efficiency (e.g., productivity, speed) in a relatively simple task and examined experimentally the effect of some small set of independent variables on the efficiency of the organization. In this tradition have been the studies of communication nets, of simulated radar warning stations, and of small problem-solving groups. Somewhat less experimental have been the studies of morale and productivity, but they also have the emphasis on a criterion of efficiency.

The final "branch" of organization theory dates in a sense from the earliest political and social philosophers. Speculation about centralization and decentralization and the problems of co-ordination can be found in pre-Christian writings (Plato, *The Laws* Book IV: *The Virtuous Tyrant*). In this case, however, modern administrative theorists generally reject with considerable vigour the earlier formulations. In particular, Barnard and Simon have argued against the excessively formalistic and unoperational analyses of early administrative theory. Much of the work in this area is directed toward viewing the organization as a clearing house through which transfer payments are arranged among participants (e.g., workers, investors, customers). It is a theory that specifies the conditions of organizational survival in terms of the methods of motivating organizational participants.

We have not attempted to give anything more than this very brief sketch of existing organization theory because we think it suffices to illustrate the major points we wish to establish. There are three such points. First, the theory focuses on a quite different set of problems from the economic theory of the firm. They are very largely non-economic; virtually nothing is said about the setting of output levels, the determination of advertizing expenditures, etc. Second, although there is considerable emphasis on the study of "process"—the study of what goes on in an organization—the processes observed tend not to be organizational decision-making. Third, unlike the theory of the firm there is no "aggregation". Indeed, there is nothing to aggregate.

Given these characteristics of organization theory—or much of it—and the theory of the firm—or much of it—it is clear to us that simple "integration" is unlikely to be fruitful. What appears to us to be needed is an approach that takes as its focus the economic decisions with which economic theory has traditionally dealt and as its research commitment the emphasis on organizational process.

Some Research Needs

We start with a very simple conception of an organizational decision as being a choice in terms of objectives among a set of alternatives on the basis of available information. This leads to an examination of how organizational objectives are formed, how decision strategies are evolved, and how decisions are reached within those strategies.

Organizational objectives of a business firm: Once we drop the concept of a single, universal organizational goal (e.g., profit maximization) and look instead at the process by which objectives are defined in organizations, we need to specify some propositions about the development of goals. What is the effect of departmental structure on the goals actually pursued in an organization? It is commonly alleged that one of the most frequent phenomena in an organization is the differentiation of sub-unit goals and the identification of individuals with the goals of the sub-unit, independent of the contribution of that goal to the organization as a whole. What difference does this make for a business firm and the decisions it makes on such things as resource allocation?

What is the effect of planning and plans on organizational objectives? Plans are a conspicuous part of organizational functioning; yet their impact on organizational goals is little understood. We would place particular emphasis on a study of the role of the budget in determining goals. Thus, we would argue for more information on the ways in which budgets are determined as a necessary part of a revised theory.

How do objectives change? If we allow goals to develop within the organization, we must also allow them to change over time. To what extent can the theories and research on individual aspiration levels be used to deduce propositions about shifts in organizational objectives?

What characterizes the objectives that are defined in an organization? Assuming that profit maximization is sometimes replaced by the use of profit surrogates, acceptable-level criteria, or other goals, can we predict under what conditions a given objective will be used? Even more awkward, how do we deal with (i.e., what are the consequences of) conflict of interest within organizations?

Decision strategies: We are assuming that the decisions made by the firm are not uniquely determined by its external environment, for example, the market. That there are situations where the external environment so completely dominates the determination of price or other major output as to make the internal decision structure largely irrelevant, we are happy to concede. They are simply outside our interest. Where the firm has discretion, we think it forms what we have called decision strategies. Many of the most important aspects of those strategies turn on the distinction between decision variables and parameters made by the firm. What is taken as given and what is treated as subject to manipulation by the firm? Here there are a number of organizational characteristics that seem to us important. To what extent are some things treated as variable only at specified points in time? What difference does such time spacing of decisions make? To what extent are one department's decision variables another department's parameters and what difference does it make?

Most important of all, we need to know what kinds of organizations in what kinds of industries under what kinds of conditions have predictable preferences among strategies. For example, is there an interaction between strategies and market position?

Decision-making within strategies: once organizational objectives and decision strategies are determined, the organization can be viewed as an information-processing and decision-rendering system. We need more reliable information on where and how organizations secure information, how that information is communicated through the organization, how authoritative decisions are reached, and finally how such decisions are implemented in the organization.

To what extent does the market serve as a source of information about consumers, competitors, etc.? What alternative sources of data exist and are used? What determines which sources of information will be used by an organization? Specifically, what predictable informational biases can be identified? If it is true that typically only a very small portion of the total available information is ever recorded by the organization, the processes by which the initial screening takes place has extraordinary (and largely ignored) importance in determining the final decision.

What happens to information as it is processed through the organization? What predictable screening biases are there in an organization? What is the effect of conflict of interest on communication? What difference does time pressure make?

What characterizes authoritative decision-makers under different conditions? What significance do their prior experience and reference group identifications have for their decisions? How are executive expectations determined? What differences are there between individual and group decision-making? How do hierarchical groups make decisions? If gradual commitment distinguishes decision-making in business firms, in what respect will the content of the decisions be affected?

What is the relation between decisions made by the responsible executives and the final "decision" implemented by the organization? How do variations in the control systems used (e.g., accounting systems) affect the implementation of decisions? What is the function and consequence of "organizational slack"? In what systematic ways do decisions get elaborated and/or changed by the organization?

In general, there are a large number of questions about the behaviour of business firms with which there is paired only a small number of answers. Existing theory is not equipped to answer most of the questions we have raised. Where an answer can be derived by brute force, it tends to be ambiguous or conspicuously inadequate.

If our objective is to devise a theory more capable of explaining the behaviour of individual firms, a possible strategy—not the only one—is to examine empirically the actual behaviour of firms. But such an approach, though frequently attempted, has generally been rather unproductive. The real world has seemed much too complicated for existing techniques of model construction.

It is tempting to announce that we have a solution to all this, that at last the theory of the firm is to be saved from the despair into which it has fallen. Perhaps it is. But missionary zeal is perennially terrifying, and simulation has a full staff of zealots. All we wish to do is to suggest that simulation has at least some virtues that conventional mathematics does not for constructing a theory of the firm.

DEVELOPMENT OF SIMULATION MODELS

The basic proposition is that *prima facie* the computer permits us to handle the kind of complex system that we have frequently said we would like to handle but could not with conventional methods. At the same time, this approach raised the ancient problems of obtaining empirical data, utilizing them in model construction, and testing the adequacy of the models.

Data for the Models

Simulation permits the construction of detailed models. It requires exact data on the decision processes in business organizations. It is quite true that decision-makers in the firm cannot tell you, in the detail needed, how decisions are made. In this sense, the economic theorist's traditional disdain toward interviewing is justified. The problem is to predict a process which involves such elements as human judgment, interpersonal communication, and expectations under uncertainty.

There are no magical solutions to the problem of finding adequate data. The methods available—interviewing, direct observation, reconstruction of past decisions—have well-established disabilities. Many of the difficulties, however, are not inherent in the methods themselves.

When used in conjunction with a detailed model, the methods are more adequate.

A Department Store Model

In order to specify the meaning of simulation as it is being used here, consider a specific example. We wish to predict internal resource allocation and pricing behaviour in a large department store. The decisions involved in such activities within the store are focused primarily on the merchandising budget and the day-to-day decision of the store buyers and the merchandising manager.

Our preliminary investigations indicate that we can identify four more or less independent phases that are actually involved in the firm's decision-making process.

The *first phase* is the allocation of a merchandising account or "open-to-buy" to a department by the executive committee. The "open-to-buy" represents the funds available to the buyer for a six-month period. He uses these funds to purchase inventory. To simulate this phase, we require two major sub-models. The first is one that predicts the estimation by the buyer of expected sales and desired stock levels for the coming period. The second is one that predicts the action of the executive committee on the request of the buyer.

The *second phase* of the model is the decision to buy specific amounts of particular categories of goods. To simulate this decision it is necessary to classify the entire inventory into categories. These categories are not necessarily the same ones that the buyer uses. The categorization is based on the homogeneity of information required to make decisions on purchases and on the type of decision rules used. For example, we need to know at this point the product mix constraints that the buyer accepts.

The *third phase* of the model is the pricing decision. Here the problem is to predict the prices assigned by the buyer during the period. The simulation introduces such factors as cost, standard mark-up, expectations about competitors' behaviour, and price-line constraints.

The *fourth phase* of the model includes the adjustments made as a result of inputs during the six-month operating period. The demand part of the model is not simulated. We can record the actual purchases made and give these data to the model as inputs. In this part of the model, we predict the reaction of the store to such standard accounting data as mark-up achieved, inventory levels, and rates of return in other stores. The model determines, first, if any action is to be taken. If action is to be taken, the model predicts what the action is.

Within this framework it is possible to introduce such observations as the following: buyers' estimates of probable sales tend to be biased downward. The Executive Committee tends to adjust the budget by across-the-board changes. Buyers are more sensitive to shifts in average mark-up attained than they are to changes in return on individual items. Search for new alternatives by a buyer tends to be relatively vigorous when average mark-up is down, relatively passive when it is up.

It is clear that we can tolerate a great deal more complexity in a model having such a form than we can in a more conventional one. It is also clear that such a model comes closer to reproducing the actual process involved in making a decision than do more conventional ones. The critical question, however, is the extent to which the model generates unique, testable, and accurate predictions of market behaviour. Any attempt to answer such a question with impressive confidence obviously must await further work. But it may be well at this point to note some of the methodological problems raised by the use of simulation in the theory of the firm.

SOME PROBLEMS

Computer models tend to reopen a number of issues most of us are inclined to view as either well-resolved or unresolvable with respect to familiar types of models.

How General is General?

Suppose that we are able to develop a computer program that simulates exactly the behaviour of Corporation A in pricing Product 1 over a class of situations X. In what sense is this a theory? Usually we distinguish between case studies and theory. We require that a theory have some properties of generality. In some cases the problem of generality is moderately straightforward. If one model can be shown to be a special case of another, the second is generally viewed as more general than the first. There are, of course, some deceptive problems involved in special-casemanship, but at least we have some feelings that we can tell a theory from an instance of the theory.

In the case of a computer model, we tend to be less sure of where we stand. The model is literally a set of instructions for a computer. Suppose that our model for the pricing of Product 1 in situations X by Corporation A consisted of 10,000 instructions in machine language. And suppose that to predict the pricing of Product 1 in situations X by any other corporation we could take the program for Corporation A and change one instruction. Then we would be inclined to say that we have a theory and that it has one corporation specific parameter. But suppose that we had to change 7,500 instructions. Would we then be prepared to say we have a theory with 7,500 parameters? Almost certainly we would want to say that we have an underidentified model. But do we have anything of general interest at all?

At the same time, there is clearly something excessively arbitrary about simply counting instructions. At least some theorists would like to maintain a distinction between what they see as the "theory" and the specific machine code by which it is fed into the computer. Consequently, one hears questions of the following general type: how much change in the "structure" of the model is needed to permit it to handle a wider range of events? And answers of the following general type: not too much: virtually none: a fair amount.

Presumably time will witness the development of a standard terminology to deal with generality in computer models. At the moment no such terminology has been widely adopted.

How Good is the Fit?
Rightly or wrongly, we think we know how to test conventional models for their goodness of fit to the phenomena they purport to predict. Standard tests involve comparing the output of the model with the output of the real world and measuring against a test model the differences between the two outputs. In the case of computer models, we are a little unsure just what to label as output and very uncertain regarding the appropriate test model.

A computer model ordinarily generates a great deal of output. Not only do we predict the prices that will be set by the department store. We also predict the budgets that will be set, the estimates of sales that will be made, and when changes in price will be considered (even if not made). Moreover, there are interdependencies among these outputs. If we are wrong on one, we are likely (if the model is a good one) to be wrong on several others. Consequently we do not know how to count outputs.

The appropriate test model is even less clear. By and large we are not well equipped for testing models with multiple outputs. Even less are we clear on what a parameter is in a computer model. The characteristic feature of such models is that they seem to have many more parameters than conventional models. Typically, some of these are estimated from the data, some are not. Even worse, the standard distinction between equations and parameters becomes surprisingly fuzzy.

CONCLUSION

It is always easier to raise problems than to solve them. But it is difficult to solve problems without first raising them. There is a problem with the theory of the firm and with organization theory as they now stand in so far as we are interested in predicting the behaviour of business firms with respect to such economic decisions as price, output, capital expenditures, and internal resource allocation. We see scant hope for a theory that does not attempt to answer the kinds of questions we have raised at the beginning of this chapter. If we are correct in our judgment that this is a framework within which the theory of the firm problem can be solved, a shift in the strategy of research in that field seems indicated. Specifically, we require greater attention to the development and testing of detailed models of firm behaviour. In turn, such attention will require the development and refinement of simulation as a language of theory.

10 Organizational Design*

with J. G. March

ORGANIZATIONAL DESIGN AND THEORY

Organizational engineering is an ancient calling. Aristotle, Machiavelli, Bentham, and Madison devoted considerable energies to the design of purposive organizations. In more recent times, Urwick, Taylor, Fayol, Mooney, Gulick, and Davis focused on the problems associated with engineering joint human effort through complex organizational systems. Out of this work has come a relatively distinctive vocabulary and some principles of design. The dimensions of organizational anatomy have been reduced to a few simple canonical symbols. In the purest form of descriptive anatomy we require only two symbols: a rectangle (representing a relationship between two positions). The relationship is normally defined in terms of such expressions as "reports to", "has authority over", "is the boss". By using these two symbols, we can construct a schematic representation of an organization—the familiar organization chart. Alternatively, we can translate the basic notation into one appropriate for graph theory or matrix manipulation. In any case, much of the basic material of classical organizational engineering represents constraints imposed on this simple chart.

Conventional practice requires that each position should "report to" one and only one other position (scalar principle); conventional practice places some constraints on the number of positions that should "report to" any given position (the span of control); conventional practice distinguishes among positions on the basis of the pattern of "reports to" relationships (e.g., the distinction between "line" and "staff". Usual organizational engineering goes well beyond these simple relations and

* Reproduced by permission from *New Perspectives in Organizational Research* ed. W. W. Cooper, H. J. Leavett and M. Shelley (John Wiley & Sons, Inc., New York, 1964).

elementary principles. We consider the design of a reward system, communication system, work flow system, etc., against the background of the organization chart (e.g., an ordering of positions according to salary is ordinarily required to be consistent with an ordering of positions according to the "reports to" relationship. Or we elaborate the chart to include additional symbols (e.g., most charts now contain at least one kind of dotted line representing some kind of relation other than the strict "reports to" relation). Or we suggest an alternative form of anatomy altogether (e.g., a sociometric chart, a means-end tree, an information processing diagram).

In the last decade, however, developments in organization design and organization theory have been remarkably independent. Except in the area of interpersonal and intergroup relations in organizations—where the research has been considerably influenced by applied problems—attempts to develop the engineering implications of modern theories of organizational decision-making have been modest. Possibly this is because the engineering implications are themselves meagre. Neither the professional journals nor the folktales of the culture report any spectacular successes; few responsible organization theorists would be enthusiastic about a major leap into the problems of design, although there are some obvious possibilities for using parts of recent work to design decision systems.

As we consider these possibilities, it should be clear that we approach the problem of design in a manner that is somewhat different from the manner characteristic of many conventional treatments of management theory. We cannot distinguish between "good" and "bad" organizations without a criterion, and we know of no general criterion function which can be used. Nor do we think it particularly useful for organizational engineers to devote their energies to looking for such a criterion. The function of the engineer, as we see it, is to design a system that will perform to certain specifications, to provide information on potential inconsistencies among specifications, or to evaluate the probable consequences of specified changes in design. Given existing knowledge and given some specifications of the kind of organization desired, we may be able to design an organization that will come tolerably close to the specifications. At least, we may be able to do this occasionally for some kinds of specifications.

In the next two sections we consider some possible directions for considering design problems. We reconsider a model that we first presented in the context of duopoly theory, and we examine some recent attempts to develop models of organizational decision-making.

ORGANIZATIONAL STRUCTURE AND BEHAVIOUR IN A MODEL OF DUOPOLY

In 1955 we suggested that "it should be possible to develop a model that specifies a meaningful relationship between significant characteristics of organizational structure and some important attributes of organizational behaviour." We then proceeded to outline four propositions about the effect of organizational structure on decision behaviour, specify two ideal-type firms exhibiting extreme organizational structures, and describe the impact on the conventional Cournot duopoly analysis of having decision-making systems such as we specified. The models were naïve in a number of ways. We have not found them particularly useful in subsequent research; but they illustrate one kind of approach that might be feasible and fruitful.

Consider the two firms we described: In Firm 1, the decision-making unit consists in a committee of equals and does not have responsibility for establishing the criteria for pricing decisions (i.e., the unit is decentralized and is subject to dicta from above with respect to price policy). At the same time, communication chains between the decision-making unit and the primary sources of information are long; and information on demand, competitor's behaviour, and official firm policy are all channelled through a relay point (e.g., an accounting department) that emphasizes the importance of costs and cost conservatism. In Firm 2, the decision-making unit is an individual and he has responsibility both for the specific decisions and for the criteria for pricing (i.e., the unit is centralized). Communication chains tend to be short, and information on demand, competitor's behaviour, and firm policy are channelled through a relay point (e.g., a sales department) that emphasizes demand and the importance of sales.

It seemed reasonable to argue that Firm 1 would be a firm in which price changes tend to be infrequent and reaction to competitors primarily passive; conversely it seemed reasonable to expect Firm 2 to exhibit frequent price changes and price leadership with respect to competitors. We then explored a modified Cournot analysis to determine the effects of these structural characteristics on market equilibrium.

Let there be two duopolists in the market (Firm 1 and Firm 2). Following Cournot, let there be no costs, let the market demand function be:

$$p = 25 - \frac{x_1 + x_2}{3}$$

where p = price
x_1 = output of Firm 1
x_2 = output of Firm 2

and assume that each duopolist expects no reaction on the part of the other in response to a change in output:

$$\frac{dx_1}{dx_2} = \frac{dx_2}{dx_1} = 0 \text{ (conjectural variation terms)}$$

The Cournot market solution is reached by setting marginal revenue for each duopolist equal to zero (i.e., the point of optimal production under the assumption of no costs) and solving the resulting equations. In this case, an equilibrium is reached at

$$x_1 = 25$$

$$x_2 = 25$$

$$p = 8.33$$

To explore some of the implications of the organizational models, we assumed that in the market specified above, Firm 1 and Firm 2 had reached the Cournot equilibrium point. We then postulated a shift in market demand, such that

$$p = 30 - \frac{x_1 + x_2}{3}$$

Under the assumptions previously outlined, it can be predicted that Firm 1 will tend to: (*a*) be slow in changing its perception of the market demand: (*b*) underestimate demand when its perception does change; and (*c*) give a positive value to the conjectural variation term. To provide a specific solution, we argued that Firm 1 might have expectations with regard to the market demand function and the conjectural variation term as follows:

$$p = 25 - \frac{x_1 + x_2}{3}$$

$$\frac{dx_2}{dx_1} = 1$$

Similarly, it can be predicted that Firm 2 will tend to: (*a*) change its perception of market demand quickly; (*b*) overestimate demand; (*c*) give a value of zero to the conjectural variation term. Thus, we asserted that Firm 2 might have the following estimates of key information:

$$p = 100 - x_1 - x_2$$

$$\frac{dx_1}{dx_2} = 0$$

Under these conditions, the market solution obviously deviates significantly from the standard Cournot solution.

$$x_1 = 10$$

$$x_2 = 45$$

$$p = 11.67$$

The effect is to make Firm 2 dominant in the market.

In our original paper we argued that the solution derived above would be stable only if the new production level and the resultant profits were acceptable to the dominant control groups of the two firms. Otherwise, some reaction—in the form of a reorganization—might reasonably be expected. Such a reorganization would have obvious consequences for the model. In point of fact, it is possible to specify a set of values for organizational structure and the aspiration level of control groups such that a market which has, under standard economic analysis, a given equilibrium point has, with the addition of the organizational factors, either a different equilibrium point or no stable equilibrium at all. Thus, under the postulated conditions, the design of organizational structure is critical to decision-making behaviour; and decision behaviour is critical to the outcome in the market.

The paper from which we have borrowed considerably was not intended as a contribution to organizational engineering. Quite to the contrary, we were exclusively concerned with the development of a positive theory of oligopoly. Nevertheless, it is clear that, if the positive theory is correct in this case, the design implications are direct and obvious. A firm organized according to the Firm 1 structure will follow a pricing policy quite different from that followed by a firm organized along the lines of Firm 2, and the relative positions of the two firms will depend on the interaction between their organizational structure and the characteristics of the market. The attributes of organizational structure specified in the model are attributes that can be manipulated deliberately in the real world; the predictions of consequences are relatively straightforward.

ORGANIZATIONAL STRUCTURE AND DECISION-MAKING: GOALS AND SEARCH

In the years that have passed since the publication of the duopoly model, we have learned some things about organizational decision-making. At least we have learned enough to suggest that the approach taken in that model was at best incomplete, certainly over simple, and quite possibly fundamentally wrong. The simplicity of the ideas in the model permits us to illustrate the way in which organizational design is implicit in parts of organization theory, but for substantively more promising work we need to turn to developments that are largely subsequent to 1955.

In general, recent studies of organizational decision-making suggest two things: first, they seem to confirm our earlier argument that the major impact of organizational structure on decision-making occurs when feasible solutions to organizational problems are nonunique. The action of an organization is constrained by external (e.g., market, governmental) forces, but at many points in a decision sequence there is more than one feasible solution. Organizational design is primarily relevant in determining what potentially feasible solutions will be discovered and how they will be evaluated. Where the external constraints are severe and feasible solutions scarce, we would not expect organizational structure to play as important a role. Second, the studies picture an organization as an adaptive, incompletely rational, political coalition. It is a political coalition in the sense that it consists of a number of individuals and groups making demands which are only partially consistent and which lead to imperfectly rationalized goals within the organization. It is incompletely rational in the sense that it acts upon imperfect and incomplete information about alternatives and the consequences of alternatives. It is adaptive in the sense that it modifies its behaviour on the basis of experience.

Since our purpose is hortatory and suggestive rather than exhaustive, we do not propose to elaborate greatly the description of organizational decision-making that we think is consistent with recent work. It will suffice to outline a quite simple framework in which the process of decision is viewed as a series of conditional steps.

1. The organization first considers whether performance is satisfactory on a particular goal.
2. If it is, the system "learns" that the procedures used were effective—thus becomes more likely to use them in future situations and the goal is modified to reflect experience.
3. If performance has been unsatisfactory, the organization searches for a solution to the problem. The search involves first defining what class of problem exists and then following a search procedure learned from previous experience with problems of that class.
4. If the search is successful, the organization "learns" to search in the same way in future cases and to be relatively sanguine about future goal failure.
5. If the search is unsuccessful, the organization learns to prefer other

search rules. It also modifies its goals. Thus, search rules, decision rules, and goals adapt to experience.

It is clear from this simple framework that two of the key concepts are "goals" and "search". If the theory is correct, organizational factors that affect either organizational goals or the procedures for search will affect organizational decisions. If the theory can be elaborated to show in more detail how goals or search procedures (and their development with experience) are influenced by organizational factors, we would have the basis for some propositions in organizational design.

Consider first the process of goal formation within an organization. One theory (our own) of organizational objectives describes goals as the result of a continuous bargaining – learning process. The bargaining is among the members of the organizational coalition and particularly among the more active members of that coalition. It is primarily through bargaining within this active group that the basic outline of what we call organizational objectives arise. Side payments among coalition members are not exclusively the distribution of a fixed, transferable booty. On the contrary, since a significant number of these payments are in the form of basic policy commitments, they represent the central process of goal specification.

These commitments are elaborated in the sense that sub-units develop specific subgoals through three internal processes:

1. A problem-solving process by which subgoals and specific performance criteria are associated with higher level goals. The organization finds over time that a certain level of attainment with respect to some subgoal (e.g., share of market volume of sales) is apparently consistent with satisfactory performance on some non-operational, widely shared goal (e.g., maximum profit). The sub-units then tend to take these subgoals as their own specific goals.

2. A learning process by which subgoals and specific performance criteria are selected by sub-units in terms of their attractiveness to the sub-units involved and converted into their own goals. The criteria of performance selected tend to be those that are rewarding either in terms of their relative ease of achievement, or in terms of their side effects.

3. A sub-unit identification process by which subgoals and specific performance criteria are linked to specific subgroups. This identification process is reinforced by the internal interaction of the members of the sub-unit. Thus, the volume of sales may become the subgoal of the sales department and its importance reinforced among the members of the sales department by their constant references to it.

These three internal processes are of particular significance because operative subgoals determine the behaviour of the organization. Thus it is not enough to design an organization to achieve some broad non-operative higher level goal. The critical question for behaviour is how the sub-units will convert the higher level goal into operative subgoals and the nature of the subgoals.

How can organizational design affect the development of goals in such a process? In classical treatments of organizational design, decisions on how to organize major sub-units (e.g., whether to organize by purpose or process) are usually described as affecting primarily the problems of efficiency in co-ordination and communication. However, if the above theory of organizational goals is roughly correct, departmental structure should have a number of important effects on operative goals. First, the structure identifies a conspicuous solution to the coalition problem. If a coalition focusing on the major sub-units of the organization is a viable coalition, it is likely to be considered before other alternative viable coalitions that cut across or outside major sub-units. Second, the structure influences the interaction among members of the organization and thus the development of sub-unit identification with subgoals. Thus, one important way of influencing the development of goals is to modify the organizational structure. At the same time, the theory suggests that modifications in reports (i.e., operational criteria) made available to the organization will—under appropriate conditions—lead to shifts in goals.

Similarly, if we examine the nature of organizational search, we can identify some ways in which organizational design can affect the decisions of the organization. We generally refer to organizational search as problemistic search. By problemistic search we mean search that is stimulated by a problem (usually a rather specific one) and is directed toward finding a solution to that problem. A problem is recognized when the organization either fails to satisfy one of its goals or when such a failure can be anticipated in the immediate future. So long as the problem is not solved, search will continue. The problem is solved either by discovering an alternative that satisfies the goals or by revising the goals to levels that make an available alternative acceptable.

We assume that rules for search are simple-minded in the sense that they reflect simple concepts of causality. Subject to learning, search is assumed to be concentrated in the "neighbourhood" of the problem symptom and in the "neighbourhood" of the current alternative. These two constraints reflect different dimensions of the basic causal notions that a cause will be found "near" its effect and that a new solution will be found "near" an old one. "Nearness", thus, refers (among other things) to organizational associations (e.g., search in the department in which the symptom was discovered), means – ends associations (e.g., search in links on the means –end chain that are adjacent to the symptom), or temporal associations (e.g., search in a time period near to the time of the symptom).

What does all this say for the effect of organizational design on search behaviour? There are at least three relevant points: First, the problems the organization attends to are partly a function of organizational design. "Gresham's law of planning" says that routine or structured activity drives out the non-routine or non-structured. Thus, for example, if planning is a desirable activity of the organization, the design has to take account of Gresham's law (e.g., by isolating planning from more programmed activity) or there will be no planning, and no planning problems on which search activity is expended. Second, organizational structure is an important device for associating search behaviour with particular problems. In effect, the structure is a surrogate for a learned, causal map of problems. It serves as one important kind of memory for the organization. We can destroy or modify the organization's memory by altering the structure. Third, the problem solution discovered by the search activity will depend upon the organizational locus of the group doing the search. Differences in training, information sources, and subgoals assure quite different search procedures by different groups. The problem of organizational design is to construct an organization such that the search stimulated by a particular problem takes place in the "right" locale.

METHODOLOGICAL PROBLEMS AND RESEARCH STRATEGY

It is hardly necessary to dwell upon the methodological problems involved in translating research on organizational decision-making into useful precepts for organizational design. They are large and they are obvious. We do not know much about the functional forms describing the behaviour of organizations. We have at best only crude guesses or broad bounds for the parameters of imperfectly identified functions. We know rather little about second- or third-order side effects. Although the availability of computer simulation as a technique permits us to relax some of the constraints we have traditionally faced with respect to allowable complexity, we still require some meaningful inputs in order to generate much in the way of meaningful outputs.

These problems or their natural progeny will be with us indefinitely. They are annoying, and hopefully they will be solved. But there are two compelling reasons for proceeding with the study of organizational design without awaiting a complete tidying of the methodological mess.

First, however incomplete and inaccurate the present models of organizations may be, they seem to have both some validity and some possible relevance to design problems. The risks of using them for design purposes seem modest; the potential gains somewhat larger. Second, organization theory will develop faster it it is built on an engineering model of research as much as on a "pure science" model. This is not simply a plea for methodological permissiveness. Many problems in complex systems are likely to be more amenable to an approach that emphasizes the design of a system to meet certain specifications than to an approach seeking a complete mapping of causal connections. It seems quite likely that such a situation holds in many areas of organizational analysis.

Part IV
Simulation

11 Computer Models in Dynamic Economics*

with Kalman J. Cohen

The development of the electronic digital computer has been an extremely significant technological innovation for science, probably ranking on a par with the inventions of the telescope and the microscope. Our experience with electronic computers is still too limited for anyone to predict the ultimate significance which these machines will have in both the natural and the social sciences. However, our knowledge has increased so rapidly from the years immediately after World War II, when computers were viewed only as larger and faster desk calculators, that it seems worthwhile to examine some of the implications which electronic digital computers have for research methodology in the social sciences.

It is undeniable that electronic computers, when used as routine calculating devices for performing statistical analyses and clerical data processing operations, can be extremely useful in social science research. The purpose of this chapter is not to consider the importance of such "routine" uses of computers in the social sciences, but, rather, to explore the possibilities of using computers to simulate the behaviour of complex social systems. The specific illustrations used are all drawn from the field of economics, but the concepts seem equally relevant to other fields of social science. We shall use the term "computer model" to refer to a formal model designed for digital computer simulation. In this chapter, we propose to examine the characteristics of computer models and to survey some of the economic computer models that have been formulated. In addition, we shall attempt to evaluate the future achieve-

* This chapter is based on research supported by grants made by the Graduate School of Industrial Administration, Carnegie Institute of Technology from the School's Research Funds and from funds provided by the Ford Foundation for the study of organizational behaviour. The authors owe a considerable debt to their colleague, James G. March, for criticisms of an early draft and for many fruitful discussions of the contents. Reproduced by permission from *Quarterly Journal of Economics*.

ments which might reasonably be expected from further work with computer models.

THEORY CONSTRUCTION (MODEL BUILDING)

The professional in any science works within a framework of definitions and concepts that becomes second nature to him. As a result, basic methodological points are frequently taken for granted. In appraising a methodological innovation, however, it is useful to re-examine such points. The explanation and evaluation of computer models can be simplified by examining the nature of theory construction (model building) itself.

A theory consists of three elements—definitions, assumptions, and conclusions. The following is a simple and familiar example of a theory:[1]

Assumptions: (1) Firms attempt to maximize profits.
             (2) The marginal revenue curves intersect the marginal cost curves from above.
             (3) The marginal curves are continuous.
Conclusion: A firm will produce that output corresponding to the point of intersection of its marginal revenue and marginal cost curves.

It is obvious that this theory depends also on a set of subject matter (extra-logical) definitions—profits, marginal cost, and marginal revenue.

There are a number of relevant points that can be noted from this example. The conclusion is a logical implication of the assumptions. The language in which the conclusion is derived from the assumptions is a matter of the theoretician's choice. In general, there are three languages that have been commonly used by economists for drawing a conclusion from a set of assumptions—ordinary prose, pictorial geometry, and formal mathematics. In the particular theory under discussion, it is obvious that the conclusion can be derived using any of the three languages. It would also, of course, be possible to state the assumptions and the conclusions in any of the three languages. Generally it is most convenient to state assumptions and conclusions in prose alone or a combination of prose and mathematics. The question of which language to use is answered quite nicely in the following quotation:

If mathematics is no more than a form of logical reasoning, the question may be asked: why use mathematics, which few understand, instead of logic which is intelligible to all? It is only a matter of efficiency, as when a contractor decides to use mechanical earth-moving equipment rather than picks and shovels. It is often simpler to use pick and shovel, and always conceivable that they will do any job; but equally the steam shovel is often the economic proposition. Mathematics is the steam shovel of logical argument; it may or may not be profitable to use it.[2]

Another point to note is that the conclusion is true only in the sense of logically following from the assumptions. The theory must be tested empirically before it can be said that the theory "proves" anything about the world. As has been said a number of times, it is not possible to "prove" by an *a priori* argument that a particular proposition is true of the real world. With most economic theories, unfortunately, testing is difficult, as it is with any non-laboratory science.[3] One important reason for this difficulty in economics is that for the most part we are dealing with static theories, whereas the world in which we must test the theory is dynamic. As a result, it is usually difficult to find satisfactory data for testing purposes. Therefore economists frequently use artefacts of one kind or another to establish a "subjective" probability of the validity of a theory. One frequently used artefact is the determination of whether or not the assumptions correspond with the facts. This procedure has provoked a sharp attack by one economist which has resulted in an interesting controversy.[4] We do not intend to be sidetracked by this controversy, other than to comment on the fact that the practice is the result of difficulties in testing directly the conclusions of most theories. We mention the issue because, as will be argued below, we feel that computer models can reduce the difficulties of developing models that can be directly tested, although some new statistical problems may arise.

An additional point should be recognized about the nature of most economic theories which is relevant to the problem of testing. The point has been effectively made by Professor Samuelson:

The general method [of economic theory] involved may be very simply stated. *In cases where the equilibrium values of our variables can be regarded as the solutions of an extremum (maximum or minimum) problem, it is often possible, regardless of the number of variables involved, to determine unambiguously the qualitative behavior of our solution values in respect to changes of parameters.*[5]

This means that the testing procedure consists in making numerical measurements to determine whether or not the direction of change of certain parameters is the predicted direction. In general, economic theory seems more successful in yielding propositions about directions of change than propositions about numerical magnitudes of particular variables.

GENERAL CHARACTERISTICS OF COMPUTER MODELS

A computer model is a model in which the implications of the assumptions, that is, the conclusions, are derived by allowing an electronic digital computer to simulate the processes embodied in the assumptions. Computer programs can thus be considered to be a fourth language in which the assumptions of a theory can be expressed and its conclusions derived. Actually, computer models might be viewed as special cases of mathematical models. We shall not pause to debate taxonomic subtleties, however, for it is more important to examine some of the features which characterize computer models.

We have stated above that there are a number of languages that *could* be used in model building. There are also a number of criteria that might be used to determine which language *should* be used. It seems obvious, however, that one important criterion is efficiency, as R. G. D. Allen argued. Computer models may be the most efficient approach when the model portrays a dynamic process and numerical answers in the form of time series are desired.

The notion of a dynamic process can perhaps be made clear by reference to the simple Cournot duopoly model.[6] In Figure 11.1 the

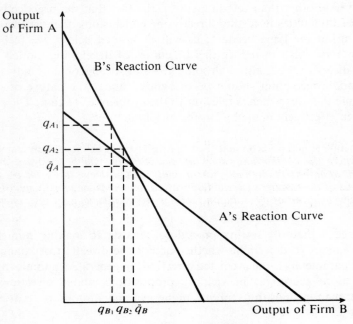

Figure 11.1: Cournot duopoly model

reaction curves for rivals A and B are given. Each reaction curve shows the optimum output for one firm as a function of the output of its rival. In accordance with the model, the curves are drawn on the assumption that the conjectural variation terms

$$\left(\frac{q_A}{\partial q_B} \text{ and } \frac{\partial q_B}{\partial q_A} \right)$$

are equal to zero. The dynamic process of the model can be started at any point. Assume that A is producing q_{A1}; then B will produce q_{B1}. In answer to this, A will produce q_{A2}. B will then produce q_{B2}, etc. If this simple model were analysed as a computer model, the computer would generate the time series of outputs for each firm. After the model had been run for a large number of periods, it would be clear that the outputs were tending towards the equilibrium values where A is producing $\bar{q}_A$ and B is producing $\bar{q}_B$.

In a model as simple as the Cournot model, we are generally not interested in tracing through the process by which equilibrium is reached, but only in deriving the equilibrium values. These values are easy to find by simple mathematical analysis. However, the addition of a few assumptions about the behaviour of the two firms can complicate the model sufficiently so that a computer simulation will be the most efficient method for determining the implications of the model. The volume of conclusions derived from a model is within the control of the model builder. However, in complicated computer models there are, generally, a large number of potential implications generated, many of these being time series of particular numerical values.

The fact that conclusions drawn from computer models may consist of a series of numerical values has in itself a number of interesting consequences. Numerical solutions should be contrasted with the analytic solutions usually derived from mathematical models. In terms of our earlier discussion on theory construction, we could say that the conclusions sought from a mathematical model are usually in the form of relations among the variables and parameters (including, frequently, derivatives or differences of the variables or parameters), while in computer models the conclusions obtained typically are in the form of time series of specific numerical values. This suggests that computer models are less general than mathematical models. The reason for this is that the amounts of input for computer models are greater than for the usual mathematical models. The increased input places greater restrictions on the relationships among the variables and parameters and, therefore, produces a less general but more specific model. One advantage to economists of computer models is that their conclusions are presented in immediately testable form.

It should be emphasized that the above characterization does not imply that computer models are necessarily less general or mathematical models necessarily less specific. Our considerations are related primarily to questions of convenience and efficiency. It is possible to use a computer model, for example, to gain insight into the effects of rates of change of particular parameters on the results of the model. This end is accomplished by varying the parameters of the model from one simulation run to another, and comparing the output time paths which are generated. If the model can be solved analytically, however, such a result could be more easily achieved by mathematical analysis.

COMPARISON OF COMPUTER MODELS WITH OPERATIONS RESEARCH SIMULATIONS AND ECONOMETRIC MODELS

In order better to understand the nature of computer models and the problems of using them, it is desirable to examine the use of simulation in the burgeoning field of operations research.[7] Additional clarification can be gained by comparing computer and econometric models.

There are two basically different approaches which can be followed in using computer simulation to study a complex system. The actual approach taken, of course, depends on the questions to be answered and the kind of information known at the time of the investigation. The approach generally taken in operations research or management science might be entitled "synthesis". This approach aims at understanding the operating characteristics of a total system when the behaviour of the component units is known with a high degree of accuracy. The basic questions answered by this approach relate to the behaviour of the overall system. In principle, the entire system response is known once the characteristics of the structural relations are specified. If the system is complex, however, it may be difficult or impossible to determine the system behaviour by current mathematical techniques. In this situation, simulation by an electronic computer can be utilized to determine the time paths traced by the system.

In social science, generally, the situation is quite the reverse. The behaviour of the total system can be observed. The problem is to derive a set of component relations which will lead to a total system exhibiting the observed characteristics of behaviour. The usual procedure is to construct a model which specifies the behaviour of the components, and then to analyse the model to determine whether or not the behaviour of the model corresponds with the observed behaviour of the total system. When this model is sufficiently complex, either because of the nature of the underlying functions or the number of variables contained in it or both, computer simulation may be the most convenient technique for manipulating the model. It is logical to call this approach to simulation "analysis". The actual output of the model is a set of time paths for the endogenous variables being studied by the model.

Traditional econometric models are essentially one-period-change models. Any lagged values of the endogenous variables are, in effect treated as exogenous variables. They are assumed to be predetermined by outside forces rather than by earlier applications of the mechanisms specified in the model. Hence the output of econometric models is the determination of the values of the endogenous variables for a given time period. To determine these values for the next period, new values would have to be assigned to the lagged endogenous variables. For this reason, most econometric models should be regarded as determining the changes which take place in the world from one period to another. They should be contrasted with process or evolutionary models which attempt to exhibit the unfolding of dynamic processes over time.

The mechanisms of a computer process model, together with the observed time paths of the exogenous variables, are treated as a closed dynamic system. In such a model, the values of the lagged endogenous variables are the values previously generated by the system. Computer models may thus be forced to operate with errors in the values of the endogenous variables made in previous periods, there being no correction at the end of each period to assure correct initial conditions for the next period as in econometric models.

The contrasts between econometric and computer models have not been offered as invidious comparisons. It is clear that economics has benefited, and will continue in the future to benefit, from work in econometrics. Rather, our analysis is aimed at showing the nature and peculiar attributes of an important new research technique for social science.

METHODOLOGICAL PROBLEMS OF COMPUTER MODELS

As with any new research technique, there are methodological difficulties connected with the efficient utilization of computer simulation. There are three basic classes of problems which arise in using computer models. These problems are the specification of functional forms, the estimation of parameters, and the validation of the models.

The problem of specifying functional forms is literally an example of the "embarrassment of riches". Most mathematical models have been formulated in terms of linear equations in order to facilitate the attainment of analytic solutions. Since this restriction is unnecessary for computer models, the way is opened for non-linear functions having a wide variety of forms. The solution to this problem will probably come from two sources. First, as our empirical information (the collection of which will be stimulated and guided by attempts to formulate computer models) increases, some clues as to the proper forms to use to explain and predict behaviour will be available. Second, technical statistical criteria will be developed to select efficiently the proper forms of the equations, presumably on the basis of predictive power.

The problems of parameter estimation have, of course, been much discussed in statistical and econometric literature. A major advance has been the proof that unbiased and efficient estimates can be obtained only by acknowledging the simultaneity of the equations of a model.[8] If this result carried over to computer process models, obtaining maximum likelihood estimates of all the parameters in such models will be a forbidding task.

A more feasible approach to the parameter estimation problem may be to restrict attention to the joint determination of only the current endogenous variables within a single period and to consider that the values of the lagged endogenous variables are subject to errors. The parameter estimation problem must then be considered within the framework of an "errors in the variables" model rather than an "errors in the equations" model. A few econometricians have investigated this kind of estimation problem, and their results may prove applicable to computer models.[9]

The likelihood of a process model incorrectly describing the world is high, because it makes some strong assertions about the nature of the world. There are various degrees by which any model can fail to describe the world, however, so it is meaningful to say that some models are more adequate descriptions of reality than others. Some criteria must be devised to indicate when the time paths generated by a process model agree sufficiently with the observed time paths so that the agreement cannot be attributed to mere coincidence. Tests must be devised for the "goodness of fit" of process models with the real world. The problem of model validation becomes even more difficult if available data about the "actual" behaviour of the world is itself subject to error.

Although the formal details have not yet been adequately developed, there appear to be at least three possible ways in which the validation problem for process models can be approached.[10] First, distribution-free statistical methods can be used to test whether the actual and the generated time series display similar timing and amplitude characteristics. Second, simple regressions of the generated series as functions of the actual series can be computed, and then we can test whether the resulting regression equations have intercepts which are not significantly different from zero and slopes which are not significantly different from unity. Third, we could perform a factor analysis on the set of generated time paths and a second factor analysis on the set of observed time paths, and we can test whether the two groups of factor loadings are significantly different from each other.

REVIEW OF THE LITERATURE

Although the notion of utilizing the computer as a tool in model building is still relatively new, there are several ongoing research projects and several segments of research in economics that have been completed which have followed this approach. A review of some of this work will give some specific indications of the versatility of computer models; our review is intended to be illustrative, rather than exhaustive, of the applications of computer models in economics which have been reported in the literature.

Simulation of households. A large-scale simulation which had as its ultimate goal the simulation of the total economy of the United States was conducted under the direction of Professor Orcutt.[11] The project was concentrated on the analysis of households. The ultimate goal was to develop a general model consisting of the ten flow-of-funds sectors used in national income accounting.

The first stem in Orcutt's approach was to develop a stratified sample of households classified along the dimensions of some twenty-three variables. These variables, such as race, age, sex, education, income, debt, stocks of assets, etc., are the inputs to the decision units in the model. The outputs of the household model include relevant data for forecasting population, purchases of durables, non-durables, services, and housing, net change in debt, and net change in assets for the household sector.

The individual decision units of the model were endowed with the values of the various input variables in accordance with the actual system being simulated. The unit is viewed as having alternative types of behaviour available. With each alternative there is associated a probability, empirically determined. Random numbers are generated to select specific actions for each unit in a manner consistent with the assigned probabilities. In this way outputs are determined for each unit. The outputs are then used to modify the inputs for the next series of decisions.

The above description is, of course, only the skeleton of the model. Orcutt discussed many other problems connected with the model such as parameter estimation, discrepancies between generated series and the actual, etc. Orcutt saw his model as providing an instrument for "consolidating past, present, and future research efforts of many individuals in varied areas of economics and sociology into one effective and meaningful model; an instrument for combining survey and theoretical results obtained on the micro-level into an all-embracing system useful for prediction, control, experimentation, and analysis on the aggregate level." [12]

Firm models. In another early work, Hoggatt has developed a simulation of a perfectly competitive industry. [13] His objective was to study the stability of a model in which entry and exit conditions, as well as the formation of price expectations, are specified. The model consists of the following:

(1) A market demand function dependent on two parameters.

(2) A long-run average cost curve dependent on two parameters.

(3) A total cost curve for each firm dependent on the same parameters as (2).

The assumption is made that entering firms will expect the then current price to prevail in the future, and they therefore select that plant size which will maximize profits given the current price. The usual neoclassical decision rules for determining output of the firms prevail. The model is ready to operate when the four parameters in (1) and (2), the initial number of firms, and the size of plant for each firm are specified.

Hoggatt begins by choosing values which give an equilibrium position for the industry. He assumes all firms to be of equal size. The output of the model is the price in the market and the production and profits for each firm. (There are also a number of other outputs which are used for analysing the system.) The demand curve is then shifted to the right by changing one of the parameters, and the results studied. One interesting conclusion the model brings forth is the "possibility that the market variables (price and industry supply) may be nearly stationary even though there is considerable entry and exit activity on the part of firms in the industry." [14] The model is particularly interesting as an example of the type of complex questions that can be asked of an old model with the technique of simulation.

Industrial dynamics. Another use of computer models has been made by J. W. Forrester. [15] He utilizes time lags within a system to demonstrate the types of fluctuations that can develop within a company as a result of a shock to the system, for example, an increase in demand. The model utilized consists of five component parts. These are factory, factory warehouse, distributors, retailers, and customers. The customers' order rate is as an exogenous variable. There are given time lags through the whole system in terms of the delivery of goods from retailer to customer, distributor to retailer, etc., back to the factory lead time for production. There is also a series of time lags in the information system. The lags are in the timing of orders for goods, transmitted from component to component. The last aspect of the model is a description of the policy followed in placing orders at each level and the rules for maintaining inventory.

Once the parameters (time lags and policies) are fixed, the system is set in motion and can be analysed for any given customer order rate. The model is non-linear and would be difficult to analyse by any method other than computer simulation.

Forrester also analyses a further model in which advertising is introduced with a similar set of time lags. It is clear that a number of additional variables can be introduced, and their effects on fluctuations in production, employment, and investment analysed for the firm. Forrester's main aim is to utilize such analysis for the improvement of business management.

Industry analysis. Perhaps the most detailed published attempt at using computer models in economics is the study of the shoe, leather, and hide industries by K. J. Cohen.[16] This work was designed to explore the usefulness of computers in economic analysis. The models in the study are based on the empirical research of Mrs Ruth P. Mack.[17] Several different models are constructed in Cohen's study, but only the outline of the general approach will be discussed here.

The industry can be divided vertically into five segments—consumers, shoe retailers, shoe manufacturers, cattlehide leather tanners, and hide dealers. The major variables on which attention is focused are the selling prices of each sector (other than consumers), the purchases of each sector (other than hide dealers), and the production of retailers, manufacturers, and tanners. The models are an attempt to explain the monthly values of each of these variables from 1930 to 1940. The major exogenous variables used are disposable personal income, the Bureau of Labor Statistics consumers' price index, and hide stocks in the hands of hide dealers. As can be seen from the above descriptions, the models are formulated in terms of two major classes of variables, prices and physical flows.

The dollar expenditure on shoes by consumers is determined by disposable personal income and a seasonal factor, both exogenous variables. The physical volume of retailers' sales is simply the consumers' expenditures divided by the retail price of shoes. The retailers' receipts of shoes are determined basically by demand considerations accompanied by some price speculation on inventories: retailers always try to have available for sale at least enough shoes to meet their anticipated demand; the extent to which they try to push their inventory levels beyond this point depends upon their changing evaluations of future market prospects. The manufacturers plan their shoe production in response to retailers' orders for shoes, spreading these orders evenly over the available lead time to obtain some smoothing of production. The leather purchases by manufacturers are designed at least to provide for their current production requirements, but the manufacturers frequently build up their leather inventories beyond current needs in response to price speculation motives. The production of finished leather by tanners depends upon the relation between their leather shipments and their leather stocks, but, because tanners attempt to smooth production rates, finished leather production is also tied to the previous month's production and hide wettings. Tanners' hide wettings depend upon the turnover rate of tanners' finished leather stocks, but again efforts are made to prevent rapid changes from occurring in the rate of production. Tanners' purchases of hides are determined by a reduced form relation which reflects both their current needs (the higher the rate of wettings, the more hides the tanners will order) and their view of the supply situation (the lower the price of hides last month, the more hides tanners will buy).

The retail price of shoes is determined in the models by a rigid markup on factory shoe prices. In setting the factory shoe price manufacturers consider both the strength of consumer demand and the costs of production, as reflected in recent leather prices. Current leather price depends upon lagged leather price and current and lagged hide prices. Current hide price is determined in the models by a reduced form relation which reflects interactions between supply and demand considerations. The supply aspects are summarized in the final reduced form equation in terms of the ratio of leather and hide stocks in the hands of buyers to the leather and hide stocks in the hands of sellers; the higher this ratio, the lower the relative size of sellers' inventories, and the higher the price the sellers require to induce them to sell hides. The demand side is reflected in the reduced form equation by actual uses of hides by tanners, i.e., by hide wettings and finished leather production, and by factory shoe price, which serves as a proxy for underlying forces causing shifts in the demand schedule for hides.

There are several important interactions between prices and physical flows in the models. The physical volume of retail shoe sales is directly affected by retail shoe price. Retailers' purchases of shoes, manufacturers' purchases of leather, and tanners' purchases of hides are affected, largely through price speculation on inventories, by prices which are endogenously determined. The most important converse effect in the models is the dependence of hide price upon the purchases of leather by manufacturers and the finished leather production, hide wettings, and hide purchases by tanners.

Both one-period-change and process models were formulated. Mathematically, the forms of the models are non-linear systems of lagged simultaneous difference equations. Simulation techniques were used to trace the time paths generated by the models for all endogenous variables. These generated series were then compared with the observed values of these variables between 1930 and 1940. While these comparisons do not result in complete agreement between the hypothetical and the actual time series for the endogenous variables, they do indicate that the models may incorporate some of the mechanisms which in fact determined behaviour in the shoe, leather, and hide industries.

Oligopoly theory. In recent years there has been an increased emphasis on studying the decision-making processes of firms. One of the difficulties has been to find a convenient language in which a model encompassing the complex of relevant variables could be constructed. An attempt at using computer models to describe firms in a duopoly market which goes into the internal decision-making mechanisms of the firms has been described by Cyert, Feigenbaum, and March.[18] It is a homogeneous duopoly, and the major decision that each firm makes is an output decision. No discrepancy between production and sales is assumed, and thus no inventory problem exists in the model. The duopoly is composed of an ex-monopolist and a firm developed by former members of the established firm.

The decision-making process postulated by the theory begins with a forecasting phase. In this phase, competitor's reaction, the market demand curve, and the firm's average unit cost curve are estimated. Concurrently, a profit goal is established (goal specification phase). An evaluation phase follows, in which an effort is made to find the best alternative, given the forecasts. If this best alternative is inconsistent with the profit goal, a re-examination phase ensues, in which an effort is made to revise cost and demand estimates. If re-examination fails to yield a new best alternative consistent with the profit goal, the immediate profit goal is abandoned in favour of "doing the best possible under the circumstances".

Specific values were assigned to the parameters and a demand curve which varied over time was assumed. The model was allowed to run for forty-five periods. To demonstrate that the model as a whole has some reasonable empirical basis, comparisons were made with the can industry, an industry having some of the structural characteristics of the model. Specifically, the ratio of the two duopolists' profits and market shares generated by the model and the corresponding actual ratios for American Can Company and Continental Can Company were compared for forty-five periods. The predictions were viewed by the authors as satisfactorily approximating the observed data.

FUTURE OF COMPUTER MODELS

We have examined the nature of computer models, the associated methodological problems, and some of the literature utilizing computer models. It is now appropriate to evaluate the role of computer models in social science research. We clearly maintain that computer models are an important new tool for the social sciences. Computer models should be viewed as a supplement to available procedures rather than as a replacement for all existing techniques.

The basic advantage of computer models is that they provide a language within which complex dynamic models can be constructed. In addition, and because of the richness of the language, such models can incorporate the relevant empirical variables. This does not imply that economists should no longer be interested in general models, but it does mean that economists are no longer forced to deal *only* with general models.

Computer models provide a bridge between empirical and theoretical work. The requirements of a computer model can provide a theoretical framework for an empirical investigation, and, in return, the empirical information is utilized in developing a flow diagram for the model. Through this process of working back and forth, it is possible to know when enough empirical information has been gathered and whether it is of the proper quality. Once the model is simulated, a more rigorous test of the validity of the model can be made, as indicated earlier, by comparing the time series generated by the model against the actual observed behaviour of the system.

Because computer models have such a large capacity for utilizing empirical data, a burden may be placed on the actual collection of empirical information. We know of no obviously optimal procedure for gathering information that exists inside firms or inside consumers' heads. Nevertheless, this is the kind of information which economists desire and which computer models can readily handle.

Once the reduction of a system to its individual decision-making units has been accomplished, there is great hope for a solution of the aggregation problem. Thus, through computer models, we see the possibility of developing working models of the economy that will have a solid empirical basis. [19]

NOTES

1. George J. Stigler, *The Theory of Price* (New York: Macmillan, 1946), pp. 4–6.
2. R. G. D. Allen, *Mathematical Economics* (London: Macmillan, 1957), p. xvi.
3. For a lucid and penetrating analysis of the problems of testing economic propositions see Emile Grunberg, 'Notes on the Verifiability of Economic Laws', *Philosophy of Science*, Vol. 24 (Oct. 1957), pp. 337–48.
4. Milton Friedman, *Essays in Positive Economics* (Chicago: University of Chicago Press, 1953), pp. 3–43. For criticism of some of Friedman's arguments see the following: Tjalling C. Koopmans, *The State of Economic Science* (New York: McGraw-Hill, 1957), pp. 137–42; Eugene Rotwein, 'On "The Methodology of Positive Economics"', *Quarterly Journal of Economics*, LXXIII (Nov. 1959), pp. 554–75; Emile Grunberg, *op. cit.*, p. 343 (fn. 26).
5. Paul A. Samuelson, *Foundations of Economic Analysis* (Cambridge: Harvard University Press, 1947), p. 21.
6. A. Cournot, *Researches into the Mathematical Principles of the Theory of Wealth*, Trans. Nathaniel T. Bacon (New York: Macmillan, 1897), Chapter 7.
7. A broad survey of the scope of operations research simulations can be found in the *Report of the Systems Simulation Symposium*, ed. D. G. Malcolm (American Institute of Industrial Engineers, 1958). The number of operations research simulation studies which have been discussed in professional meetings or journals is too numerous to permit us to undertake here any further discussion of them (e.g., at the Sixteenth National Meeting of the Operations Research Society of America in Pasadena, California, November, 1959 there were approximately twenty papers presented dealing with computer simulation).
8. See, e.g., Lawrence R. Klein, *A Textbook of Econometrics* (Evanston, Illinois: Row, Peterson and Co., 1953), Chapter III.
9. Surveys of the state of econometric methodology regarding errors in the variables models can be found in J. D. Sargan, 'The Estimation of Economic Relationships Using Instrumental Variables', *Econometrica*, Vol. 26 (July 1958), pp. 393–415, and in Albert Madansky, 'The Fitting of Straight Lines When Both Variables Are Subject to Error', *Journal of the American Statistical Association*, Vol. 54 (Mar. 1959), pp. 173–205.
10. These have all been suggested by Professor Jack Johnston in private conversations with the authors.
11. Guy H. Orcutt, Martin Greenberger, and Alice M. Rivlin, *Decision-Unit Models and Simulation of the United States Economy* (Lithograph draft, Harvard University, 1958). See also Guy H. Orcutt, Martin Greenberger, John Korbel and Alice M. Rivlin, *Microanalysis of Socioeconomic Systems: A Simulation Study* (New York: Harper and Brothers, 1961).
12. *Ibid.*, p. 36.
13. Austin C. Hoggatt, *Simulation of the Firm*, I.B.M. Research Paper, RC-16 (Aug. 15, 1957).
14. *Ibid.*, p. 62.
15. Jay W. Forrester, 'Industrial Dynamics—A Major Breakthrough for Decision Makers', *Harvard Business Review*, Vol. 36 (July–August 1958), pp. 37–66.

16. Kalman, J. Cohen, *Computer Models of the Shoe, Leather, Hide Sequence* (Englewood Cliffs, N.J.: Prentice Hall, 1960).
17. Ruth P. Mack, *Consumption and Business Fluctuation: A Case Study of the Shoe, Leather, Hide Sequence* (New York: National Bureau of Economic Research, 1956).
18. R. M. Cyert, E. A. Feigenbaum, and J. G. March, 'Models in a Behavioral Theory of the Firm', *Behavioral Science*, Vol. 4 (April 1959), pp. 81–95.
19. A more detailed discussion of the problems of and of the potential for combining individual micro-level models into an aggregate level computer model is contained in Kalman J. Cohen, 'Simulation of the Firm', *American Economic Review, Papers and Proceedings*, L (May (1960), 534–40.

12 A Description and Evaluation of Some Firm Simulations*

The term "simulation" means many things to many people. In the context of the title to this chapter, it would therefore be possible to focus upon any of a variety of issues. I will attempt to do three things;

1. Clarify the concepts of simulation, illustrating the variety of techniques which have been so labelled.
2. Review some of the simulation studies that have been made, with particular emphasis upon business applications.
3. Look into the future, pointing to the new opportunities that exist as a result of the availability of electronic computers and related techniques of analysis.

The concept of simulation has, for at least a brief period of time, captured the imagination of men. Its appeal is as basic as our desire to understand the present and to foretell the future. Simulation has been portrayed as the magic technique by which these ends can be accomplished—the method by which large, complex systems can be run through their paces and evaluated. How much of this is fact and how much is fiction? What is the promise of the emerging techniques and where are the pitfalls?

The term "simulation" has been used to identify two distinct products of research: (1) a *description* of the dynamic processes underlying the behaviour of an individual or system, for example, models of the ordering and pricing behaviour of a department store buyer and the

* This paper draws freely from another written with Kalman J. Cohen (Cohen and Cyert, 1965). Reprinted by permission from Proceedings of the I B M Scientific Computing symposium on Simulation Models and Gaming, held on December 7–9, 1964, at the Thomas J. Watson Research Center, Yorktown Heights, NY. Copyright © 1964 by International Business Machines Corporation.

process of information flow and decision-making in an organization, and (2) a method of *evaluation* in which alternative courses of action are examined in terms of their probable implications for the system under study, for example, models of a firm's distribution system capable of ascertaining the effects of various inventory policies upon lost sales and storage costs.

Originally, the term "simulation" was applied only to dynamic models, that is, mathematical or logical descriptions of the behaviour of processes over successive periods of time. In contrast, the term "model" was used more broadly to also include static descriptions of systems or relationships among variables. Economists, for example, have long used static models in an attempt to describe the price-quantity demand relations presumed to exist at a point in time. A current review of the literature on simulation would, however, be complicated by the fact that the term has been applied to such a wide variety of methodologies as to make the term almost synonymous with "evaluation". Because of the magic of the term "simulation", many researchers have found it convenient to use this label in merchandising their wares, thereby associating them with the most up-to-date analytic methods. As a result, some simple computational procedures which are little more than the computerization of calculations too time-consuming to be performed manually are now frequently referred to as simulations. Although such computer applications can be of great value to management, they do not fall within the use of the term in the balance of this chapter. To be sure, it is difficult to draw a clear line between what is and what is not a simulation. I will, however, attempt to limit the term to models which describe or incorporate the behaviour or mechanics of processes which include some element of the time dimension. Within this framework, the time path of a process might be described, or the time sequence of steps used by humans solving specific problems could be programmed for a computer to follow.

The essence of a simulation is the study of a process over time and the reduction of that process to a series of logical steps. In general, simulation models are deterministic because the behaviour of human beings in the processes simulated is reducible to a logical structure. But rather than attempt to philosophize about simulation, it is probably better to look at some examples which illustrate the various categories of simulation.

The four major classes into which we divide simulations of organizational behaviour are differentiated according to the purposes for which the models were formulated. First, there are descriptive simulation studies of existing organizations. The purposes of this type of computer models are to formulate theories which explain why existing organizations have behaved in particular ways, to test these theories by comparing the observed past behaviour with the simulated behaviour generated by the model, and to predict how these organizations will behave in the future. Second, there are illustrative (or "intellective") simulation studies of quasi-realistic organizations. The purposes of this type of simulation models are to explore the implications of reasonable assumptions about organizational behaviour, in order to determine what the world would be like if these assumptions were true. Third, there are normative simulation studies for designing organizations. The purposes that models of this type serve are to allow us to determine which of several possible forms of organizations are in fact best suited to particular goals we want these organizations to fulfil. Finally, there are man-machine simulations, which are intended to train people to function better in organizational settings.

EXAMPLES OF DESCRIPTIVE SIMULATION STUDIES OF EXISTING ORGANIZATIONS

Simulation of a Department Store Buyer
Cyert, March, and Moore have found that the department store buyer makes relatively independent price and output decisions. There are loose connections between these decisions, but for the most part they are made with reference to different goals in response to different stimuli. There are two general goals that the department pursues: (1) A sales objective. The department expects (and is expected by the store) to achieve an annual sales objective. (2) A mark-up objective. The department attempts to realize a specified average mark-up on the goods sold. Organizational decision-making occurs in response to problems (or perceived potential problems) with respect to one or the other of these goals, so that the behaviour of the department is problem-oriented.

The buyer in a department forms sales "estimates" that are consistent with its sales goal and develops a routine ordering plan for advance orders. These orders are designed to avoid overcommitment, pending feedback on sales. As feedback on sales is provided, results are checked against the sales objective. If the objective is being achieved, reorders are made according to standard rules. This is the usual route of decisions.

Suppose, however, that the sales goal is not being achieved. In such circumstances a series of steps is taken.

First, the department's buyer attempts to change its environment by negotiating revised agreements with either its suppliers or other parts of its own firm, or both. Within the firm, the buyer seeks a change in the promotional budget that will provide greater promotional resources for the goods sold by his department. Outside the firm, he seeks price concessions from manufacturers that will permit a reduction in retail price. If either of these attempts to relax external constraints is successful, reorders are made according to appropriately revised rules.

Second, the buyer considers a routine mark-down to stimulate sales generally and to make room for new items in the inventory. The buyer ordinarily has a pool of stock in his department available for markdowns, and he expects to have to reduce mark-up in this way on some of the goods sold. He will attempt to stimulate sales by taking some of these anticipated mark-downs. Once again, if the tactic is successful in increasing sales sufficiently, reorders are made according to slightly revised rules.

Third, the buyer searches for new items that can be sold at relatively low prices (but with standard mark-ups). Most commonly such items are found when domestic suppliers are eliminating lines or are in financial trouble. Another major source is in foreign markets.

In general, the buyer continues to search for solutions to his department's sales problems until he finds them. If the search procedures are successful, all goes well. In the long run, however, a solution may be found in another way. The feedback on sales not only triggers action; it also leads to the re-evaluation of the sales goal. In the face of persistent failure to achieve the sales goal, the goal adjusts downward. With persistent success, it adjusts upward.

The buyer's reaction to the mark-up goal is analogous to, but somewhat different in impact from, his reaction to the sales goal. On the basis of the mark-up goal (and standard industry practice), price lines and planned mark-up are established. Feedback on realized mark-up is received. If it is consistent with the goal, no action is taken and standard decision rules are maintained.

If the mark-up goal is not being achieved, the buyer searches for ways in which he can raise mark-up. Basically the search focuses on procedures for altering the product mix of the department in the direction of increasing the proportion of high mark-up items sold. For example, the buyer searches for items that are exclusive, for items that can be obtained from regular suppliers below standard costs, and for items from abroad. Where some of the same search efforts led to price reduction (and maintenance of mark-up) when stimulated by failure on the sales goal, here they lead to maintenance of price and increase in mark-up. At the same time the buyer directs his department's major promotional efforts toward items on which high mark-ups can be realized. In some instances, the buyer has a reservoir of solutions to mark-up problems (e.g., pressure-selling of high mark-up items). Such solutions are generally reserved for problem-solving and are not viewed as appropriate long-run solutions. Finally, as in the case of the sales goal, the mark-up goal adjusts to experience gradually.

In order to explore the implications of their analysis of the department store buyer's decision processes, the authors formalized these decision processes by developing a computer model to describe the processes. The model was programmed for a computer, and by letting the model run on the computer, it was possible to simulate the decisions of the department store buyer under a wide range of circumstances. In this manner, the properties of the model and the type of behaviour it produces could be explored in as much depth as desired. It was also possible to test the empirical validity of the model by presenting it with the facts about a number of actual decision situations that the real department store buyer faced and then comparing the simulated decisions of the model with the actual decisions made by the buyer in these circumstances.

In general the tests support the notion that a buyer's decisions can be programmed. In pricing, for example, the computer simulation model predicted about 95 per cent of the buyer's prices, correctly to the penny. By elaborating the program to take into account special cases that do not occur frequently, the authors contend that 100 per cent of the decisions could be simulated correctly.

Simulation of a Trust Investment Officer

Similarly, good results have been obtained in a program to simulate a trust investment officer. Clarkson [1962] developed a model to simulate a trust inventor in a bank and tested it by comparing the computer's selection of stocks in four trust portfolios with that of the trust investment officer.

Both the computer model and the trust officer selected a total of five common stocks for the first portfolio. Three of the common stocks selected were the same in both cases, in name as well as in number of shares. The same fourth common stock was selected in both cases, but the number of shares differed slightly (50 shares were bought by the trust officer, but only 45 shares were chosen by the computer model). The computer model chose a different fifth stock for this portfolio than did the trust officer.

For the second portfolio, both the trust officer and the computer model selected a total of nine common stocks. Seven of these were identical, both in name and in number of shares. The other two stocks chosen by the computer model were not the same ones actually bought by the trust officer.

There were eight common stocks selected by both the computer model and the trust officer for the third portfolio. Seven of these stocks were exactly the same, even to the number of shares, both for the trust officer's and for the computer model's portfolios. The remaining stock differed in the two cases.

A similar result was obtained for the fourth and final test portfolio. There were seven common stocks in both portfolios. Six of these were exactly the same stocks with the same number of shares in both the simulated portfolio selected by the computer and the actual portfolio chosen by the trust officer. The only discrepancy was with the seventh stock, which was not the same in both cases.

EXPERIMENTAL SIMULATION STUDIES

Balderston and Hoggatt Study

Balderston and Hoggatt [1962] have developed a quasi-realistic computer simulation of the West Coast lumber industry. We choose to classify this as an illustrative or intellective simulation study, rather than a descriptive simulation study of real organizations, because Balderston and Hoggatt intended their model to bear only a loose resemblance to the actual industry, and they did not attempt to study in detail the decision processes of several firms in that market.

The Balderston-Hoggatt model is a study of the dynamic behaviour of firms in a two-stage market. In this model, supplier firms sell to wholesale intermediaries, and these wholesalers in turn resell to customer firms. There are flows of information, materials, and money between firms at the different vertical stages of this market, but no horizontal communication within the same stage is allowed in this model.

The model is driven by the wholesalers. They send search messages to suppliers (manufacturers) to discover the quantities the supplier is prepared to sell and the price he is asking. Similarly the wholesalers send messages to the retailers to determine the quantity demanded and the price. If the transaction is profitable to the wholesaler on the basis of his tests, the transaction is completed. The material is shipped directly to the retailer. The wholesalers carry no inventory but handle the financing of the transaction.

A market period ends when all the wholesalers have completed their searching; that is, there is no longer any wholesaler who wishes to send a search message. At the end of the period two important categories of action take place. First, price and output decisions are made by manufacturers and retailers for the next period. For the retailer, the decision includes not only bid prices and quantities but also the price and quantity for selling in the final market. Second, decisions to enter and leave the industry are made at this time. The decision criterion in each case is quite simple. If a firm has a negative cash position, it leaves the industry, and if average profits for any class of firms is higher than some given level, a new firm enters.

There are two basic parameters in the model which can be changed without affecting the other relations. One of these parameters is the cost of sending a message. There is only one cost for sending a message, regardless of which of the three classes of participants sends the message. In developing an experimental design for testing certain hypotheses of the model, four different message costs were used—0, 12, 48, and 192. The second basic parameter of the model is the method of formulating a criterion by which a firm in one class decides with which firm in another class it will deal. Thus a manufacturer must have a preference ordering of wholesalers to decide to which one he will sell. Retailers must also have a preference ordering of wholesalers, and wholesalers must have preference orderings for both manufacturers and retailers. The authors have used two methods in the model. One preference ordering is based on experience. It is a number which depends on the relation of transactions to orders and the actual quantity shipped. The higher the number, the more preferred is the particular firm. The second method is to determine a preference ordering on the basis of random numbers. The experimental design then consists of a complete run of the model for each cost and each method of preference ordering. This gives a total of eight runs, which form the basic data for analysis. These data are used in the testing of a series of hypotheses the authors have constructed.

The first set of hypotheses ignores the potential interactions among variables and concentrates on the relationship of one variable to another. Accordingly, these are called elementary hypotheses. These hypotheses are concerned with three factors: (1) market stability, (2) the effect of changing message costs, and (3) the effect of the alternate methods of preference ordering.

The hypotheses on market stabilization are generated from classical economic theory for the most part. Thus the authors examine the three sets of prices in the model—offer prices, bid prices, and retail prices—for evidence of a trend toward equilibrium. In addition, hypotheses concerning the flow of the physical commodity through the system, the number of firms in each class, and the amount of profit were tested. In the case of the other two classes of hypotheses, the attempt was made to determine the effects of parameter changes in message cost and preference ordering on the same set of variables as above.

In addition to the elementary hypotheses, certain hypotheses related to specific characteristics of the internal structure were tested. In particular, the effects of changing the two parameters—message cost and preference ordering—on the average firm size were tested. The authors then go further and attempt to isolate the various casual mechanisms in the model. This is done in lieu of an analytical reduction of the model which in the case of most simulation models is not possible.

NORMATIVE SIMULATION STUDIES FOR DESIGNING ORGANIZATIONS

Simulation of Information and Decision Systems in the Firm

Bonini [1963] formulated a computer model to study the effects of certain informational, organizational, and environmental factors upon the decisions of a business firm. This can be regarded as an exploration of the effects of changing the informational format and flows and the decision processes in a firm upon the firm's performance, and hence as a prelude to suggesting particular design changes for the firm to improve its performance.

Bonini's simulation is a model of only one firm which is divided into three major areas: manufacturing, sales, and an executive committee for planning and control of the whole firm. The organization in each segment is based on rough empirical evidence. The manufacturing division of the firm is headed by a vice-president. In addition, there are a plant supervisor, five foremen, and an industrial engineering department. The sales group has a general sales manager, seven sales district managers, and forty salesmen. The executive committee of the firm includes the vice-president for manufacturing, the general sales manager, and the controller of the company. The functions of the committee are those of planning, control and co-ordination. The accounting department is the major information source for the committee.

In general, Bonini's firm plans by making forecasts; it operates by setting price and output, incurring costs and administrative expenses, and making sales; and it controls by using standards and quotas.

The forecast of sales for the total firm is a summation of the individual forecasts of the salesmen. The latter are made by trend extrapolation. Quarterly budgets for administrative expenses are normally estimated to be the same as previously. However, if pressure, which is a parameter in the model, has been at a continued high level, the budget is decreased by a small amount. If the pressure has been low, the budget will be increased slightly. The total cost per unit of production is estimated as the average of the previous period's cost and the established standard cost.

The executive committee is responsible for the planning of the company. The planning process takes place in the following manner:

1. The committee sets a profit goal
2. The estimates described above are used to estimate profit.

3. If the estimate is equal to or greater than the profit goal, the goal stands; if the estimate is less than the profit goal, step 4 is used.
4. Re-examine the cost estimate. If the profit goal still cannot be met, step 5 is used.
5. Re-examine the sales estimate. If the profit goal still cannot be met, step 6 is used.
6. Re-examine the price which has been set. If the profit goal still cannot be met, step 7 is used.
7. Modify the profit goal.

This process is followed until a satisfactory solution (estimated profit equal to or greater than profit goal) is found. The final estimates of cost, sales, and price are then put into the company's quarterly plan. The output goal is determined by the vice-president of manufacturing. The goal is a function of sales for some past periods and the current inventory level.

The first step in the control procedures used in Bonini's simulated firm is the establishment of standards of performance (i.e., salesmen's sales quotas and manufacturing standard costs for foremen) against which actual performance can be compared. Comparisons of past performance in relation to standards are then converted into a set of "indices of felt pressures". These pressure indices, in turn, are the major control mechanisms through which feedback concerning past results affects future actions.

The actual manufacturing costs and sales levels are randomly determined by drawings from specified probability distributions, although foremen and salesmen have some control over the means and standard deviations of the distributions. Changes in the distributions are the result of pressures felt by the foremen and salesmen. In general, foremen react to great pressure by cutting the mean cost level. Thus if pressure is low, mean costs rise. Each of the four types of salesmen reacts somewhat differently by pressure. Administrative expenses are also determined in an analogous way.

One question that arises in a model of this kind concerns the method of simulating the economic environment. Specifically, in this model it is of interest to know how sales and costs are determined. In the case of sales, a function of three variables has been devised. The three variables are growth, price, and the abilities of the salesmen in relation to the potential for the various sales districts. Costs are determined on an accounting basis. A normal output is established which has a standard cost, including overhead. A formula which is a function of the difference between actual output and normal output then is used to increase or decrease the normal cost as the actual output is greater or less than the normal output.

In order to understand the implications of his model for the problem of how to design efficiently operating firms, Bonini chose to study the effects on the firm's performance of eight different types of variations in the model. Two of the changes (External World Variability and Market Growth Trend) relate to factors external to the firm. By making these changes, Bonini was able to study the reasonableness and stability of the model, as well as the direct effects of the changes themselves.

Three of the alterations (tightness of Industrial Engineering Standards, Sensitivity to Pressure, and Contagious Pressure) relate to changing sets of decision parameters which are of crucial importance in the model. Another change (Average Cost versus LIFO) relates to a decision rule but is also closely related to the information system.

The final two changes (Use of Present versus Past Information in Control and Sales Force Knowledge of Inventory) relate to the information system within the firm.

While this is a relatively small number of changes, it was possible for Bonini to achieve a limited degree of generality by studying the effect of any particular change over all the combinations of other changes.

Bonini adopted a fractional factorial experimental design as a means for making these eight types of systematic changes in his model and analysing their implications. Using only 64 different runs of his model, Bonini was able to measure and analyse the main effects of each model change, as well as the first-order interactions and the effects of four different sets of starting conditions. There were enough degrees of freedom to permit statistical tests of significance to be made.

We will not discuss Bonini's results in detail. The analysis was designed primarily to test the effects of a series of two-valued variables. These variables were quite diverse in nature. Some related to accounting, some to psychological variables, and some to organization variables. Bonini's experimental design did allow him to get good tests of most of his hypotheses, however.

MAN-MACHINE SIMULATION STUDIES FOR TRAINING PEOPLE

A man-machine simulation study involves the use of a computer model framework within which some human actors or decision-makers are embedded. The computer is used to simulate the behaviour of the environment within which the humans are performing. This is a feedback system in which the actions of the people will affect the simulated environment, which in turn leads to new actions by the people, etc. The purpose of having "live people" interacting with a computer in this manner may either be our inability adequately to model some particular aspects of human decision-making or else it may be our desire to provide a training exercise which will improve the humans' performance.

In this section, we shall discuss in detail two different man-machine simulations which have been used to improve the performance of people in particular organizational settings. One of these, the Carnegie Tech Management Game, has been devised to help train future business executives. The RAND Air Defense Simulation has proved to be very useful in training crews for air defence direction centres.

The Carnegie Tech Management Game

Complex business games, such as the Carnegie Tech Management Game [Cohen *et al.*, 1960; Cohen *et al.*, 1964], illustrate the use of man-machine simulations for training people to become more effective business managers. The Carnegie Tech Management Game has been developed to mirror more realistically than earlier business games the problems of running a company. It provides the participants with a wealth of both quantitative and qualitative information about the particular firm they are managing, other firms in the industry, and the economy in general. On the basis of this information and their own managerial skills, the participants make a large number of related business-type decisions. After these decisions have been made for all firms in the industry, they are fed into a computer model which simulates the resulting actions and interactions for all firms. The quantitative results are then reported to the participants, serving as the basis for another round of decision-making. The Carnegie Game is realistic enough so that it elicits from the participants a great deal of emotional as well as intellectual involvement. In many respects, it serves for business students somewhat as a simulated cockpit trainer serves for fledgling aircraft pilots.

A month is the basic decision period in the Carnegie Tech Management Game. Each simulated month, a team is called upon to make several hundred interrelated decisions about its firm's operations. At the end of each decision period, every team will receive almost 2000 items of information about their own performance, about their competitors, and about the environment in which they are embedded. Much of this information is automatically and freely provided, but some of it must specifically be purchased in the Game.

The packaged detergent industry is the general setting for the Carnegie Tech Management Game. However, this is not intended as an exact simulation of the detergent industry. Only those features of the real world which were considered by the designers to be useful in terms of their fundamental educational and research purposes have been incorporated in the Game.

For Game purposes, the packaged detergent industry is composed of three competing firms. The participants play the roles of the top executives in these companies. The country is divided into four different marketing territories, and each firm may market as many as three separate brands of detergent at any time.

All three firms' factories are located in the same marketing territory. In addition to having production facilities on which different product mixes of detergent may be produced and packaged, each firm's factory also has separate warehouses for storing raw materials and finished goods. Any firm may expand its production capacity or storage capacity for raw materials or finished goods by investing in new facilities; the construction of these require six months for completion, however, so that advanced planning is essential. Maintenance expenditures must be large enough to cover the repair and renovation of existing facilities.

The firms compete against each other for the detergent market in each marketing territory. The sales of the firms consist of shipments to wholesalers and to those large retail chains which perform their own wholesaling function. The orders for detergent placed by wholesalers and large retailers are simulated by the computer model, as are the orders by the retail stores at the next level and the ultimate purchases of different brands of detergent by consumers. The marketing decisions of each firm, the availability of different brands in the stores, and general economic conditions simulated by the computer model interact to influence the demand for each brand of detergent.

Each firm leases a district warehouse in every marketing territory for storing finished goods. Deliveries of detergent to the firm's customers are made only from these district warehouses. Additional space in the district warehouses may be rented as needed so that a firm incurs storage charges based upon the amount of inventory it holds in these warehouses.

There are a total of seven raw materials from which all products may be manufactured. Any one product, however, usually requires only a few different types of material. Since there are delivery lags ranging from one to three months, raw materials must be ordered from the suppliers ahead of time. The prices of raw materials may fluctuate from month to month. By paying suppliers promptly, the firms may earn sizeable cash discounts.

In order to produce any finished product, players in the Carnegie Tech Management Game must make a host of related decisions. They must schedule production by product and by warehouse destination; they must purchase raw material ahead of time; they must ensure, through their employment and overtime policies, that enough workers are on hand;

and, through maintenance and capital investment expenditures, they must provide adequate equipment and facilities. Finished goods may be consigned either to the factory warehouse or to one of the four district warehouses. Excess inventory at one warehouse may be shipped to another warehouse. If stockouts occur at the district warehouses, the firm's future sales demand may suffer.

There is a one-month lag between production and the availability of finished goods for delivery to a firm's customers. The sales of the various brands of detergent will be strongly influenced by the consumers' reactions to such product characteristics as sudsing power, washing power, and gentleness and by the various firms' decisions regarding selling price, advertising expenditures, and distribution outlays.

Firms can generate potential new products by expenditures on product research and development. Only a few of the new product ideas thus obtained may be worth marketing, however. The laboratory reports on a potential product's physical characteristics may help decide this, but to get more information on the marketability of a new product idea, a firm may spend money for product comparison tests. Other types of market research reports which may be purchased provide estimates of competitors' prices, advertising expenditures, retail sales, and retail stockouts for each brand in every marketing territory.

Firms must plan ahead to ensure their having sufficient cash to meet their financial commitments. Additional funds may be obtained on short notice by selling any government securities they may be holding, by not discounting their accounts payable, or by negotiating ninety-day bank loans. If applications are filed several months in advance, firms may obtain term loans from their banks or new equity funds by issuing common stock. The terms upon which outside financing is obtainable in the Game depend upon the same types of considerations as would apply in the real world.

In order to perform well, players in the Carnegie Tech Management Game must plan and budget carefully and thoughtfully. In some areas, such as the development and introduction of new products, plans must be made at least one year ahead in order to obtain the desired results.

Active participation in the Carnegie Tech Management Game has proved to be useful training for future businessmen [Cohen *et al.*, 1964]. Students playing the Game are challenged to deal effectively with many of the same types of problems faced by real executives. The Game helps students understand that decisions made in different functional areas and at different dates are interrelated, and it helps them realize that their organization and procedures for decision-making have consequences for the quality of performance which results.

There are many other ways in which the Game helps students develop managerial skills. It provides them with experience in seeking and evaluating meaningful information from the mass of data that exist in a complex and diffuse environment. It tests their ability to organize this information so that it provides a useful guide to future decisions. To do well in the Carnegie Tech Management Game, the participants must be able to forecast, plan, and take action to achieve desired outcomes in a situation where there are literally hundreds of variables which need to be co-ordinated and controlled. This provides the students with opportunities for exercising quantitative techniques of management-decision analysis and for discovering in an unstructured setting problems to which these techniques can usefully be applied. Players in the Game are asked to combine the roles of generalists and specialists and to handle both decision problems whose solutions rest on imaginative, thorough analysis, and decision problems for which fast, intuitive judgments are appropriate. Finally, participants in the Game must be able to work effectively with other people on their team and with outside groups. The Game provides opportunities for students to improve their ability to communicate with other people, both by written reports and in face-to-face situations. Since the participants are grouped into teams of five to ten players, problems of decision-making within an organizational context are very important in the Carnegie Tech Management Game.

Debriefing sessions were held after each experimental run so that the operating results that had been obtained could be reviewed. Chapman and others thought that these discussions were essential to the organizational learning that led to improved crew performance. As the task load on the crews became increasingly difficult, some signs of bad morale on the part of the participants emerged. Rather than being a harbinger of impending failure, however, the "griping" of the participants seemed to serve as a form of tension release, frequently followed by procedural changes which permitted the crews to cope with their heavier task load.

Even though the task load which they were called upon to handle increased threefold during these experiments, the crews continued to operate very effectively. One of the most striking things which the participants learned which enabled this was the ability to distinguish between the information which was useful for task accomplishment and the information which was not. As the experiments progressed, the crews differentially focused their attention on the important classes of stimuli at the expense of the unimportant classes.

SOME PROBLEMS OF COMPUTER MODELS

In the previous sections, we have emphasized the power and versatility of computer models and simulation techniques. Now we would like to examine some of the difficulties associated with use of these procedures. The first problem concerns the amount of explanatory power gained when computer models are used. As we have already indicated, a computer model of organizational behaviour can be regarded as a series of logical relations which describe the process by which decisions are made and modified on the basis of previous information and the way in which these decisions affect the state of the environment. A tendency which is sometimes displayed in the formulation of simulation models is to embed as much of the real world as possible in the models. This is motivated by the feeling that the more complicated a model is, the better able it is to describe special cases, and hence the better will be its predictions.

As a model becomes more complicated, however, it becomes more difficult to determine which variables have significant effects on the model's behaviour. In other words, the model may become almost as complex as the real world, and, therefore, the model may become almost as difficult to understand (although at least it may be experimentally manipulated and intensively observed in a way which is usually not possible with the real world). In practice, many of the same types of techniques may be used in the analysis of the model's output as are used in the analysis of data from the real world. For the Cohen-Cyert-March-Soelberg model [Cyert and March, 1963, pp. 149–82], for example, multiple regression techniques were used in an attempt to reduce the model to a small set of critical variables. In Bonini [1963], statistical tests of hypotheses were used to identify the causal mechanisms operating in the model.

Unfortunately, however, these statistical methods have the same weaknesses in analysing data from the models as they do for the analysis of real-world data. The use of multiple regression techniques implies linearity in the model, and we have no knowledge to indicate that such an assumption is justified. Hypothesis-testing can, at best, isolate significant variables, but it will not determine the form of the mathematical relationships between these variables and model behaviour.

We thus find ourselves in a dilemma. The power of computer simulation technique stimulates the formulation of very complex models, but models which are too complex defeat the purpose of model construction, which is to simplify the world so that it can be understood. We caution the users of computer models, therefore, to try to find the middle ground where the model is complicated enough to deal with reality but not so complicated that it impedes our comprehension of this reality.

A second major problem in the use of computer models arises in testing the models. Computer models are generally designed to explain a dynamic process. Therefore, the usual direct output from these models takes the form of a time series of values for each variable. A first difficulty in testing the model is to determine which of the time series are relevant for this purpose. This selection is presumably made on the basis of the questions the model is designed to answer. A more critical difficulty relates to the specific methods for testing the "goodness of fit" of the model. Testing the conformity of generated time series to actual data is a problem because of the many possible dimensions which could meaningfully be used. For example, any of the following measures might be appropriate:

(a) number of turning points
(b) timing of turning points
(c) direction of turning points
(d) amplitude of the fluctuations for corresponding time segments
(e) average amplitude over the whole series
(f) simultaneity of turning points for different variables
(g) average values of variables
(h) exact matching of values of variables.

More dimensions should readily be added.

At present, there is no single test which will consider all the relevant time series dimensions at once. The only recourse is to use individual tests for particular properties. This means, in fact, that a great deal of judgement must enter into the evaluation of computer models. Some specific suggestions for ways of testing have been made [Cohen and Cyert, 1961, pp. 120–1]. Where the computer model does not generate time series but rather a point prediction, the testing problem can be handled by classical statistical methods [Cyert and March, 1963, pp. 146–7].

Other methodological problems have been discussed in the literature [Cohen and Cyert, 1961, pp. 119–20]. In particular, the problem of specifying the functional forms and the problem of parameter estimation have been emphasized.

Previous literature has not stressed one important defect of the way in which some computer models are of necessity specified. This problem is confounded by the complexity of the model and our ignorance of the world. Complex computer models which attempt to describe organizations contain many parameters which relate to a variety of processes. For many of these parameters, especially when we are dealing with general models, there are no real-world data available for estimation purposes. Therefore, these parameters must be set *a priori* by the model builder [Cyert and March, 1963, pp. 84–93; Balderston and Hoggatt, 1962, pp. 161–9]. In a model having many such parameters, the conformity of the model to the real world my be helped significantly by a judicious choice of parameters. Unfortunately, the theory being modelled is usually not detailed enough to dictate even broad limits for some of these parameters. Thus it is necessary to use a large number of computer runs if one is to vary the parameters appropriately until the model seems to perform well. In the end, one may not know whether his model describes the real-world process properly or whether he has merely judiciously set enough parameters to allow the model to fit the existing data.[1] One possible test, of course, would be to use only part of the available real-world data for the process of tuning the model's parameters and then to use fresh data as a basis for determining if the output of the now completely specified model conforms to this new information about the world.

When simulation techniques are used for the design of new organizations or for training people to perform more effectively in organizations, the ultimate validity test of the simulations is, of course, how well they work in practice. When the new organizational designs which are suggested as a result of the simulation experiments are adopted, is the improved performance of the system as great (or at least in the same direction) as expected? Do people who have had man-machine simulation experience as part of their training in fact function more effectively when they are asked to perform in real organizations? The statistical problems involved in designing suitably controlled experiments to answer such questions may be difficult to solve, but they are not unique to the field of simulation.

We hope that in pointing out some problems which are involved in using computer models, we will not be regarded as condemning simulation. We intend this discussion to serve as a series of cautions to the prospective computer-model builder. Every research or training methodology has its difficulties, but the mark of the professional is that he either avoids the pitfalls or else discovers devices for turning them into advantages.

NOTES

1. Forrester [1961, p. 122] points out that when the purpose of the simulation model is organizational design, the problem may not be to estimate the current values of parameters in the real world, but rather to control these parameters so that they assume a new, known set of values: "We are then much more interested in whether the new system can be made to conform to the model than in whether the model conforms to the old system. Here the validity test takes the form of whether or not the actual system is being controlled to agree with the model." The methodological point we are making in the text is entirely applicable, however, both to descriptive and analytic simulation studies.

REFERENCES

Balderston, F. E. & Hoggatt, A. C., *Simulation of Market Processes*. Berkeley: University of California, Institute of Business and Economic Research, 1962.
Bonini, C. P., *Simulation of Information and Decision Systems in the Firm*. Englewood Cliffs, New Jersey: Prentice-Hall, 1963.
Clarkson, G. P. E., *Portfolio Selection: A Simulation of Trust Investment*. Englewood Cliffs, New Jersey: Prentice-Hall, 1962.
Cohen, K. J., & Cyert, R. M., 'Computer Models in dynamic Economics'. *Quarterly Journal of Economics*, 75 (1), pp. 112–27, 1961.
—— 'Simulation of Organizational behaviour' *in Handbook of Organizations*, ed. J. G. March. Chicago: Rand McNally, 1965.
—— Dill, W. R., Kuehn, A. A., Miller, M. H., Van Wormer, T. A. & Winters, P. R., 'The Carnegie Tech Management Game'. *Journal of Business*, 33, pp. 303–27, 1960.
—— *The Carnegie Tech Management Game: an Experiment in Business Education*. Homewood, Illinois: Irwin, 1964.
Cyert, R. M. & March, J. G., *A Behavioral Theory of the Firm*. Englewood Cliffs, New Jersey: Prentice-Hall, 1963.
Forrester, J. W., *Industrial Dynamics*. New York: Wiley, 1961.

DISCUSSION

P. M. Morse: I understand that you were not including random variables in your model. Is this because it was not appropriate for your particular model or because you didn't think it was important for models in general?

R. M. Cyert: No, what I said was that the simulations that fall into the classification that I made tend to be deterministic. They were constructed by observing a particular process and trying to develop criteria within the model which might, in fact, replicate that process. What I'm saying applies primarily to the first classification. It's clear that normative simulations or training simulations are not necessarily deterministic.

P. M. Morse: It seemed to me that in the training simulation there might be some advantage in introducing an element of randomness.

A. E. Saffer: I have a question about the first simulation. You have tried to generalize a set of rules from the case of one buyer, but now you have introduced two other buyers. Is this a theory about one buyer, or is it a general theory applicable to all buyers?

R. M. Cyert: This particular model was developed as one test of a broader theory of decision-making and is one attempt to see through intense observation how well the general theory explained the real world. We were not interested in developing generalized rules for buyers. But I think, if you turn it around and look at it from the normative side, there are some places where this study could be used in improving the operation within the firm. That is why in many cases the sharp distinction of the categories I've made is false. It's foolish to distinguish normative from descriptive.

J. C. Ornea: Was there any indication from the performance of the department store buyer that as a result of the close surveillance he changed and perhaps improved his behaviour patterns?

R. M. Cyert: Yes, this is of course a concern. I would answer your question on two levels. What happens is that you try to define the person you're observing, by going thought the report of his boss on how well he does a job, and try to establish good rapport. Second, you do get some opportunity to test out the program, from observing and interviewing him and looking at past detail. This is the best test, probably, that you have as to whether he is really behaving differently. This is not 100 per cent successful, because some of the past data that you pick up may well be exceptions to the program. You have to make sure that the discrepancies aren't due to his changed practices.

L. S. Joel: Did you draw any conclusions as to the precision of this new method? For instance, did you decide that a buyer doesn't have to be very imaginative? I was suspicious of the fact that both the models you cited seemed to be basically the same, and I wonder how closely they applied to personality.

R. M. Cyert: In other words, do you get conformity in the descriptive type of model between the model and reality because of the personalities of the individuals involved? Do they like to make an explicit program and use it to make decisions?

In both cases we searched around, with the help of the president and the general merchandising manager, for the more intelligent buyers, in particular, for the buyer who could articulate what he was doing. This may be the key: that he can articulate, know what he's doing, and thereby formalize rules and act consistently. This may be a personality factor, but my own feeling is that, in any of the tasks, in any of the so-called decisions where "thinking" takes place, there is in fact a large element of the program which can be written down, time and time again. For instance, if you look at research papers in any particular discipline, you'll find there are certain general classifications of behaviour both in terms of the kind of problem that was used and the paper that was written. I personally think that we'll be getting some research done in a variety of areas through computer simulation, where computers will be writing research papers. I don't put the personality factor very high.

H. Guetzkow: As I understand your four purposes, you wish to create more knowledge about organizations. Why do we devote energies to simulation of organizations, rather than doing field work in these organizations? Can we perhaps achieve all four objectives more adequately by conducting experiments in the organizations in which we work, as the Civil Aeronautics Board has done recently? For example, the board created new organizational forms for inclusion in their elaborate experimental design, achieving important heuristic outputs. Further, in executing their experiments, they found themselves training their executives.

My query is whether we might not gain more leverage, as social scientists, by working in experimental situations we can create in the field as managers of ongoing organizations than by using simulation procedures which contain the difficulties you indicated at the end of your presentation.

R. M. Cyert: That's a very good and appropriate question. Let me say, first of all, that I don't look upon simulation as a substitute for field studies. In fact, the first type of study can be made only by extensive observation of actual organizations. I think the same can be said of all the other categories. The reasons that they go hand in hand, however, are rather important. Simulation is a great methodological contribution to field studies. The reason for this is that field studies in the past have tended to be, when they've finally been published, pretty amorphous and qualitative in the kind of things they say. When you plan to simulate the results of a field study, you are led to ask more precise questions and to develop more detailed information about the actual processes. I have been very discouraged, for instance, by the number of field studies that are described in very broad terms: how the decision-maker looks at such-and-such data, how these data are important to him, and how these variables are combined and go into the final decision process. I think that with simulation you can go much further, and this is why I think it's important, in the first type of study at least, for simulation and field studies to go hand in hand. Similarly, if you look at the normative type of study, the value of effective simulation is that you can predict ahead of time what the results from a prospective change are going to be. Furthermore, you can search through many more alternatives than if you try to make a change and observe it, after some period of time. With simulation, you have more flexibility and more power. So simulation and field studies do go hand in hand. I think all of the categories are involved.

P. M. Morse: I can think of a few operational situations where there seems to be some reluctance to do experimentation in the field and thus where simulation is the only possible experimental procedure. For example, in a traffic network one might ask whether a certain change would increase the number of accidents. I think there are also certain tactical experiments in wartime conditions that some generals are reluctant to carry out.

Part V
Philosophy of Economics

13 Towards a Better Micro-economic Theory*

with Garrel Pottinger†

INTRODUCTION

Our objective in this chapter is to suggest some approaches to the problem of improving microtheory in economics. We emphasize at the outset that it is not our main concern to rekindle the perpetual argument about profit maximization. Nevertheless, issues involved in that controversy will need to be discussed.

Though microtheory has been subjected to a great deal of criticism over the years, it is still true that most economists spend their time developing the orthodox theory and efforts to produce a better theory are rare.[1] We endorse the view that the objective of microtheory is to develop a positive theory of market behaviour. We will try to show that our criticisms are in accord with good scientific methodology and that the alternative approaches we suggest are consistent with the objectives of economic theory.

We will begin by summarizing the evidence and arguments usually employed against the use of the profit maximization assumption in micro-economic theory, and then pass directly to consideration of the methodological arguments with which we are mainly concerned. Two arguments will be considered. The first summarizes positions which have been taken in print by various proponents of classical theory who defend it on grounds that critics are confused. In order to rebut this position, we develop a scheme for classifying theoretical assumptions and show that

* Received June 1978; revised August 1978. Reprinted by permission from *Philosophy of Science*, 46, No. 2 (June, 1979) pp. 204–22.
Copyright © 1979 by the Philosophy of Science Association.
† This research was supported in part by the National Science Foundation under grant SOC 77–07548. The original draft of this paper was considerably improved by virtue of the comments of two unknown referees and the suggestions of our colleague Alan Anderson. We are grateful for their help.

the plausibility of the argument of such defenders derives, in part at least, from ignoring these distinctions between types of assumptions. The second argument we will consider is one we have not seen in print but believe is the implicit argument of most defenders of the classical theory. The argument is that a better theory is more likely to be attained by continuing the development of the orthodox theory than by trying directly to construct a theory that will give an empirically more satisfactory account of micro-economic events. We will use an argument due to G. Tintner in order to show that this view is mistaken and will then go on to describe the steps which have already been taken in the direction of developing a better theory and to speculate about the form such a theory may take.

CRITICISMS OF THE PROFIT MAXIMIZATION ASSUMPTION

It is a standard part of economic theory to assume that firms maximize profits. The assumption is precise. It does not mean that firms try to maximize but rather that they do. It is this assumption (and its counterpart utility maximization for consumers) that has allowed economists to utilize the calculus extensively in building models of economic phenomena.

It is clear that if the firm is to maximize profits the entrepreneur must have a great deal of knowledge. On the cost side he must know the marginal cost curve d(total cost)/d(output). This knowledge in turn implies knowledge of the total cost curve and, in fact, the whole retinue of cost curves. There can be no uncertainty about the prices of inputs nor about the production function which relates inputs to outputs. It is also crucial that the quality of inputs be known and that their performance be unvarying. Without such knowledge the firm may make a decision that is not a profit-maximizing one.

On the demand side the entrepreneur must know the demand curve facing the firm. The extent of this knowledge will vary depending on the type of market facing the firm. If the market is perfectly competitive all the firm needs to know is the market price. If the firm has a monopoly, then the entrepreneur must know the complete demand curve in order to maximize profits. For oligopolistic markets there is no simple description of the knowledge needed because of the uncertainty of the actions and reactions of competitors.

The usual criticisms of the use of the profit maximization assumption in the theory of the firm are essentially of two kinds. One set of criticisms is built around the notion that the entrepreneur is interested in a number of things besides profits. In this vein one writer has suggested that one ought to maximize a general preference function rather than merely the profit function.[2] A second set of criticisms questions directly the use of maximization techniques.[3] The authors of this set of criticisms propose alternatives to maximization such as satisfactory profits, target profits, or acceptable level goal. In all cases the proposals imply a specific target for the firm as opposed to a process of maximization.

Criticisms of the first sort can be supplemented by empirical data indicating inefficiencies with respect to the problem of cost minimization and, hence, non-maximization of profits. One way of making this point is by referring to situations in which the actions of firms in cutting costs under the pressure of a bad market indicate that previously costs must have been excessive. Another way of making it is by referring to decision-making techniques that can be proved to be inadequate for maximization of profits. The area of capital budgeting, in which the payback period may be used rather than discounted cash flow, is an example of this type of reference.

The most radical criticism of the second sort is due to G. Tintner. He argues that in a situation where decisions must be made subject to uncertainty (e.g., in real life) the notion of profit maximization makes no sense. Alchian's summary of his position is excellent:

Attacks on [profit maximization] are widespread, but only one attack has been really damaging, that of G. Tintner. He denies that profit maximization even makes any sense where there is uncertainty. Uncertainty arises from at least two sources: imperfect foresight and human inability to solve complex problems containing a host of variables even when an optimum is definable. Tintner's proof is simple. Under uncertainty, by definition, each action that may be chosen is identified with a *distribution* of potential outcomes, not with a unique outcome. Implicit in uncertainty is the consequence that these distributions of potential outcomes are overlapping ... each possible action has a distribution of potential outcomes, only one of which will materialize if the action is taken, and that one outcome cannot be foreseen ... there is no such thing as a maximizing distribution.[4]

STANDARD DEFENCE

We find these empirically based complaints against the profit maximization assumption persuasive. The criticisms in question have been made with vigour and conviction by a number of people over a long period of time. Despite the force of these complaints and their long history, the profit maximization assumption continues to play a central role in contemporary micro-economic theory, and it seems that most economists are singularly uninterested in trying to develop a theory based on empirically more satisfactory assumptions about the behaviour of firms.

Most economists agree that economics is a positive science. Consequently, the apparent conflict between micro-economic theory and practice raises one important question. According to basic methodological principles, a positive theory not in accord with relevant empirical findings is unsatisfactory and, when a theory is shown to be unsatisfactory in this way, it is incumbent on scientists working in the field to try to replace the theory in question with one that does accord with relevant empirical information. Henceforth, we will call these principles *the principles of empiricism*. Micro-economic practice usually is defended against criticisms based on these principles by means of the following sort of argument.[5]

Scientific theories must be both general in scope and formally manageable. Theories which have these properties necessarily will involve simplifications, abstractions, and idealizations. While a decent regard for empirical findings is essential in positive science, empiricism must not be pushed so far as to make attainment of generality in scope and formal manageability impossible.

The usual empirically based criticisms of the employment of the profit maximization assumption in micro-economic theory are naive and misguided because they ignore these points. Micro-economic theory is concerned with explaining and predicting the behaviour of markets, and it is empirical findings about market behaviour which are relevant to determining whether the theory is satisfactory, not collections of reports about the internal workings of individual firms. So long as the theory provides a satisfactory account of market behaviour (as it does in many cases), and so long as there is no reason to believe that replacing the profit maximization assumption by more realistic assumptions about the behaviour of firms would lead to a better account of market behaviour (and there is no such reason), it is legitimate to proceed on the basis of this assumption.

Henceforth, we will call this argument *the standard defence*. It relies both on some quite general claims about scientific methodology and on some specific claims about the current state of micro-economic theory. The remainder of this section will be devoted to examining the general methodological views involved in the standard defence. The specific claims about current micro-economic theory will be dealt with in a later section.

It is well known that when scientific practice is considered in the light of the principles of empiricism, many difficulties arise. One that is particularly important in the present context is the fact that scientists often proceed by assuming things which they know (or have good reason to think) are not true. Furthermore, such assumptions are by no means peculiar to the social sciences. Physicists, for example, have often arrived at theoretical conclusions by assuming that gasses are perfect, fluids are incompressible, processes are infinitely slow, etc. The standard defence amounts to an attempt to derive comfort for the orthodox economist from these general features of scientific practice by arguing that his employment of the profit maximization assumption is on a par with the employment of fictive assumptions by non-economists in works which must be viewed as paradigms of good scientific procedure.

The effect of this ploy is to confront the empirically motivated critic of micro-economic theory with a dilemma. He must either bite the bullet and say that scientists who employ such assumptions (e.g., Clausius, Maxwell, and Boltzmann) are not doing their job properly or give an account of the use of such assumptions that explains why their use is sometimes legitimate, distinguishes cases where it is legitimate to use such assumptions from cases where it is not, and allows him to argue that the micro-economic cases with which he is concerned are of the illegitimate variety. The first horn of this dilemma is singularly unattractive, so we will attempt to do what the second requires.

TYPES OF THEORETICAL ASSUMPTIONS

Scientists often employ fictive assumptions in works that must be viewed as paradigms of good scientific procedure. The situation is even more puzzling than this statement indicates because scientists employ assumptions which are not merely fictive but are in fact inconsistent with the laws of the theories they are investigating. A simple example from physics will serve to illustrate this point. In deriving the formula $s = 1/2gt^2$ from the laws of Newtonian mechanics and gravitation, one employs a number of fictive assumptions (e.g., that the motion of the system of Cartesian co-ordinates which has its origin at the centre of mass of the body under consideration at the instant it is dropped, and has its z axis running through the centre of mass of the earth and rigidly attached to the centre of mass of the earth is uniform and rectilinear) to arrive at the equation

$$dv_z/dt = -kM/|\bar{r}|^2 = -g$$

where k is the gravitational constant, M is the mass of the earth, and $\bar{r}$ is the vector running from the centre of mass of the body to the centre of mass of earth. One then assumes that $|\bar{r}|$ is constant and arrives at the desired formula by integrating twice. But this last assumption is clearly inconsistent with the logical implications of the laws of the theory (and in fact is inconsistent with the desired result). Such examples can be multiplied at will.

What this example shows is that in deriving conclusions from theoretical assumptions, scientists do not proceed by simply drawing out the logical consequences of those assumptions. The standard view that one determines whether a theory fits the facts by logically deducing statements with observational content from the laws of the theory and then checking to see whether these statements are true does not accord with scientific practice. It, therefore, appears that if we are to complete successfully the general methodological task we have set ourselves at the end of Section 3, we must produce a scheme which, besides explaining satisfactorily the use of fictive assumptions in science, allows for the features of scientific procedure just noted.

We begin by establishing a scheme for classifying theoretical assumptions. It will be seen that this scheme is pragmatic in character. The distinctions involved can be made only on the basis of information about the state of knowledge in a given field of scientific inquiry at a specific time. Furthermore, these distinctions rely on the notion of theoretical contexts, which are assumed to be determined by the particular theoretical problems being addressed. On this account an assumption which is legitimate in one theoretical context may be illegitimate in another. Since we do not know how to say in a precise, general way how problems determine theoretical contexts, this feature of the scheme will make it somewhat vague. But the degree of vagueness introduced in this fashion will not be intolerable for present purposes.

Substantive assumptions are those which must be taken into account in all theoretical contexts and which determine the language of theory. These will usually consist of general laws (e.g., in the physics of the late seventeenth through the late nineteenth centuries, Newton's laws of motion and gravitation), but may include specific, non-nomological information about particular entities or classes of entities (e.g., in current physics, that the source of stellar energy is hydrogen fusion). By saying that these assumptions must be taken into account in all theoretical contexts we mean that in each context their implications must be heeded, unless special features of the context in question can be shown to make it legitimate to ignore such implications (as, for example, it can be shown that it is legitimate to ignore the third law of motion when one is deriving Kepler's laws of planetary motion from Newton's laws of mechanics and gravitation).

Approximating assumptions are those which are made in a particular context to facilitate the drawing of conclusions from substantive assumptions, are known (or for good reasons are suspected) to be false, and are stated in the language of the theory. In contrast to substantive assumptions, no special justification need be given for ignoring in one theoretical context an approximating assumption made in another. (For example, in deriving Kepler's laws one need not worry at all about the assumption that gravitational force is constant which is involved in treating Galileo's law for freely falling bodies on the basis of Newtonian mechanical and gravitational theory.) Within the class of approximating assumptions we distinguish *calculational* assumptions, which have a purely mathematical character (e.g., that pi = 3.14159), from *material* assumptions which attribute properties to entities or systems of entities considered in the theory (e.g., in the kinetic theory of gasses, that molecules are perfectly elastic spheres).

Finally,[6] we consider *heuristic* assumptions which serve to suggest conclusions and other types of assumptions, are not stated in the language of the theory, and may be metaphorical in character (e.g., the assumption that gas molecules behave as if they were tiny billiard balls).

Several features of this classifications scheme must be emphasized in order to prevent misunderstanding before we apply it. First, assumptions which are substantive in one context may be approximating in another (e.g., in physics Newton's laws of motion are now approximating assumptions, whereas, prior to Einstein, they were substantive assumptions). Second, it is not assumed that substantive assumptions will be present in all contexts. It can happen at times that all assumptions which are known to provide an ultimate basis for theoretical arguments are also known to be false (e.g., this was the situation in the kinetic theory of gasses from around 1890 until the development of quantum theory and the statistics of Bose and Fermi). Third, in the kind of situation just described the distinction between material approximating assumptions and heuristic assumptions can become fuzzy, because what counts as the language of a theory will not be clear if the theory lacks substantive assumption (e.g., in current physics physicists are uncomfortable with assumptions about fundamental particles, because in the absence of satisfactory substantive assumptions about nuclear processes it is unclear whether "particle" is part of the language of the theory and whether statements involving this term are to be taken as metaphors).

The principles of empiricism may now be restated by saying that a theory with substantive assumptions that do not accord with relevant empirical findings is unsatisfactory and that it is incumbent on the scientist to try to replace such a theory by one that has substantive assumptions that do accord with relevant empirical information. The rationale behind these principles is clear from the description of substantive assumptions. It would be irrational to take an assumption into account in all theoretical contexts if relevant empirical evidence sufficed to demonstrate the incorrectness of that assumption. Similarly, it is clear what determines whether empirical findings are relevant—they are relevant if they disagree with *any* theoretical conclusion to an extent greater than a correct estimate of the inaccuracies introduced *via* approximating assumptions will allow.

The trouble with the standard defence can now be stated clearly. The profit maximization assumption is empirically refuted, but it is a substantive assumption of orthodox micro-economic theory. If the standard defence is to be effective, it must do more than simply point to the use of fictive assumptions in paradigmatically good non-economic science. Cases involving empirically refuted substantive assumptions with which non-economists are willing to rest content must be produced. We do not know of any such cases. In particular, the physical examples of perfect gasses and incompressible fluids amount to highly articulated ways of dealing with bodies of material approximating assumptions which are useful in many theoretical contexts, and assumptions about infinitely slow processes in thermodynamics are used to establish ideal limits on the properties physical processes can have rather than to furnish conclusions about the properties they do have.

This concludes our rebuttal of the standard defence, but before leaving the subject it will be worthwhile to recast and clarify in terms of our scheme for classifying assumptions a point made in Section 2. We remarked there that we take the profit maximization assumption to mean that firms in fact act in such a way that their profits are at a maximum. This assumption is different from the assumption that things happen *as if* firms were seeking rationally to maximize their profits. The former assumption is a substantive assumption of orthodox micro-economic theory, but the latter is an heuristic assumption of that theory. Let us call the latter assumption *the heuristic profit maximization assumption*.

It seems to us that the standard defence has seemed plausible to many people precisely because it is so easy to confuse the profit maximization assumption with the heuristic profit maximization assumption and because the heuristic profit maximization assumption has at least two evident virtues. First, it (together with the corresponding assumption about utility maximization) has guided the development of economic theory in such a way as to produce results of undeniable interest and beauty. (Consider, for example, the elegant treatment of general equilibrium theory given in Debreu (1959).) Second, (as Debreu points out) it provides a way of "interpreting" economic theory by giving us a body of concepts for thinking about the abstract developments of the theory which flushes them out and makes us comfortable with them. By giving us a story to tell about the theory the heuristic profit maximization assumption allows us to make sense of the theory in the way we make sense of a story, and for many purposes an appropriate chapter of the story will do almost as well as the corresponding theoretical developments and will be much less difficult to tell and understand. (Consider, for example, the discussion of short-run equilibrium given in Cohen and Cyert (1975, pp. 52–5). It is quite informative and intelligible to the economic novice. Imagine what would be involved in recasting this discussion in terms of the theory of Debreu (1959) by introducing appropriate approximating assumptions.)

There is, of course, nothing at all wrong with using such a powerful heuristic assumption in context where the second virtue is what is required, and assumptions which have the first virtue noted above must be treated with due respect. But one cannot logically pass from this recognition to the conclusion that the profit maximization assumption is a satisfactory substantive assumption of economic theory. We do not charge that the proponents of the standard defence are guilty of equivocating in this way (though much evidence of such confusion can be found, for example, in Friedman (1953)), but we do believe that many have been convinced by this defence because they have unconsciously so equivocated.

THE PRACTICAL DEFENCE

Returning to the main point at issue, we are led to the conclusion that the apparent conflict between micro-economic practice and the principles of empiricism is a real conflict which the standard defence does not resolve. Even granting this, however, the defender of orthodoxy might fall back to the following position.

Admitting that you are right about these abstract methodological issues, let us consider practical matters. It is still true that orthodox micro-economic theory provides a decent account of market behaviour in many cases, and we have no reason to think that at the present time one could develop a theory that employs more realistic assumptions about the behaviour of firms and accounts for market behaviour as satisfactorily as the orthodox theory. Indeed, it seems that a better theory is more likely to be obtained by pushing ahead with the development of the current theory (which is formally manageable and in some respects empirically satisfactory), rather than by trying to make up a new theory based on a welter of reports about what actually goes on in firms (and, almost certainly, getting bogged down in a mass of indigestible descriptive detail).

Remember that physicists knew how to deal with perfect gasses and spent a lot of time discussing them long before they managed to construct theories within which such talk could be understood as consisting of "highly articulated ways of dealing with bodies of material approximating assumptions," and recall that physicists working on gas theory did not spend every bit of their time trying to develop such theories as soon as it was known that real gasses are not perfect (which was known practically from the time of origin of the kinetic theory of gasses). It seems only reasonable that the search for a better micro-economic theory should proceed in a similarly indirect way, even if that means we will continue working with "empirically refuted substantive assumptions" for the foreseeable future.

You aren't likely to persuade many economists to give up the profit maximiza-tion assumption unless you can provide convincing reasons for thinking striking progress is likely to be made by doing so. This is as it should be. Bacon (an empiricist if there ever was one) said that truth arises more readily from error than from confusion. The policy your remarks suggest amounts to advising economists to plunge into massive confusion rather than working for the time being on the basis of an error we know to be fruitful.

Though we have never actually seen this argument anywhere in print, it strikes us as the sort of thing those who use the standard defence probably would say if they were convinced that they could no longer rely on the standard defence. We will christen it the *practical defence* and set about rebutting it.

PROSPECTS FOR A BETTER THEORY

The practical defence makes the same claims about the current state of micro-economic theory which are involved in the standard defence but goes beyond these to make claims about the prospects for developing a better theory. After a remark about the first set of claims, we will devote the remainder of this paper to consideration of the second set.[7]

The basis for arguing that standard micro-economic theory provides a good account of market behaviour is weak. It consists chiefly of remarks which point out unspecifically that in a limited variety of situations there is a qualitative agreement between what orthodox micro-economic models predict and what goes on in markets. Furthermore, the cases chosen for exhibiting this kind of agreement between theory and reality typically are picked out in the light of careful hindsight. Awkward disagreements between theory and reality tend to be swept under the convenient rug provided by the *ceteris paribus* clause which is a pervasive feature of the models being considered. Consequently, the enterprise of showing that orthodox micro-economic theory provides a satisfactory account of market behaviour amounts almost to an exercise in special pleading rather than to a genuine attempt to determine the extent of agreement between theory and what is going on in the world. For these reasons we are not convinced by the claims shared by the standard and practical defences, and we think it is clear that no economist should be. We turn now to the claims which are peculiar to the practical defence.

The practical defence claims that the best way to go about trying to produce a better micro-economic theory is by continuing the development of the orthodox theory. The methodological arguments we have given and the arguments summarized in Section 2 can be combined to show that this is not so. This conclusion is arrived at in the following way.

According to our methodological arguments the profit maximization assumption must be given up because it is an empirically refuted substantive assumption, and the arguments of Section 2 make it clear that this assumption fails under empirical scrutiny chiefly because decisions made under uncertainty will almost never lead to maximization of profits. It is reasonable to infer from this that the prospective better theory will have to incorporate a satisfactory treatment of the problem of decision-making under uncertainty, and Tintner's argument shows that it is precisely this which is ruled out by adherence to the profit maximization assumption. To contend that a theory which incorporates a better account of what economic actors will do in conditions of uncertainty is likely to be arrived at if one doggedly insists on attributing to those actors motivations which *cannot* make sense in such conditions is bizarre, and in the light of Tintner's argument it is clear that this is exactly what the practical defence advises. Such advice should be shunned.

We believe that these remarks show that the research strategy suggested in the practical defence cannot lead to the production of a theory which will escape condemnation under the methodological strictures we have applied to the orthodox theory, but in arguments about policy it is insufficient to point out that a policy is bound to be impotent in order to root it out. In order to do down an established policy (and, certainly, the research strategy outlined in the practical defence is established policy among economists) one must go on to present an alternative policy which has some prospect of leading to success. We will now try our hand at laying out such a policy.

According to the methodological arguments we have presented, orthodox micro-economic theory must be replaced by a different theory because its account of the behaviour of individual firms is at odds with the facts about how firms behave, and we have also argued that its account of the behaviour of individual firms fails in this way chiefly because decision-making under uncertainty cannot be handled sensibly in a theory which has the profit maximization as a substantive assumption. It is therefore reasonable to guess that the way to go about searching for a better theory is to begin by trying to get hold of an empirically satisfactory account of how firms make decisions under uncertainty. This being accomplished, one would hope then to be able to arrive at a theory of market behaviour based on this account. Such is the policy we suggest. We admit that it seems logically possible that some other policy would be better than our suggestion but we are unable to conceive of such a policy at this time and we can provide evidence that the policy we advocate has some prospects of leading to the desired result. We will now adduce this evidence.

There are a variety of ways in which economic theory can deal with uncertainty. One of these is to retreat from analysis of the individual units and rely on an analysis of market forces.[8] This approach is somewhat akin to the use of the environment by the biologists to explain adaptation of species. It has merit and might be used to provide an explanation for certain kinds of behaviour in the long run and at an aggregate level. The approach in question is, however, bound to lead to theories which are deficient in one important respect—such theories will not give us an account of the behaviour of individual firms. This deficiency is important for two reasons. First, one must have an account of the behaviour of individual firms in order to deal with monopoly and oligopoly. Second, although we are concerned with micro-economics as a positive science, it must be remembered that micro-economic theories are intended to have normative uses and that one of these is to help in the making of public policy decisions. Theories which do not give an account of the behaviour of individual firms will not be helpful in deciding things like this. Still, some progress has been made by looking at micro-economics in this way and we think it is well worth pursuing. There is no conflict involved in implementing the policy we have suggested by simultaneously pursuing global approaches of this sort and pursuing approaches which involve explicit treatment of the behaviour of individual firms. In fact, to do this would be to employ a both-ends-against-the-middle strategy, which is usually a good plan in conducting the sort of search being considered.

A second method of handling the problem of decision-making under uncertainty, which brings to bear the existing techniques of mathematical analysis, is to assume that the firm can develop subjective probability distributions of profit for decision alternatives. In addition it is necessary to assume that the firm has a utility function that enables it to convert probability distributions of profit into utilities, and that the firm makes decisions so as to maximize the utility function. This may well be a useful approach if by empirical work the process by which businessmen establish probability distributions can be determined and if the form of the utility functions used by businessmen can be discovered. It is, of course, notoriously difficult to get empirical information about such matters, so we suspect that the advantages of this way of treating decision-making under uncertainty are not likely to extend much further than the formal ones we have pointed out. These advantages are not to be taken lightly, however, and, as in the case of the preceding approach, we point to what has been achieved[9] and recommend further development.

A third method, and one of which we are proponents, is to study empirically the way that businessmen make decisions in the face of uncertainty, to embed the decision process into a theory of the firm,[10] and then to construct a theory of market behaviour based on the resulting theory of the firm. We will dub this approach the *behavioural approach* and discuss it at some length. The first problem to be considered is that of constructing the desired theory of the firm.

The construction of such a theory will require the making of many observations. We will begin by saying something about what is involved in doing this.

"Observation" can be viewed as a process in which a trained scientist watches and records the actual process of making a decision. The observations will include being present at meetings, interviewing relevant participants, analysing written documents, and any other steps designed to lead to understanding of the criteria being used to make the decision and the goals these criteria are intended to serve. Such an approach requires the co-operation of the firm and the co-operation of the participants in the decision-making process. There are difficulties (e.g., the problem of getting an accurate picture of the process rather than a formalized, polished one developed for external purposes), but it is possible to make such observations.[11]

The critical problem involved in constructing the theory of the firm required by the behavioural approach is to determine the goals of the firm and to understand the process by which decision rules are learned and modified in the face of feedback from the environment in the interest of serving these goals. This problem is critical because one of the main ideas behind the approach is that the way to get a better theory of the firm is by viewing it as an adaptive mechanism that can learn from its environment, and it seems clear that the features of this sort of learning which will lend themselves to theoretical treatment are the decision rules used in the firms.

As an adaptive mechanism the firm is able to learn about its environment by taking actions and analysing the results. The actions it takes—raising price, increasing output, etc.—are selected from a limited number of alternatives. The actions are designed to achieve a goal—a particular level of profit, a certain market share—and the results of the actions are analysed in terms of achieving the goal. The results of the analysis are then stored within the organization's memory and the demand curve or the cost curve begins to take on certain characteristics as a result. Thus if price is increased on a number of different occasions and demand does not slacken, it is likely that the demand curve will be characterized as highly inelastic. This example is a simple one and is designed to illustrate what we mean by the firm as an adaptive mechanism. The firm is capable of learning under far more complex conditions and adapting appropriately.

We note that there is reason to think that the goals which drive this process are pretty much the same from firm to firm, when considered in general terms, though different firms will consider these goals to have been achieved by quite different levels of performance and a given firm will alter the desired levels of performance over time. [12] This similarity of goals should make it easier to do the job we are projecting, but we also note that we do not intend to rule out the possibility that a firm may acquire new goals and discard old ones in the course of time. If this process of acquiring and discarding goals is found to be an important aspect of the working of firms, then it will have to be studied in detail.

In treating the processes to be studied, careful attention will be given to the fact that the firm (even with computers) has a limited capability to process information and, therefore, may not reach the position that hindsight analysis demonstrates to have been optimum. The recognition of limited information processing insures that the ability in the firm theory will avoid the sorts of empirically based complaints which have been lodged against the orthodox theory of the firm.

We will call the decision rules to be studied *behavioural rules*. The firm develops these rules of thumb as guides for making decisions in a complex environment with uncertainty and incomplete information. Behavioural rules incorporate the decision-makers' assumptions about the nature of the environment and the nature of the firm itself which suffice to allow a decision to be reached in such circumstances. The aim of the behavioural approach to the theory of the firm is to make business judgment susceptible of rational, theoretical treatment by analysing what is essential to the process of judgment in terms of sets of behavioural rules.

Turning from the theory of the firm to the problem of constructing a micro-economic theory based on the theory of the firm, we note that we are not recommending that the baby be thrown out with the bath water. Indeed, we lay it down as a requirement both for the theory of the firm and for the theory of market behaviour that as the behavioural theory is applied to situations in which uncertainty gives way to certainty and knowledge increases without limit the results derived from the behavioural theory should approximate more and more closely those derived by *a priori* reasoning about the simplified situation treated by the orthodox theory.

A scientific theory is supposed to provide an account of what will happen in a variety of possible worlds, and we acknowledge that the orthodox theory works admirably for an extensive set of worlds which differ from the one that we live in chiefly by not involving decisions made under uncertainty and incomplete information. Clearly, in such a world the firm operating in the framework of the competitive system with market prices, the marginal cost curve, and the average variable cost curve known has no need for behavioural rules other than those derived by the usual marginalist reasoning. In these circumstances the firm must determine prices and output by the intersection of the price and marginal cost curve. It is the firm operating under conditions of ignorance of its demand and cost curves which must find other methods of decision-making. We are aiming at a theory which, both with respect to the behaviour of individual firms and with respect to the behaviour of markets, will explain what is going on in the latter situation and establish clearly the relations between this and the existing account of what is going on in the former.

The next order of business is to say something about the form the behavioural theory is likely to take. It seems probable that, at least in the beginning, the formal development of the theory will proceed by means of computer simulation. The hope would be to produce a manageable and empirically well-grounded class of computer models of individual firms which can be incorporated naturally into simulations of markets. This would be a rigorous way of proceeding, but it must be acknowledged that so long as the development of the theory proceeds exclusively by means of computer simulations, the kinds of general theorems which are regarded as the chief glory of the orthodox theory will not be forthcoming. We will now offer some comments about computer simulations in general and about the second point stated in the preceding sentence.

The advantage of computer simulation over ordinary mathematical modelling is that more complex relations can be developed in the simulation than in a model which employs ordinary analytic methods. This obviates the tendency, which is given free rein in the orthodox theory, to over-simplify reality so that a model which is mathematically tractable can be developed and, therefore, suits our purposes exactly. It must be admitted, however, that simulation models are prone to certain defects. For one thing they are usually too complicated. Because of the power of the computer it is possible to make a simulation model nearly as complex as the real world. As one would expect, such models become as difficult to analyse as the real world and, consequently, are of little explanatory value. Clearly, the simulation models to be used in the behavioural theory will have to be built with appropriate restraint.

General theorems will not be forthcoming so long as the development of the theory proceeds exclusively *via* computer simulations. The lack of existing mathematical techniques sufficient to furnish general theorems in the context of the theory we are proposing should not be regarded as an evident defect of that theory. If the behaviour of the computer models to be used in the theory is sensible, this will furnish the strongest possible evidence that techniques sufficient for the desired theorems can be developed. Assuming that models of this type can be constructed, it is clear that the fact that we do not currently possess mathematical machinery of the sort necessary to produce general theorems about them should be viewed as an exciting challenge.

Finally, we point out that the concept of behavioural rules is not new to economics. Every determinate model developed under conditions of some uncertainty utilizes a behavioural rule. In the cobweb model, suppliers are assumed to determine the current period's supply on the basis of the last period's price, $s(t) = f(p(t-1))$. In the Cournot duopoly model, each firm assumes that it is independent of its rival, in particular, that changes in its output will have no effect on its rival. In the kinked demand curve model, each firm assumes its rival will always behave in the way that will hurt it the most. Thus a price increase will not be followed by rivals but a price decrease will. For other models where uncertainty exists in the situation being modelled but is eliminated in the model, some form of behavioural rule can be shown to be present. Our proposal amounts to saying that economists should stop viewing such rules as *ad hoc* devices introduced to enable the finding of determinate solutions of neo-classical models and instead consider them as part of the central subject matter of their discipline. We hope that we have made it clear how we have been led to make this proposal by general methodological considerations and by what we can understand about the way the world is and what economics ought to be like.

CONCLUSION

Studies of decision-making behaviour in organizations have produced conclusions that bear on the problem of handling uncertainty and at the same time illustrate the way in which a behavioural approach may contribute to model building. Our hope is that such an approach will lead to better micro-economic theories.

In most business decisions involving price and output in the short run the decision-maker confronts uncertainty with no way to dodge it, and no ordinary forecasting model or application of orthodox economic theory will give him the answers he needs. This situation exists in every firm producing multiple products about which production decisions must be made before the market has decided which items will be most in demand. The problem is handled in most cases by some form of sequential decision-making process in which the firm bases its decisions on a sample of buyer preferences. The firm collects information until it can satisfice on the product mix and, depending on the production process, will continue to collect information and repeat the process for subsequent decision.

It is hardly credible that much further progress in micro-economic theory can be made if these facts are ignored. We believe that the most reasonable policy for economists is to accept these facts and, with the help of the psychologist and organization theorist, to try to construct a micro-economic theory based on a theory of the firm which explains the decision processes involved in these facts. In order to do this the economist must understand more about the activities of the decision-maker or decision-making group. The emphasis in economic theorizing must be on understanding processes as opposed to making simple assumptions about motivation and proceeding to develop models without reference to their empirical correctness, if theoretical activity in economics is not to become sterile.

It is clear that the firm wants to make as much profit as it can subject to the constraints that any individual or organization must face in making decisions, and an astonishing amount of progress in economic theorizing has stemmed from this simple insight. But it is not reasonable to believe that much further progress will be forthcoming on this basis. In our view the job of the economist is to demonstrate through the use of all the knowledge available to him why the firm stops its search process when it does, to explain how the forces within the organization and the market have combined to make the level of investment in the plant what it is, and to show how the effects of the various competing groups within the firm and the market forces have worked to determine price changes and output in particular cases. This is a formidable task, but it is nowhere written that the doing of science must be easy.

We hope we have made it clear that we are not arguing that theory should be discarded in favour of pure description but, rather, that a micro-economic theory which takes into account empirical information about processes taking place within the firm should be developed. We believe that a micro-economic theory which includes a theory of decision-making within organizations that will take into account both the internal variables of the firm and the market forces operating on firms in particular market structures can and should be developed. Progress, albeit limited, *has* been made towards the development of such a theory. We have written this chapter in order to encourage continued work in this direction in the face of energetic, but misguided, defences of the conventional approach.

REFERENCES

Alchian, A., 'Uncertainty, Evolution, and Economic Theory'. *Journal of Political Economy*, 58, pp. 211–22, 1950.

Cyert, R. M. and DeGroot, M. H., 'Bayesian Analysis and Duopoly Theory'. *Journal of Political Economy*, 78, pp. 1168–84, 1970a.
———— 'Multiperiod Decision Models with Alternating Choice as a Solution to the Duopoly Problem'. *Quarterly Journal of Economics*, 84, pp. 410–429, 1970b.
————'Interfirm Learning and the Kinked Demand Curve'. *Journal of Economic Theory*, 3, pp. 272–87, 1971.
———— 'An Analysis of Cooperation and Learning in a Duopoly Context'. *American Economic Review*, 63, pp. 24–37, 1973.
Cyert, R. M., DeGroot, M. H. and Holt, C., *Capital Allocation within a Firm*. Technical Report No. 109, Department of Statistics, Carnegie-Mellon University, 1976.
Cyert, R. M. and Hedrick. C. L., 'Theory of the Firm: Past, Present, and Future; and Interpretation'. *The Journal of Economic Literature*, 10, pp. 398–412, 1972.
Cyert, R. M. and March, J. G., *A Behavioural Theory of the Firm*. Englewood Cliffs, New Jersey: Prentice Hall, 1963.
Cyert, R. M. and Simon, H. A., 'Theory of the Firm: Behavioralism and Marginalism'. Working Paper, Graduate School of Industrial Administration, Carnegie-Mellon University, 1971.
Debreu, G., *Theory of Value: An Axiomatic Analysis of Economic Equilibrium*. Cowles Foundation Monograph 17, John Wiley & Sons, 1959.
Friedman, M., 'The Methodology of Positive Economics'. In *Essays in Positive Economics*, University of Chicago Press, 1953.
Gordon, R. A., 'Short Period Price Determination'. *American Economic Review*, 38, pp. 265–88, 1948.
Grunberg, E., 'Notes on the Verifiability of Economic Laws'. *Philosophy of Science*, 24, pp. 337–48, 1957.
Machlup, F., 'Theories of the Firm: Marginalist, Behavioral, Managerial'. *American Economic Review*, 57, pp. 1–33, 1967.
Margolis, J., 'The Analysis of the Firm: Rationalism, Conventionalism, and Behaviorism'. *Journal of Business*, 31, pp. 187–99, 1958.
Papendreou, A., 'Some Basic Problems in the Theory of the Firm'. In B. F. Haley (ed.), *A Survey of Contemporary Economics*, Vol. 2, pp. 183–219, Richard D. Irwin, 1952.
Simon, H. A., 'A Behavioral Model of Rational Choice'. *Quarterly Journal of Economics*, 69, pp. 99–118, 1955.
Williamson, O. E., *Corporate Control and Business Behavior*. Prentice-Hall, 1970.
Winter, S. G., 'Economic Natural Selection and the Theory of the Firm'. New Haven, Connecticut: Yale University Press. *Yale Economic Essays*, Vol. 4, pp. 224–72, 1964.
———— 'Optimization and Evolution in the Theory of the Firm'. In R. H. Day and T. Groves (eds), *Adaptive Economic Models*, pp. 73–118. New York, New York: Academic Press, 1975.

NOTES

1. As one can see from the survey given in Cyert and Hedrick (1972).
2. See Papendreou (1952).
3. See Gordon (1948), Margolis (1958), and Simon (1955).

4. See Alchian (1950, p. 212).
5. We have in mind chiefly Friedman and Machlup. The classic statement of Friedman's view is his (1953). Machlup's ideas about this issue are summarized in his (1967).
6. We do not claim that our scheme for classifying assumptions is exhaustive. The categories defined here are sufficient for present purposes, but there may be others.
7. Some of the material in this section is taken from Cyert and Simon (1971).
8. Alchian (1950) and Winter (1964 and 1975) are examples of this approach.
9. See Williamson (1970), and Cyert and DeGroot (1970a, 1970b, 1971 and 1973).
10. As in Cyert and March (1963). See also Grunberg (1957).
11. As one can see from Cyert and March (1963), and Cyert, DeGroot, and Holt (1976).
12. See Cyert and March (1963, pp. 40–3).

14 The Behavioural Approach: With Emphasis on Economics*

with Herbert A. Simon

A recent article by a philosopher of science defends economists against attacks on the profession stemming from the many conflicting and inaccurate predictions made in recent years. The defence may not be satisfying to economists, however. The argument is that it is unfair to expect relevant policy predictions since economics is not an empirical, but rather a deductive discipline that might better be viewed as a branch of applied mathematics (Rosenberg, 1982).

The behavioural approach that we are espousing is one methodology that can be used in empirical science and, indeed, we believe is the approach that must be used to make economics an empirical science. Before we make the positive argument it is useful to clear away the allegation that empirical evidence advanced over the last ten to twenty years has validated the deductive approach of neo-classical theory.

To be sure, some economists have argued that it does not matter whether individual firms *in fact* make their decisions along marginalist lines (that is, incremental) as long as aggregative phenomena behave *as though* they did (Friedman, 1953). We will discuss this issue below but we want to emphasize that at least *one* of the goals of economics is to understand and explain economic phenomena of all kinds and at all levels of aggregation or disaggregation. However unnecessary a theory of the firm's decision processes might be for economic policy (and we do not here prejudge this issue one way or the other), it is undubitably necessary in order to explain an important area of human, rational behaviour. We will restrict ourselves in this chapter, therefore, to the scientific question of how far a particular theory is supported by empirical data.

Following that argument we will re-examine the major alternative

---

* Reprinted by permission from *Behavioral Science*, Vol. 28, No. 2, April, 1983.

paradigm to marginalism: behaviouralism. Despite the fact that this alternative has been explicated by articles and books, there is significant evidence of failure to understand its role, present and potential, in economic theory.

THE EMPIRICAL CASE FOR MARGINALISM

Strong claims have been made over the years by some economists for the conclusiveness of the empirical evidence for the neo-classical theory of the firm. Among the strongest claims are those of Jorgenson and Siebert who assert in their 1968 paper that "the evidence is so largely favorable to the theory that current empirical research emphasizes such technical questions as the appropriate form for the production function and the statistical specification for econometric models of production based on this theory" (Jorgenson & Siebert, 1968). In the same passage, Jorgenson and Siebert refer to "the entire econometric literature on cost and production functions, all of which is based on the neoclassical theory of the firm", and cite "a recent survey of the literature by Walters ... [that] enumerates 345 references, almost all presenting results of econometric tests of the neoclassical theory which are overwhelmingly favorable to the theory."

In the face of this mountain of evidence, it would seem that for an economist to test the basic theory further would be as redundant as an engineer running experiments on Newton's Laws of Motion before daring to use them to design a bridge. But perhaps before we accept this conclusion as final, we should have one last look at the evidence.

We cannot consider here all the kinds of evidence that have been adduced, at one time or another, in support of the theory (Earley, 1956). Instead, we will focus on the three kinds of studies upon which Jorgenson and Siebert rely in making their claims of overwhelming empirical verification of the neo-classical theory. These are:

1. The demonstration that the exponents in the labour term of fitted Cobb-Douglas functions are usually nearly equal to labour's share of income;
2. Evidence that firms' short-run and long-run cost curves are U-shaped; and
3. Evidence that firms' investments are best explained by regressions whose form is derived from neo-classical theory.

Topics 1 and 2 are covered in the review article by Walters that Jorgenson and Siebert cite, and the latter do not themselves add new evidence on these points. Topic 3 is the central theme of the econometric work that these authors report in their own paper.

THE COBB-DOUGLAS FUNCTION AND LABOUR'S SHARE

Since most of the relevant evidence has been summarized conveniently for us by Walters, and since the important issues have to do with the interpretations attached to the findings, and not the findings themselves, we can use Walters's survey as our evidential base (Walters, 1963). Our first task is to review briefly the reason that the data on production functions have been thought to provide significant support for the marginalist theory. (The argument in this section has been further developed and formalized in Simon, 1979b.) The next two pages borrow freely from Sections I and II of that paper.)

Fitting Cobb-Douglas functions to data with just-identified regression models proves nothing, of course, about the validity of the classical, or any other, theory of the firm. It is of the nature of a just-identified model that it can always be fitted (more or less well) to the observed data, and that the fitted regressions will provide unique estimates of the model's parameters. A just-identified model, taken by itself, is a tool for estimating parameters of an accepted theory, not a tool for testing theories. (It is true that extensive hypothesizing about a model prior to fitting the model to the data enables the investigator to gain information from even a just-identified model.) Unless a model is over-identified, so that the data could be inconsistent with it, it cannot—with any conceivable data, real or imaginary—contradict the theory, and, hence, cannot test it.

The fact, therefore, that a considerable part of the variance of outputs can be explained by fitted, just-identified Cobb-Douglas functions with quantities of labour and capital as inputs has no implications for the question before us. What does have implications are two further empirical generalizations that can be induced from the many such parameter-estimating studies that Walters reviews:

1. When the exponent of the labour factor of the fitted Cobb-Douglas function is compared with the labour share of income, there is usually reasonably good agreement between these two numbers; and
2. In a majority of cases, the sum of the exponents of the labour and capital factors of the fitted function is close to unity—the fitted Cobb-Douglas functions are nearly homogeneous of the first degree.

Let us consider, very briefly, the theoretical import of these findings.

The Cobb-Douglas function can be written:

$$P = YL\alpha C\beta, \qquad (1)$$

from which we obtain the marginal productivities of labour and capital:

$$\partial P/\partial L = \alpha P/L; \; \partial P/\partial C = \beta P/C. \qquad (2)$$

But, in marginalist theory, these marginal productivities must equal wages, w, and the price of capital, r, respectively, so that:

$$w = \alpha P/L; \; r = \beta P/C. \qquad (3)$$

However, if labour's share of income, Lw, plus capital's share, rC, equals total income, then:

$$wL + rC = \alpha P + \beta P = P, \qquad (4)$$

from which it follows immediately that

$$\alpha + \beta = 1. \qquad (5)$$

Thus, classical marginalist theory, combined with the assumption that the production function is Cobb-Douglas, demands (Equation 3) the equality observed in the data between α and labour's share of income $(wL)/P$. Further, if the labour and capital shares of income exhaust total production (Equation 4), as the data usually indicate they nearly do, then the Cobb-Douglas function must be homogeneous of the first degree.

The first of these results has been regarded as a very important piece of evidence supporting classical theory. The theory predicts that the labour exponent should equal labour's share of income, and if we reject the theory, we appear to be attributing the observed equality to coincidence —an implausible and unsatisfying alternative.

So it would be, that is, if coincidence were the only alternative explanation. But it is not. The observed equality can be derived from assumptions whose *a priori* probability is at least as high as that of the classical theory (Walters, 1963), as we will show.

We need to distinguish three classes of data to which the Cobb-Douglas function has been applied: 1) cross-section data (intra-industry or inter-industry) from a single country; 2) international cross-section data; and 3) time-series data.

The implausibility of the classical Cobb-Douglas interpretation of the single country cross-section studies has often been noted. Since the cogent analysis by Phelps Brown is well known, it needs only brief review here (Brown, 1957). What Brown observed is that output measures in these cross-section studies were basically measures of the labour and capital costs of goods sold. Hence, if variations in wages and capital charges were small—as would be the case within a single economy—what was being fitted in the regressions was chiefly the variation in output against variation in amounts of labour and of capital employed in different firms and industries—what Bronfenbrenner had earlier called the "interfirm function" (Bronfenbrenner, 1944)—rather than anything that might legitimately be regarded as a production function in the classical meaning of the term. Brown showed that, in these circumstances, the exponents of the erroneously fitted Cobb-Douglas function would sum approximately to unity and the labour exponent would be equal to labour's share. (See also the derivation and extension of these results by Simon & Levy, 1963; Simon, 1979b.) The empirically observed fact that the sum of the two exponents is usually close to unity— sometimes smaller, sometimes larger—has always been something of an embarrassment for the classical theory. For, as is well known, decreasing returns to scale are essential to standard demonstrations of competitive equilibrium (Lucas, 1967). The alternative explanation produces the observed result without implying anything about whether returns to scale are decreasing, constant, or increasing (Lucas, 1970). Hence, it is compatible with competitive equilibrium, while marginalist explanation is not whenever the sum of the coefficients equals or exceeds unity.

So much for inter-firm and inter-industry cross-section studies. The principal international cross-section study is the well-known paper by Arrow, Chenery, Minhas and Solow (1961). Here, the analysis just given does not apply, since there is wide variation in w and r over the observations. On the other hand, since that study does not test the constancy of labour's share, it is irrelevant to the issue before us—the validity of marginalist theory. Most of the paper is an exercise in estimating, rather than theory testing. Its principal empirical finding is that output per unit of labour input varies from country to country approximately with the eight-tenths power of wages, a result consistent with classical theory and with many other theories as well.

We come, finally, to the time-series studies, the most important of which are summarized by Walters on page 26 of his article. Here Mendershausen as long ago as 1938 provided an alternative to the Cobb-Douglas explanation that fits the data equally well, takes into account the high degree of collinearity among the variables, and avoids the unacceptable assumption (embedded in the Cobb-Douglas analysis) of no technological change (Mendershausen, 1938). Mendershausen showed that the time series for output, labour, and capital could be represented by exponential functions, each with a different exponent, and that if the exponent for output fell between the exponents for capital and labour—as was the case for the time series used in the empirical studies—all of the observed results would follow from fitting a Cobb-Douglas function mistakenly to the data.

Given this alternative interpretation of the data, as well as the other difficulties in the Cobb-Douglas explanation mentioned by Walters, we cannot but say "amen!" to Walters's own summary (1963, p. 28) that: "One cannot conclude from this survey of time series estimates that the simple single-equation Cobb-Douglas specification has been uniformly successful."

As Solow has shown in a celebrated study (Solow, 1957), most of the variation through time, of w must be attributed to a shift in the production function due to technological change. Suppose now that we have a savings function that makes C nearly proportional to $P, (C = sP)$, at least over the narrow range of variation that is observed in r. Then, from Equation (4), $w = (P - rsP)/L$ will, of course, increase with a shift in the production function, as demanded by the observed data. But then, $(wL)/P = (P - rsP)/P = (1 - rs)$ will also remain constant. (See Simon, 1979b, Section VI, for a more complete derivation of this result.) This derivation depends on the constancy of r and of the savings ratio, which are assumed, not derived. But perhaps this assumption is no more gratuitous (and perhaps even less) than the assumption of neutrality of technological change which is required to draw any of the classical conclusions from the fitting of Cobb-Douglas functions.

In passing, we remark that Walters reports nothing like the solid proof of marginalist theory from the data he reviews that Jorgenson and Siebert aver at second hand. See especially his qualifications, qualms, and warnings on pages 11 ("After surviving the problems of aggregation one may easily doubt whether there is much point in employing such a concept as an aggregate production function."), 17, 19 (both referring to "meagre evidence" on crucial estimating assumptions), 27–8 (leading to the summary statement quoted above), 34, 35, 37 (on the interfirm function), 38, and 39 (Walters, 1963).

Thus we see that the empirical findings that have been heralded as decisive evidence for the validity of the marginalist theory of the firm lend themselves to a quite different—and more plausible—interpretation. The entire body of work on the Cobb-Douglas function does not lose its interest, but it does lose its crucial significance as a test of the neo-classical theory.

THE SHAPE OF THE COST CURVE

If the studies surveyed by Walters of production functions fail to validate neo-classical theory, the empirical data that he cites on cost curves are no more helpful to that end. (In this section, we follow closely Simon, 1979b, Section VIII.) To indicate why this is so, we cannot do better than quote Walters himself (Walters, 1963):

> To summarise, the theoretical arguments suggest that the short run average cost curve has the typical U shape, although Menger has added several reservations. Theory is reasonably clear on the proposition that long run average costs may be expected to decline at first with increasing scale. But for high outputs the theoretical arguments do not seem to be so convincing. Choice between the alternatives must depend on the empirical evidence.

Of course, if empirical evidence must decide the actual shape of the long-run cost curve, and if any shape evidence may disclose is consistent with neo-classical theory, then that same evidence is useless to validate or invalidate the theory. But the situation is not much better with respect to the short-run curve. While (subject to the reservations mentioned) empirical evidence that the actual curves are *not* U-shaped might be taken as a reason for distrusting the theory, logic does not force the converse on us (Gold, 1981). If the actual curves *are* U-shaped, this finding is consistent with the neo-classical theory, but does not imply the validity of the theory.

We need hardly debate, however, what such a finding would imply, since the empirical data, as summarized by Walters, are so inconclusive. In his paper, he opines "that the evidence in favour of constant marginal cost is not overwhelming. Certainly the revision of theory to include this phenomenon is not an urgent matter" (Walters, 1963). And on the following page, we find the following, curiously weak, defence of the classical theory (Walters, 1963):

> For "competitive" industries, the U-shaped hypothesis does not inspire great confidence. But this is *not* because it has been refuted by direct empirical evidence. On the contrary, this lack of faith is occasioned by the very few *opportunities* for collecting evidence to refute the theory directly. Instead we are driven to indirect and circumstantial evidence. But at least there is no large body of data which convincingly contradicts the hypothesis of a U-shaped long run cost curve and the fruitful results which depend on it.

Our review began with the bold reference of Jorgenson and Siebert to Walters's "345 references, almost all presenting results of econometric tests of the neo-classical theory which are overwhelmingly favorable to the theory" (Jorgenson & Siebert, 1968). Apart from the fact that less than half of these references are to empirical studies, the rest being theoretical and methodological, we now find that Walters himself makes no such claim to evidence "overwhelmingly favorable" to classical theory. Instead, he makes the mild claim that the data on cost curves, though generally not supportive of the U-shaped curve usually thought to be necessary for classical theory, are not so conclusive as to require the theory to be abandoned!

INVESTMENT BEHAVIOUR

Having found that nothing in Walters's review can properly be interpreted as empirical support for the neo-classical theory of the firm, we turn to other kinds of evidence that have been put forward—in particular, the evidence of regression models fitted to data on business firm investments. The paper of Jorgenson and Siebert will serve as our specific example in discussing the issues.

For a proper analysis of the interesting work that has been done on business investment behaviour, we must be more precise than was necessary in the previous sections in defining what is meant by "marginalist" or "neo-classical" theory. There does not appear to be any single authoritative definition in the literature, and not all authors sweep the same collection of models into this category. Ordinarily, such ambiguity does no harm—we would find the scope of such a term as "Newtonian mechanics" no less indefinite. But since we are concerned with choosing here between neo-classical theory and some of its alternatives, we must be a bit more specific in drawing the boundaries.

Following Jorgenson and Siebert, we consider a number of different models for explaining investment behaviour, all of them within the following framework:

1. The firm is taken to have a desired level of capital, determined by long-run considerations. (Jorgenson & Siebert, 1968)
2. Capital is adjusted toward its desired level by a certain proportion of the discrepancy between desired and actual capital in each period. (Jorgenson & Siebert, 1968)
3. Total investment is the sum of this adjustment and replacement investment. "Replacement is proportional to actual capital stock." (Jorgenson & Siebert, 1968)

Within this framework, alternative models of investment behaviour can be specified which differ only with respect to their assumptions about how the firm determines its desired level of capital. Jorgenson and Siebert compare, in particular, five alternative theories of investment behaviour: neo-classical (two versions), accelerator, expected profits, and liquidity. In the neo-classical I model, desired capital is proportional to the value of output divided by the price of capital services including capital gains. The neo-classical II model is identical, except that capital gains are excluded. In the accelerator model, desired capital is assumed to be proportional to output. In the liquidity model, desired capital is assumed to be proportional to liquidity (profits after taxes plus depreciation less dividends paid, deflated by the investment goods price index). In the expected profits model, desired capital is proportional to the market value of the firm.

To what extent, if at all, can these several models be said to follow from marginalist assumptions—from the assumption that the firm is investing at that level which will maximize profits? All five models postulate a notion of "desired capital", which could (but need not) be interpreted to mean the profit-maximizing level of capital. In this interpretation, the models differ only in the assumed method whereby the firm estimates what the optimal level of capital is. (We disregard here the question of whether the adjustment path from the actual to the desired quantity of capital is optimal. The issues we wish to explore can be illustrated without introducing this additional complication.)

If the view be accepted that "desired capital" in all of these models is identical with the optimal level of marginalist theory, then it would be proper to call all of them "neo-classical". Jorgenson, however, uses the latter term in a stricter sense. He calls a theory neo-classical if the equation defining the desired amount of capital is itself derived from profit-maximizing assumptions. Thus, his two neo-classical models are derived as the steady-state profit-maximizing equilibria of particular capital theories. He does not consider the remaining three models to be neo-classical because the relations determining desired amount of capital are not so derived, or, at best, are derived in some rather vague and not fully formalized way.

Jorgenson and his colleagues, in this and other papers, then proceed to show that, by certain criteria, regressions based on the neo-classical models (in the narrower or Jorgensonian sense) give better estimates of the actual levels of investment than do regressions based on the other models. Not all students of these matters accept these views of the empirical superiority of the neo-classical models, but this again is a question that need not concern us at the moment. Many issues relating to the statistical methods employed have also been raised (Cyert, DeGroot & Holt, 1979). We shall disregard these, too.

We come now to the crux of the matter: to what extent and in what way do these empirical studies validate the neo-classical theory of the firm? This validation is claimed by Jorgenson to follow from the superior success of the neo-classical models over other models in estimating the level of investment. But we cannot accept this easy inference without examining it more closely.

Such excellence as the empirical estimates provided by the neo-classical models exhibit might be attributable *either* to (1) a Friedman-like and as-iffish coincidence between these estimates and the decision of the firm, the latter being reached by quite different and unknown processes, or (2) to the fact that the regression equations actually capture the main feature of the firm's decision-making processes. We have already indicated that our emphasis is on understanding and explaining economic phenomena of all kinds and we infer that Jorgenson and Siebert have the same goal and thus intend the second approach. In the first place, they employ data from individual firms, and fit each of the regressions individually. In the second place, if the agreement is only coincidence, it does not provide us with an explanation of the behaviour of the firm, nor give us any confidence in using the fitted parameters to predict the firm's reactions to new conditions—e.g., a change in taxes or in the interest rate.

We proceed, therefore, on the assumption that the neo-classical theory (as used by Jorgenson and Siebert) is to be interpreted as an actual description (if only an approximate one) of the procedures the firm uses to make its investment decisions, and that the parameters in the fitted regressions are approximations to the parameters used by the firm. (Of course, the firm might express the equations in a different form, but one that would allow the parameters of the econometrician's fitted regressions to be computed as functions of the parameters used by the firm.)

This assumption is one that is at the heart of an empirical science. The description of a procedure should correspond to the actual procedure (we deal with the "as-if" argument below) as is the case in the natural sciences. Process analysis, the emphasis on description of the decision-making process, in some sense avoids the controversy over motivation which has plagued economics. On the other hand, it makes it difficult to do economics without observing economic actors. Thus we are interested in the degree to which the Jorgenson-Siebert investment function describes the actual decision procedure.

DO FIRMS USE NEO-CLASSICAL MODELS OF INVESTMENT?

Is it at all reasonable to attribute to the firm a particular neo-classical model of optimal investment behaviour? Let us start out with the most favourable conditions for the firm using a neo-classical model. Let us suppose that the managers of the firm are all as dedicated to profit maximization as are neo-classical economists. Let us suppose additionally that they are as well trained in economics and econometrics as the ablest members of the profession. What then would be their decision procedure?

Tinbergen is credited with having proposed, in 1939, the first econometric model of investment behaviour along neo-classical lines (Tin-bergen, 1939). As Jorgenson points out, this model used the theory of optimal capital accumulation "mainly to provide a list of explanatory variables for regressions", and did not deduce the regression equations in any strict sense from the optimizing model (Jorgenson, 1965).

Since no neo-classical econometric model of investment behaviour, even at this relatively crude level, was available prior to 1939, any fit of firm data for an earlier period to such a model would have to be regarded as purely coincidental. It could not "explain" the actual decision-making behaviour of the firm, and if a good fit were actually obtained, it would have to be viewed with great puzzlement and not greeted as a success of scientific theory. To explain rational optimizing behaviour prior to that date, we would have to know, or discover, how a rational man would make investment decisions in the absence of a neo-classical theory. Only by using an "as-if" approach and, thereby, rejecting the goal of explaining actual behaviour by the actual reasons for the behaviour, does the Jorgenson-Siebert approach make any sense. To follow that approach, however, rejects the goal of making economics a true empirical science.

Similarly, there has been a progression of successively improved theories of investment up to Jorgenson's publication of his model in 1963. And even this appears not to be the end of the advancement of knowledge in this realm. Gould (1969), for example, has pointed out a flaw in Jorgenson's model and has attempted to build a model that avoids the error. The logic of this changing situation would seem to call for the rational decision-maker employing at any given point in time, the best investment theory available at that time—the best current state of the art. The econometric model the businessman uses is, so to speak, one of the determinants of his production function, and a change in model will cause changes in some or all of the parameters of that function.

A consequence of this logic is that, if we believe that firms behave rationally, the econometric models we fit to their behaviour at different points in time should not be invariant, but should reflect the state of knowledge of economic theory at the time interval to which they are applied. To explain the data adequately, it might even be important to introduce distributed lags, not for investment, but to allow for the time required to diffuse new knowledge into actual practice. As the work of Griliches (1957), Mansfield (1973), and others on the diffusion of new technology shows, these time lags are likely to be non-negligible. There is no reason for supposing, *a priori*, that decision theories are adopted more rapidly than, let us say, aluminium beer cans.

Where Jorgenson and Siebert, therefore, use a theory first published in 1963 to "explain" the investment decisions of 15 American firms over the period 1949–1963, their explanation itself demands explanation.

The mystery would be solved, of course, if it could be shown that the executives in these firms understood and applied an investment model similar to Jorgenson's. We do not like to think that business practice is so far in advance of sophisticated economic theory, but if the fact could be proved that it is, we would have to bow to that fact.

In fact there is no direct evidence that business firms use such theories and a good deal of evidence that they use simpler rules of thumb to guide their investment decisions. Joseph Bower, one of the many scholars who have made detailed empirical observations of investment processes, reports much data of the following kind from his interviews with managers (Bower, 1970):

One product manager commented, however: Ideally, if you didn't have so many problems to worry about, that were always cropping up, the product manager's job would consist of long-range product-marketing plans. But you really just don't have time to worry about the long-range as long as you have so many short-range crises to deal with in several different product areas. We are measured against our plan for the year, and with all the problems we are having, getting close is taking most of my time.

In other words, "it would be nice to plan and be market oriented but that's not what I'm being paid to do." Other examples of this sort of phenomenon abound.

A plant expansion was planned that involved more or less duplicating a high-cost facility. The reason was that no competitive standards were available to provide information that such was the case—until outside consultants hired to revise the work flow indicated that the facility concept was outdated.

The accounting system treated depreciation as a corporate expense thereby putting a premium on new facilities when return on investment criteria were used. Where managers had the time and inclination, they attempted to persuade their management whenever incremental development of existing facilities would be more profitable than an entire new facility from the corporate point of view. But often there was no time, and equally often a manager did not wish to be saddled with facilities that involved him in an annual fight with the accountants. Thus while the manual of Capital Appropriations Procedure explained that an important objective of the company was the maximization of return on stockholder's equity, there were other stronger influences on the decisions of subordinate managers.

In the face of such data, we must consider the other possible reasons models like Jorgenson's fit the empirical data as well as they do. We might, for example, look more closely at the large number of degrees of freedom of these models (five to seven typically) in relation to the brevity of the time series to which they are fit (Cyert, DeGroot, & Holt, 1979).

The difficulty of attributing, to firms, decision processes more sophisticated than those yet invented by economists, is even graver than we have suggested. The businessman's task of behaving in the manner called for by a neo-classical model like Jorgenson's is far more complex and difficult than the econometrician's task of fitting the neo-classical model, *a posteriori*, to the firm's data. Assume that both the businessman and the econometrician use the same neo-classical theory, the former to make his investment decisions, the latter to explain the former's behaviour. Both, then, use optimization theory to deduce the forms of the functions he fits. The econometrician, however, can use the firm's data, after the fact, to estimate the parameters of these functions. The businessman must estimate these parameters before the fact, and from other data.

If we examine the structure of Jorgenson's model, for example, we see that the estimating burden it places on the businessman is not inconsequential. In addition to estimating his firm's distributed lag function for investment, the interest rate and the taxes on capital, and the prices of his output—all of which he might guess reasonably accurately from information available to him—he must also estimate the exponent of the capital factor in the Cobb-Douglas function. In the previous section, we have seen that attempts to fit the Cobb-Douglas function, or other production functions for that matter, have given highly ambiguous results with respect to the shape of the function. It is not at all obvious that businessmen (or econometricians) know how to estimate the marginal productivity of capital in the aggregate from data actually available to the firm.

At this point one might be inclined to retreat to an "as-if" version of neo-classical theory. But then, in the absence of any evidence that the firm's production function is actually Cobb-Douglas, one would need to explain why the total of investments determined by making evaluations of a whole series of individual projects would be equal to the optimal investment calculated from a purely hypothetic Cobb-Douglas function. Note that desired capital in Jorgenson's model is proportional to capital's share of income in the Cobb-Douglas theory. Hence, any estimation error in fitting the (hypothetical) Cobb-Douglas function will have major consequences for the estimate of desired capital.

Our suspicions of conclusions based on this tenuous chain of assumptions can only be increased by the observed failure of the fitting procedure to yield reasonable estimates for the coefficient of the capital factor in the Cobb-Douglas function. As estimated from Jorgenson's regression equations, this coefficient is generally only about ten per cent as large as it would be if estimated directly from the data on payments to capital. Stated otherwise, the "desired capital" terms in the regressions are only carrying ten per cent of the weight, in the explanation of the phenomena, that one would expect from theory. The theory calls for much larger fluctuations in desired capital, hence, proportionally even larger fluctuations in investment, than are actually observed.

We can only conclude that, irrespective of the successes of Jorgenson's curve-fitting exercises, no case has been made that the fitted functions describe business investment decision-making rules. On *a priori* grounds, it is hard to see how procedures can be followed that have not yet been invented. On empirical grounds, critical parameters in the estimated functions are an order of magnitude lower than we would expect from other data.

UNCERTAINTY AND DECISION-MAKING

We alluded earlier to the fact that there is now a growing body of evidence, from direct empirical observation, as to how business firms make their investment decisions. This body of evidence does not contradict the assumption that firms behave rationally, but it provides us with a picture of what rationality in real life (as distinguished from rationality within the framework of simple models) actually means.

The rationality of the business firm is a rationality that takes account of the limits on its knowledge, on its information, on its capacity for computation, and on its understanding of theory (Nelson & Winter, 1982). It is a rationality that makes extensive use of rules of thumb where a more exact application of theory is impossible, whether because the theory is not understood, because the data needed for estimating its parameters is not available, or because the decision must be made under conditions of uncertainty.

Since "uncertainty" is a time-honoured word in economics, let us gather all of these imperfections and limits upon rationality—incomplete knowledge, inadequate means of calculation—under the umbrella of "uncertainty".

The problem of decision-making under uncertainty has long been recognized as one of major concern to economists. In particular, economists have been aware of the fact that the concept of profit maximization under uncertainty is exceedingly vague because of the lack of uniqueness attaching to any method of maximizing profits under these conditions. Alchian has made an excellent summary of the situation (Alchian, 1950):

Attacks on this methodology [profit maximization] are widespread, but only one attack has been really damaging, that of G. Tintner. He denies that profit maximization even makes any sense where there is uncertainty. Uncertainty arises from at least two sources: imperfect foresight and human inability to solve complex problems containing a host of variables even when an optimum is definable. Tintner's proof is simple. Under uncertainty, by definition, each action that may be chosen is identified with a *distribution* of potential outcome, not with a unique outcome. Implicit in uncertainty is the consequence that these distributions of potential outcomes are overlapping. It is worth emphasis that each possible action has a distribution of potential outcomes, only one of which will materialize if the action is taken, and that one outcome cannot be foreseen. Essentially the task is converted in to making a decision (selecting an action) whose potential outcome distribution is preferable, that is, choosing the action with the *optimum distribution*, since there is no such thing as a maximizing distribution.

There are a variety of ways in which economic theory can deal with the problem of uncertainty. One of these is to retreat from the analysis of the individual units and rely on the analysis of market forces. This approach is somewhat akin to the use of the environment by the biologist to explain the adaptation of the species. The approach has merit and might be used to provide an explanation for certain kinds of behaviour in the long run and at an aggregate level. It does not give us an understanding at the firm level.

A formal method of handling the problem is to assume that the firm can develop subjective probability distributions of profit for decision alternatives. In addition, it is necessary to assume that the firm has a utility function that enables it to convert probability distributions of profit into utility and that the firm makes decisions so as to maximize the utility function. This may well be a useful approach if by empirical work the process by which probability distributions are established by businessmen can be determined and if the form of the utility functions used by businessmen can be discovered.

A third method is to study empirically the way that businessmen make decisions in the face of uncertainty and to embed the decision process into a theory of the firm (Cyert & March, 1967). If such an approach is taken, it is also critical to understand the process by which decision rules are learned and the way in which such rules are modified in the face of feedback from the environment. This approach takes the view that the firm is an adaptive mechanism that can learn from its environment (Caves, 1980). At the same time the approach assumes that the firm (even with computers) has a limited capability to process information and, therefore, may not reach the position that hindsight analysis demonstrates to have been an optimum.

As a result managers have developed behavioural rules for making decisions. Behavioural rules (rules of thumb) are modes of behaviour that the firm (or individual) develops as guides for making decisions in a complex environment with uncertainty and incomplete information (Baumol & Stewart, 1964). These rules generally incorporate the decision-makers' assumption about the nature of the environment and the nature of the firm itself. In general the "thing" we refer to as judgment is capable of being decomposed into a set of behavioural rules. As uncertainty gives way to certainty and as knowledge increases, the behavioural rules change and move closer to those derived by *a priori* reasoning about a simplified situation. For the firm operating in the framework of the competitive system with the market price, the marginal cost curve, and the average variable cost curve *known*, there is no need for behavioural rules, other than those derived by the usual marginalist reasoning. The firm must determine output by the intersection of the market price and its own marginal cost curve. For the firm operating under conditions of ignorance of its demand and cost curves, other methods of decision-making must be found.

The concept of behavioural rules, however, is not new to economics. Every determinate model developed under conditions of some uncertainty utilizes a behavioural rule. In the cobweb model, suppliers are assumed to determine the current period's supply on the basis of last period's price, $S_t = f(p_{t-1})$. In the Cournot duopoly model, each firm assumes that it is independent of its rival, and in particular, that changes in its output will have no effect on its rival. In the kinked demand curve model, each firm assumes its rival will always behave in the way that will hurt it the most. Thus, a price increase will not be followed by rivals, but a price decrease will. For other models where uncertainty exists but is eliminated in the model, some form of behavioural rule can be shown to be present.

In most cases these behavioural rules were inserted by economists on the basis of empirical observation or in some cases by an *a priori* argument in which the behavioural rule led to behaviour consistent with other empirical observations.

The use of behavioural rules has occasionally been rationalized by arguing that such rules lead to the same result as profit maximizing behaviour. This argument is generally false (as we shall see) and ignores, moreover, the basic reason for the firm having recourse to such rules. The use of these rules is the way that the firm deals with the problem of uncertainty. If maximizing behaviour could be defined operationally in such situations, the firm would maximize. With a simple environment, where the feedback to the firm from the market is unconfounded, the firm, given enough time, might find the profit maximizing solution. For such a solution to prevail nature must provide ideal conditions for an experimental design and the firm must be able to absorb the costs of running the experiment.

When such ideal conditions do not prevail the firm must make inferences from the feedback it gets and develop behavioural rules for action in the face of inadequate information. Satisficing is one such rule that has been inferred from observed behaviour (Simon, 1955). It is a process by which a decision-maker defines the criteria for a solution that will satisfy him (Radner, 1975). If the set of possible solutions is completely known, then clearly there is no need to satisfice. When the total set is unknown and the rate at which new solutions are being revealed is also unknown, then assuming some time constraint, a decision rule for the cessation of search for new solutions must be established for a decision to be made.

To argue that this formulation is merely profit maximization is to miss the point. For maximization we must reformulate the decision in terms of the marginal costs of search and the marginal gains expected from additional search. Search proceeds, so the argument goes, until the marginal costs equals the marginal expected gain. In the real world, however, this simple procedure will not work because of the nature of the search process and the nature of the solution set. There is a large component of ignorance in each that makes the measurement problem difficult or impossible. The net result is that rules such as satisficing must be invoked to make a decision.

Finally, will behavioural rules lead to the same behaviour as profit maximizing without them? Of the many ways of showing they will not, we will mention just two. First, the various alternative models of investment that Jorgenson and Siebert examine—neo-classical or not—are equivalent to a corresponding set of behavioural rules. The fact that they can undertake to choose among these models is equivalent to saying the behavioural rules make a difference in behaviour, and an observable difference, at that.

But the point is much broader and deeper. As our reference to oligopoly theory indicates, the differences between competing economic theories are most often precisely describable as differences in assumptions about the limits of rationality—about the specific ways in which incomplete information and inability to compute affect the calculations of the economic actors. Substantially all assumptions of market imperfections and "sticky" adjustments are assumptions of behavioural rules attuned to imperfections of rationality.

Thus business cycle theory depends sensitively, as a generation of debates about Keynes has shown, on assumptions about the stickiness of wages and interest rates—assumptions that require, in turn, further assumptions about the inability of economic actors to calculate, perfectly and with perfect foresight, where their economic interests lie. These kinds of assumptions are as clearly present in the business cycle theories of rational expectationists as they are in Keynesian theory. Tax incidence theory teaches the same lesson: that conclusions depend critically upon assumptions about price stickiness and tax capitalization—that is to say, upon assumptions as to who is perfectly rational and to what degree. But the same claim can be made and supported for virtually every area of application of economic theory to real human behaviour.

CONCLUSION

We emphasize this point of the limited rationality of economic actors both because of its theoretical importance and because it represents a place where inferences from observed behaviour may contribute knowledge that can aid economic analysis. Studies of decision-making behaviour in organizations have produced conclusions that are relevant for handling the problem of uncertainty and that illustrate at the same time the way in which a behavioural approach may contribute to model building. In most business decisions involving price and output in the short run, the decision-maker confronts uncertainty with no way to dodge it. At the same time no forecasting model or economic theory will give him the answers he needs. This type of situation exists in every firm producing multiple products in which production decisions must be made before the market has decided which items will be most in demand. The problem is handled in most cases by some form of sequential decision-making process in which the firm bases its decisions on a sample of buyer preferences. The firm collects information until it can satisfice on the product mix and, depending on the production process, will continue to collect information and repeat the process for subsequent decisions. Are these decisions profit-maximizing ones? The question cannot be answered, since no unequivocal definition of profit maximizing can be given under the circumstances. Even if one could, by some juggling of definitions, argue that the decisions are profit maximizing, nothing would be added to our knowledge by that redefinition. In particular, calling behaviour "profit maximizing" gives us no way, under conditions of uncertainty, to predict it without knowledge of actual decision processes.

Our task as social scientists in these circumstances is to discover and explain the decision process (Tversky & Kahneman, 1974). In order to do this we must understand more about the activities of the decision-maker or decision-making group. The emphasis must be on understanding the process as opposed to making simple assumptions of motivation, and proceeding to develop models with reference to their empirical validity (Simon, 1979a).

It is clear that the firm generally wants to make as much profit as it can subject to the constraints that any individual or organization has in making decisions. The job of the social scientist who is committed to a behavioural approach is to demonstrate through the use of all the knowledge available why the firm stops its search process when it does; to explain how all of the forces within the organization as well as the market have combined to make the level of investment in the plant what it is; to show how the effects of the various competing groups within the firm and the market forces have worked to determine the price change in any particular case.

Progress has been slow with the behavioural approach. Firms are reluctant to allow academic observers and the latter are reluctant to leave their desks. Arm-chair theorizing is not only pleasant but is higher in economists' rank ordering of activities. Yet some progress has been made, usually in Ph.D. theses where a student can be forced to go into the field and gather data. The work of Joskow (1973), Eliasson (1974) and of Nelson and Winter (1982) are excellent examples. Understandably, progress is slow but is being made (Cyert & Hedrick, 1972).

We have not argued that theory is impossible (though completely *a priori* theory generally is), but are rather arguing that theory should correspond to the process that is taking place within the firm. Every decision cannot be explained by the simple assumption of profit maximization—especially when that concept has no unique meaning under uncertainty. A theory of decision-making within organizations that combines both the internal variables of the firm and the market forces of the particular market structure the firm is operating within can be developed (Simon, 1979a, b). Indeed progress has been made toward such a theory, and it is to encourage continued work in the face of fallacious but tenacious defences of the conventional approach that we write this chapter.

REFERENCES

Alchian, A. A., 'Uncertainty, Evolution and Economic Theory'. *Journal of Political Economy*, 1950, 58, pp. 211–22.

Arrow, K. J., Chenery, H . B., Minhas, B. S., & Solow, R. M., 'Capital-labor substitution and economic efficiency'. *Review of Economics and Statistics*, 1961, 43, pp. 225–50.

Baumol, W. J. & Stewart, M., 'Rules of Thumb and Optimally Imperfect Decisions'. *American Economic Review*, 1964, 54, pp. 23–46.

Bower, J. L., *Managing the Resource Allocation Process: A Study of Corporate Planning and Investment*, Boston, Massachusetts: Harvard University, 1970.

Brown, E. H. P., 'The meaning of the Fitted Cobb-Douglas Function'. *'Quarterly Journal of Economics*, 1957, 71, 546–60.

Bronfenbrenner, M., 'Production Functions: Cobb-Douglas, Intrafirm, Inter-firm'. *Econometrica*, 1944, pp. 35–44.

Caves, R. E., 'Industrial Organization, Corporate Strategy and Structure'. *Journal of Economic Literature*, 1980, 18, pp. 64–92.

Cyert, R. M., DeGroot, M. H., & Holt, C. A., 'Capital Allocation within a Firm'. *Behavioral Science,* 1979, 24, pp. 87–95.

Cyert, R. M. & March, J. G., *A Behavioral Theory of the Firm.* Englewood Cliffs, New Jersey: Prentice-Hall, Inc., 1967.

Cyert R. M. & Hedrick C., 'Theory of the Firm: Past, Present, and Future', *Journal of Economic Literature*, 1972, 10, pp. 398–412.

Earley, J. S., 'Marginal Policies of Excellently Managed Companies'. *American Economic Review*, 1956, 46, pp. 44–70.

Elliasson, G., *Corporate Planning—Theory, Practice, Comparison*. Stockholm: Federation of Swedish Industries, 1974.

Friedman, M., *Essays in Positive Economics*. Chicago, Illinois: University of Chicago Press, 1953.

Gold, B., 'Changing Perspectives on Size Scale, and Returns: An Interpretive Study'. *Journal of Economic Literature*, 1981, 19, pp. 5–33.

Griliches, Z., 'Hybrid-corn: An Exploration in the Economics of Technological change'. *Econometrica*, 1957, 25, pp. 501–22.

Gould, J. P., 'The Use of Endogenous Variables in Dynamic Models of Investment'. *Quarterly Journal of Economics*, 1969, 83, pp. 580–600.

Jorgenson, D. W., 'Anticipation and Investment Behavior'. In J. S. Dusenberry, E. Kuh, G. From, & L. R. Klein (eds), *The Brookings Quarterly Economic Model of the United States*. Chicago, 1965.

—— & Siebert, C. D., 'A comparison of Alternative Theories of Corporate Investment Behavior'. *American Economic Review*, 1968, 58, pp. 681–712.

Joskow, P. L., 'Pricing Decisions of Regulated Firms: A Behavioral Approach'. *Bell Journal of Economics*, 1973, 4, pp. 118–40.

Lucas, R. E. Jr., 'Adjustment Costs and the Theory of Supply'. *Journal of Political Economy*, 1967, 75, pp. 321–34.

Lucas, R. L., 'Capacity, Overtime, and Empirical Production Functions'. *American Economic Review*, 1970, 60, pp. 23–7.

Mansfield, E., 'Determinants of the Speed of Application of New Technology'. In B. R. Williams, (ed.), *Science and Technology in Economic Growth*. New York: John Wiley & Sons, 1973.

Mendershausen, H., 'On the Significance of Professor Douglas' Production Function'. *Econometrica*, 1938, 6, pp. 143–62.

Nelson, R. R. & Winter, S. G., *An Evolutionary Theory of Economic Change*. Cambridge, Massachusetts: Harvard University Press, 1982.

Radner, R., 'Satisficing'. *Journal of Mathematical Economics*, 1975, 2, pp. 253–62.

Rosenberg, A., *If Economics Isn't Science What is It?* Working Paper, Department of Philosophy, Syracuse University, 1982.

Simon, H. A., 'A Behavioral Model of Rational Choice'. *Quarterly Journal of Economics*, 1955, 69, 99–118.

—— 'Rational Decision Making in Business Organizations.' *American Economic Review*, 1979, 69, pp. 493–513. (a)

—— On Parsimonious Explanations of Production Relations'. *Scandinavian Journal of Economics*, 1979, 81, pp. 459–74. (b)

—— & Levy, F. K., 'A note on the Cobb-Douglas function'. *Review of Economic Studies*, 1963, 30, pp. 93–4.

Solow, R. M., 'Technical Change and the Aggregate Production Function'. *Review of Economics and Statistics*, 1957, 39, pp. 312–20.

Tinbergen, J., *Business Cycles in the United States of America 1919–1932*. Geneva: League of Nations, 1939.

Tversky, A. & Kahneman, D., 'Judgment under Uncertainty: Heuristics and Biases'. *Science*, 1974, 185, pp. 1124–31.

Walters, A. A., 'Production and Cost Functions: An Econometric Survey'. *Econometrica*, 1963, 31, pp. 1–66.

Index

Abramovitz, M., 3
accountancy and electronic data-processing, 22–30
accountants and collusion, 102
acquisitions by companies, 38, 51–3, 84
administrative theories of organization, 142, 143
advertising, 50, 63
agriculture, 61
Alchian, A., 203, 233–4
altruism, 68
American Economic Association, 59
American Economic Review, ix, 61, 74
analysis
  industry, 173–5
  planning phase, 82–3
  and synthesis, 168–9
Anderson, W. H. L., 64, 70
antitrust law and enforcement, 98, 106–7
approximating assumptions, 206–7
Armstrong, A. G., 38
Arrow, K. J., 224
Asch, S., 104–5
aspiration level, 34
  model, 133–4
automobile industry, oligopoly price behaviour in, 11–16
Averch-Johnson model, 65–6

Balderston, F. E., 194
Balderston-Hoggatt model, 184–6
banks' demand for excess reserves, 71
bargaining
  in coalition, 128–31, 157
  function, 96, 97, 103–5
Barzel, Y., 63
Baumol, W. J., 64, 113, 234
Bayesian analysis, xi, 67
Bayes's formula, 117
behavioural theory, 60, 65, 86–9, 213–14
  and dynamics, 112–15
  examination of, 220–38
  and generalized maximization techniques, 66–7, 70–1
  illustrative model, 115–20
  non-maximizing models, 68–9, 71
  research, 139–50
  rules, 88–9, 112–13, 214–16, 234–6
  see also control; decision-making
Bonini, C. P., 186–8, 193
Bower, J. L., 231
Bronfenbrenner, M., 224
Brown, E. H. P., 223–4
budgets, 132, 144
bureaucracy, 142
business cycle
  downturn phase, collusion and, 105

management, 79–82
changing, as control action,
84–5
and collusion, 97, 99, 100,
101, 105
and efficiency, 36, 39, 44, 51–4
evaluation of, 44
game, Carnegie Tech, 189–92
hospital, 65
quality of, 51, 83
and research and development,
39–40
see also decision-making;
objectives; planning
Management Science, 74
managerial approach to theory of
the firm, 60, 64–6, 70, 71
Mansfield, E., 230
Mao, J. C. T., 71
March, J. G., ix–x, 126, 133,
134, 137, 175–6, 181–3, 193,
194, 234
marginalism, 221–2
mark-downs, 182
market
as control mechanism, 37
structure, 37–9
and theory of the firm, 60
marketing *see* advertising
markups, 101, 174, 181–3
Mendershausen, H., 224
merger, 38, 51–3, 84
Meyer, J., 45
micro-economics
orthodox theory, 201, 205–16
criticisms, 202–3
defence, 203–5, 209–10
views of, 59–73
see also behavioural; control;
neo-classical
Middleton, R., 22–30, 34
military forces, 130
Miller, M. H., 71
Miller, R. L., 68
Minhas, B. S., 224
Minz, A., 100
Mitchell, W. C., 3

models
Averch-Johnson, 65–6
Balderson-Hoggatt, 184–6
behavioural rules, 115–20
cobweb, 89, 113, 216, 235
Cournot duopoly, 89, 92–3,
113, 153–5, 166–7, 216, 235
department store, 147–8, 181–3
dominant firm, 78, 114
econometric, 168–9
investment, 183–4, 227–33
kinked demand curve, 3, 78,
89, 109, 114, 216, 235
neo-classical, 60, 78–9, 111,
227–8
non-maximizing, 68–9
Trust Investment Officer,
183–4
monetary policy, 41
monopoly, 92, 141
in neo-classical theories, 62, 63
and new products, 62
solution, 96, 99
in UK, 38
Morse, P. M., 196–8
Myers, R. H., 61–2

National Bureau of Economic
Research, 6–7, 11, 15
Nelson, R. R., 233
neo-classical theories, 37, 61–62,
70, 85–6
examined, 220–38
extensions of, 62–7, 70–1
investment models, 229–33
marginalism, 221–2
models of the firm, 60, 78–9,
111, 227–8
and revisionist theories, 60–1
Newell, A., 72
Newhouse, J. P., 65, 70
non-profit organizations, 65
normative theory, 125–6, 186–8

objective function, 69
modification of, 64–6, 70, 71
profit as, 60, 61